Chaucer's London

NEW DIMENSIONS IN HISTORY

Historical Cities

Series Editor: Norman F. Cantor

John Wiley & Sons, Inc.   New York · London · Sydney · Toronto

CHAUCER'S LONDON

D. W. ROBERTSON, JR.

Turn again, Whittington!

10 9 8 7 6 5 4 3 2

Library of Congress Catalog Card Number: 68-30920
CLOTH: SBN 471 72730 X   PAPER: SBN 471 72731 8
Printed in the United States of America

To the memory of

EMMA JONES ROBERTSON

who lovingly taught her small

son to read, to write, and to

enjoy poetry, music, and painting.

PREFACE

This book offers the student of Chaucer and the general reader an elementary account of the City of London during the second half of the fourteenth century. In the first chapter a number of general principles are stated, in an effort to establish a point of view. Writers about the past frequently seek to reassure their readers that people have always been like themselves, that human nature is universal, and that the special periods with which they are concerned are in many respects like the period in which they live. I have sought to point out on the contrary that people in the late Middle Ages were different, that their world was very much unlike ours, and that in general human nature has changed considerably, but without any implication that during the years since Chaucer lived things have grown very much worse or very much better. This attitude will disappoint only the sentimental.

The second chapter forms a brief introduction to the outward aspects of the medieval city. As the footnotes sometimes reveal, much more information than is presented here is available about some topographical features. In other instances, our information is extremely limited. The chapter will be much easier to follow if it is read in conjunction with the map provided here. Serious readers may wish to consult the more detailed map of London under Richard II by Marjorie B. Honeybourne, published by the London Topographical Society in 1960, which is based on many years of study of primary materials. There is also a more detailed map in C. L. Kingsford's edition of Stow's *Survey of London,* but it was designed to represent a later period in the history of the city.

The chapter on city customs presents only a very concise account of the government of the city and the *mores* of its people. The surviving city records are voluminous, and large extracts from or summaries of their contents have been published. Aside from Sylvia Thrupp's extremely informative book, *The Merchant Class of Medieval London,* little effort has been made to synthesize the information thus made available in a systematic way. I sincerely hope that my efforts may serve to stimulate renewed interest not only in the printed materials, but also in the records themselves, which must eventually be reexamined when a more detailed history of the city is written.

The fourth chapter, "A Brief Chronicle," is, as the title indicates, a chronicle and not a history. It presents some of the chief events in the history of the city in chronological order against a background of related events in the kingdom. The reader should be warned, therefore, that the chapter does not pretend to be a short history of England in the late fourteenth century. Many important matters are not mentioned. Only those events that bore directly or indirectly on the history of London are considered. The reader should be warned that much of English history in the later fourteenth century is controversial. That is, estimates of the principal figures involved, like King Edward III, or King Richard II, or John of Gaunt, or, in London, Nicholas Brembre, vary considerably, not only among medieval chroniclers but also among modern historians. During the last years of King Richard, the principal facts themselves elude us. It is obvious that much work needs to be done before a definitive history can be written. Generally events are presented here from what would have been in the fourteenth century a conservative point of view, consistent, presumably, with attitudes displayed by Chaucer. Men of the time did not know what we know about subsequent history. Illegal acts and subversive attitudes in the fourteenth century may look forward to subsequent developments now widely regarded as steps in progress toward our own enlightened society. But to obtain a reasonable perspective for the discussion of any period of the past it may be best to avoid the assumption that attitudes appearing then, which, if widely held, would have destroyed the social order, are "good" because they have been useful at later times under very different conditions.

I have occasionally used the rather unsatisfactory word *feudal* to indicate in a general way the legal and social traditions of the hierarchical society in England and France during the later Middle Ages. It is not a medieval term and it is not used consistently by modern writers. But I have been at a loss to find a substitute. The word *chivalry,* which was a medieval term, is here used to suggest those ideals, attitudes, conventions, and practices then thought necessary to the successful military support of national interests. During our period chivalry was also thought of as a "virtue," which, like other virtues, was felt to have a reality outside the individual that might be reflected more or less imperfectly in actual persons. Generally, I have sought to avoid the cynicism that often characterizes modern accounts of the fourteenth century, as well as the novelistic sensationalism that often accompanies it.

The last chapter on London as an intellectual center breaks new ground. It is my hope that the information here presented will at least convince historians that there may be such a thing as the intellectual history of the city and that it deserves treatment in more detail. Insofar as Chaucer is concerned, some readers may recognize the fact that what is here said about him is unconventional. Literary historians have tended sometimes to neglect both the larger currents of intellectual history in the Middle Ages and the immediate intellectual and social background of Chaucer's work. If the present book succeeds in stimulating further interest in all of these matters, I shall consider it a success.

No one who writes about medieval London can fail to pay tribute to the scholars both in this century and the last who labored so assiduously to make primary materials available to the student or to render detailed accounts of particular places and their history, especially to H. M. Colvin, Marjorie B. Honeybourne, C. L. Kingsford, H. T. Riley, R. R. Sharpe, and A. H. Thomas. A. B. Emden's remarkable Biographical Registers of Oxford and Cambridge are indispensable guides to the essential facts concerning the lives of many distinguished men in the fourteenth century. Materials from these registers are often used without specific acknowledgement in the pages below, so that it is only proper to

say here that they are among the most valuable works of reference at our disposal for the study of England during the later
Middle Ages. Finally, I wish to express special gratitude to Urban
Tigner Holmes, Jr., who first aroused my interest many years ago
in the daily life of medieval people.

Princeton University   D. W. ROBERTSON, JR.
Princeton, New Jersey
July, 1968

CONTENTS

LIST OF ILLUSTRATIONS

ONE

Introduction

In the reigns of Augustus and Tiberius it is possible that a trading center developed on the northern bank of the River Thames where two small hills separated by a stream and flanked on the west by a river and on the east by a marsh afforded harbor facilities and convenient natural defenses. If it existed, we may imagine ships from Gaul and Italy sailing up the misty estuary to the mouth of Walbrook and the Fleet, sewers today, and to other inlets along the shore, bringing wine and luxury goods in exchange for grain, cattle, gold, silver, iron, hides, slaves, especially young females, and dogs. This early center is conjectural, but after the invasion of Claudius in 43, the Romans took advantage of the site, built a city around the small gravel hills, and instituted the history of London. The vengeful Boudicca sacked and burned their city in 60, but it was soon rebuilt, a web of military roads radiated from it to other parts of the country, and, during the second century, it became a center of finance and religion. Among its buildings was a great basilica, over five hundred feet long, used as a court, exchange, and community center. Fire devastated the city in about 125, but it rose again, and a wall eight feet thick and a little over two miles long was constructed around its perimeter. In the fourth century the city was called "Augusta." The retreat of the Romans in the fifth century left Augusta deserted. Its walls crumbled and its buildings fell into ruin. But King Alfred (d. 900) repaired the walls and established the medieval city that could properly be described in the fourteenth century before the Court of the Mayor as "the capital city and watch-tower of the whole realm." Invasion might waste it and fire destroy it, but London's position at the intersection of great roads, solidly placed by the Romans, and the fine natural highway of the Thames assured its economic importance and continued life.[1]

Chaucer's contemporaries viewed the origin of their city somewhat differently. Since a people's conception of their own history is a key to their ideals and aspirations, we should do well to accord this older view respectful attention. "In the year from the beginning of the world 4032," wrote John Carpenter in an early fifteenth-century handbook of City customs, "and before Our Lord's Incarnation 1200, the city that is now called 'London,' founded in imitation of Great Troy, was constructed and built by King Brut, the first monarch of Britain, being at first called 'New Troy' and afterwards 'Trinovant:' of which foundation, building, and construction the River Thames was the cause."[2] Carpenter goes on to describe and quote the traditional laws and customs that gave the city control over nets and kiddles in the Thames and the Medway, for the river was a source of food as well as a convenient means of transportation. Elsewhere in Carpenter's book we are told, with an echo of a famous description of the city written in the twelfth century by Fitz-Stephen, that the city is "the one principal seat of the realm of England . . . happy in the salubrity of its climate, in the enjoyment of the Christian religion, in its liberties so well deserved, and in its

[1] On early London, see Ralph Merrifield, *The Roman City of London* (London, 1965); R. G. Collingwood and J. N. L. Myers, *Roman Britain and the English Settlements* (Oxford, 1937); R. R. Sharpe, *London and the Kingdom*, Vol. 1 (London, 1894). For the quotation, see H. T. Riley, *Memorials of London and London Life in the XIII, XIV, and XV Centuries* (London, 1868), p. 492.

[2] *Liber Albus: The White Book of the City of London*, ed. H. T. Riley (London, 1861), p. 427. The *Chroniculi S. Pauli London ad annum 1399*, printed in W. Sparrow Simpson, *Documents Illustrating the History of Saint Paul's Cathedral* (Camden Soc., 1880), records that Brutus, a nobleman of Trojan origin, conquered the Isle of Albion, inhabited in those days by giants, and called the new land "Britain." The same Brutus constructed the first city of Britain, now called London, in memory of fallen Troy, calling it Trinovantem or New Troy. It was long called Trinovans. Cf. Geoffrey of Monmouth, *Historia regum Britanniae*, ed. Griscom (London, 1929), pp. 251–253, and J. S. P. Tatlock, *The Legendary History of Britain* (Berkeley and Los Angeles, 1950), pp. 30, 111–112.

foundation at a most ancient date." We are assured, moreover, that London is older than Rome and that it "possesses the liberties, rights, and customs of the ancient city Troy and enjoys its institutions."[3] In a poem written by Richard of Maidstone to celebrate the reconciliation of Richard II with the city in 1392, London is "Trenovant" or "Nova Troja," and King Richard is styled "Troilus," or "Little Troy," a convention reflected in Shakespeare's play, where the Queen calls her deposed husband "the model where Old Troy did stand." When the chronicler Thomas Walsingham wished to compliment the Black Prince, he called him "another Hector," and John Gower elaborated the figure of London as Troy in Vox clamantis.[4]

To Englishmen of the fourteenth century the Trojan origin of their nation and of their capital city was both an inspiration and a warning. The *pietas* of Aeneas, or "Ennias the athel," as he was called at the opening of *Sir Gawain and the Green Knight*, was subject to dangers, like the warm pleasures of Dido or the cold enmity of Turnus. It nevertheless triumphed in the end to serve as an inspiration to every Roman schoolboy. It also inspired Geoffrey of Monmouth, who gave it a new incarnation in the person of the Christian King Arthur, the exemplar of the chivalry of England. Chivalric ideals were not alien to the free citizens of London, who thought of themselves as tenants in chief of the Crown and as peers of the noblemen of the realm. They had some justification for feeling, during the earlier part of the reign of King Edward III, that they were subjects of the most chivalrous ruler England had enjoyed since the days of King Arthur. At the same time, however, it was remembered that Old Troy was burned by the Greeks, having first weakened itself through lust,[5] and that Britain had suffered "blysse and blunder," or pros-

---

[3] *Liber Albus*, p. 54.

[4] See Wright's earlier edition of Maidstone's *Concordia inter Regem Ric. II et civitatem London* (London, 1838), pp. 31, 32, 35; Walsingham, *Historia Anglicana*, ed. H. T. Riley (London, 1863), I, 321.

[5] The fall of Troy was widely held to have been the result of a neglect of Pallas, or wisdom, and a reversion to fleshly lusts and idolatry. For example, see the commentary on *The City of God* by Raoul de Presles (Abbeville, 1468), I, Sig. A viii *recto*, and, for a general discussion, John P. McCall, "The Trojan Scene in Chaucer's *Troilus*," *English Literary History*, XXIX (1962), 263–275.

perity and adversity, through recurrent weaknesses of its own since its foundation by "Felix Brutus." Political stability was, for fourteenth-century Englishmen, the fruit of moral stability, rather than the result of farsighted policy or long-range planning. History was a manifestation of the Order of Providence, carrying with it implications for the daily conduct of life. These implications were more important than the facts behind them.

There are numerous other ways in which medieval Londoners differed in habit of mind from their twentieth-century successors. As H. G. Richardson once wrote, "Medieval realities . . . did not include political parties."[6] This does not mean that medieval Londoners were not from time to time divided into factions. They most certainly were. But their factions were usually based on close personal ties with men of rank and power whose interests might conflict. In a brilliant book M. H. Keen has recently stressed the importance of personal relationships in medieval warfare.[7] They were, however, equally important in time of peace. Medieval society was structured in a complex system of personal obligations, typically arranged in small hierarchies within the great hierarchy of the realm. Almost everyone belonged to one or more small familial groups, owing some sort of personal allegiance to the leaders at the top. At the same time, he had a "degree," or place in the hierarchy of society as a whole. A society of this kind has no "classes" in the modern sense, only a long series of "degrees." Hence there is no possibility of its being torn by a "class struggle." As we shall see, the leaders of the peasants' uprising in London in 1381 were not confined to one class, and the peasants themselves originally wanted a return to what they thought were earlier customary relationships with their overlords. There are a few indications that the servants and yeomen of some of the London guilds sought separate organizations, but in general the guilds managed to include within a single company rich and poor alike. Successful London merchants did not think of themselves as belonging to "the middle class,"

6 "The Commons and Medieval Politics," *Transactions of the Royal Historical Society,* XXVIII (1946), 29.
7 *The Laws of War in the Late Middle Ages* (London and Toronto, 1965), esp. Ch. VI. This work is an excellent introduction to the legal and practical side of chivalry.

and they usually shared the ideas and attitudes of the nobility. Sir John Wroth, Fishmonger of London, could be a welcome guest at Christmas in the London residence of the Bishop of Ely, third son of Richard, Earl of Arundel.[8] And Sir John Philpot, Grocer of London, had been among Earl Richard's executors. The tendency of some historians to see anticipations of "democracy" in medieval parliaments, in craft guilds, or in the revolt of the peasants has led to some very odd conclusions indeed. There were, in the fourteenth century, no "masses," and the romantic ideals that inspired later revolutionaries in France had not yet been enunciated.

We should expect, then, to find in medieval London an hierarchical classless society, strongly conscious of degree, bound into groups by strong personal ties. The individuals in that society were individuals, each with his own peculiar character, talents, and disposition; but they lacked something that most of us enjoy today: "personality."[9] Our personality is the result of our participation in a loosely organized society in which the individual is relatively isolated and has no set place. Political and social equality bring with it an increased concern for the self, and for "psychology," or the exploration of inner life and inner reality. Medieval scholastic philosophy did adapt to its own needs various "psychological" ideas, especially from Aristotle; and medieval medical theory concerned itself with humors and with such matters as memory, the imaginative faculty, the will, and reason. But where practical applications are made in realms that we would consider to be "psychological," medieval writers concern themselves with morality, that is, with the evaluation of behavior within a group rather than with the potentialities of the individual. Medieval men thought of one another, therefore, not as personalities with deep inner drives and tensions, but as moral characters whose virtues or vices were apparent in their speech and actions. Such evaluations can change abruptly

---

[8] Margaret Aston, *Thomas Arundel* (Oxford, 1967), pp. 203–204.
[9] The word *personality*, used to mean the peculiar inner characteristics of an individual, is a development of the later eighteenth century; ideas like the "force" or "depths" of personality are still more recent. Medieval Latin *Personalitas* simply means those characteristics that distinguish human beings from inanimate objects.

for the simple reason that moral behavior can also change abruptly.[10] Hence Walsingham's treatment of John of Gaunt, which made him a villain up until 1389, when he is said to have repented his sins, and a hero thereafter, although it may not represent a just evaluation, is at least comprehensible.[11] Again, in discussing the death of Edward III and making a final estimate of his worth, the same author calls him "glorious, benign, clement, and magnificent" (i.e., willing to undertake great works), but after a long eulogy concludes that his death was the result of lechery.[12] Walsingham does not indicate any inner conflict in the King as a result of this vice (as, indeed, there probably was none), and he does not seek to explain it in psychological terms. The difference between a human being with a character and another with a personality is somewhat difficult to grasp, and its implications are elusive.[13] But the fact remains that neither Greeks, Romans, nor medieval Englishmen had any concept of personality or treated one another as though they were personalities.

Perhaps the situation may be clarified if we pause for a moment to consider the observations of a great modern sociologist, Elton Mayo. He is discussing Durkheim's theory of *anomie*: "His central claim is, first, that a small society lives in an ordered manner such that the interests of its members are subordinated to the interests of the group. He does not mean anything that is political, or, in any explicit sense, moral by this subordination. His reference is rather to the fact that an individual born as a member of such a community can, during infancy and adolescence, see ahead of him the function he will unquestionably fulfil for the group when he is adult. This anticipation regulates his thought and action in the developing years and in adulthood culminates in satisfaction and a sense of function for, and neces-

---

[10] Moral transformation is one of the great themes of medieval literature, from the *Confessions* of St. Augustine to the *Rime* of Petrarch.

[11] Cf. Anthony Steel, *Richard II* (Cambridge, 1941), p. 291.

[12] *Historia Anglicana*, I, 326 ff.

[13] An early perception of this difference, somewhat overburdened with value judgments, appears in D. H. Lawrence, *Apropos of Lady Chatterley's Lover* (London, 1931), pp. 91–93.

sity to, the society. He is throughout his life *solidaire* with the group. Modern development, Durkheim claims, has brought to an end this life of satisfactory function for the individual and the group. We are facing a condition of *anomie*, or planlessness in living, which is becoming characteristic both of individual lives and of communities."[14] As other sociologists have pointed out, the kind of "small-group" solidarity here described was characteristic of medieval life.[15]

There is no reason to regard this situation with nostalgia, either Marxist or sentimental. It cannot now be revived, and the industrial economy that finally replaced it in the course of the eighteenth century, even where it has been burdened by various forms of statism, has considerably improved the material welfare of Western society as a whole. However, members of small-group societies tend to make their special groups what we might call, reversing the historical process, "extensions of their personalities." The welfare of the group occupied a dominant position in the individual's attention. Thus medieval society did not dedicate itself to the "free development of the individual," but rather to the stability of the group. This fact helps to account for the insistent medieval emphasis on morality. Living as we do in comparative freedom and isolation, we find moral questions of the kind that occupied our ancestors dull and irrelevant. Industrial society developed its own morality, at first seeking moral justification for the acquisition of wealth and later constructing a social morality designed to protect the less fortunate and to condemn heedless exploitation. Neither of these developments in moral theory has any relevance to medieval conditions. On the other hand, medieval writers are obviously concerned with "vices" and "virtues" that bear on the behavior of the individual as it affects the group to which he belongs and of which he forms an integral part. The old virtues and vices which seem meaningless to us, and which we sometimes dismiss as the prod-

[14] *The Human Problems of an Industrial Civilization* (Cambridge, Mass., 1933; paperback ed., New York, 1960), pp. 124–125.
[15] For example, see the quotations from G. H. Sabine and G. C. Homans in J. F. Scott and R. P. Lynton, *The Community Factor in Modern Technology* (UNESCO, 1952), pp. 13–14.

ucts of semantic naïveté, were not only meaningful to medieval men, but, in the context of their society, genuinely practical. They had, in other words, an operational validity.

Individuals who are members of small communities in which they have an obvious functional position are likely to feel that their group solidarity is an imperfect reflection of a larger order outside of themselves and independent of their personal thoughts. Modern philosophies and modern styles in art tend to locate reality within the individual. Even among neopositivists solipsism lurks as an ever-present implication difficult to face squarely. But medieval men tended to locate reality outside of themselves, not in the confusion of the physical world, which they too could recognize, but in an hierarchical realm of what seem to us to be abstractions. Hence it was relatively easy for medieval Englishmen to accept, or to desire to accept, traditional teachings concerning Divine Providence. The manifold implications of a Providential Order are difficult for us to understand today, but before we consider some of them, it will be helpful to examine briefly a common medieval distinction that has confused historians and puzzled literary critics: that between Providence and Fortune.

The meaning of these terms is the theme of that favorite medieval book, often found in records of fourteenth-century libraries and translated by Chaucer, *The Consolation of Philosophy* of Boethius. Briefly, Boethius urges his readers to distinguish between two kinds of goods: material or "worldly" goods that are generated and perish and "true" or spiritual goods that do not change in time. To love goods of the first type, which are Providentially "temporal," is to become subject to Fortune, that is, to the flux of material things, which always disappoint those who attach themselves to them for the very reason that they are transient. Fortune is the seeming irrationality of material events, which lead sometimes to prosperity and at other times to adversity, regardless of the merits of the individual. However, as Boethius explains, there is no reality behind the word *chance*. What happens in the world happens Providentially. So-called changes in Fortune test the virtuous and punish the vicious, whether Fortune is "good" or "bad." He who recognizes, through reason, the Providential Order cannot be harmed by Fortune, which is to him a mere illusion, since his heart is set on intangible realities, that is, on God and on manifestations of God, like the virtues, which do not change. This general attitude, we should notice, holds no room for any kind of humanitarianism except that which concerns itself with the welfare of the spirit. Physical or social "good Fortune" indeed constitutes a kind of temptation to forget what was thought of as the true reality. Too great concern for it was thought to be "effeminate."

In view of attitudes such as these it is not surprising that medieval writings and medieval men in the pages of history shock us by their lack of humanitarianism, which has become, in one form or another, the great religion of the modern world.[16] Humanitarian sentiments arise most readily among the isolated, who feel themselves menaced in a hostile world and eager to love, not Tom, Dick, and Harry, who are somehow strange and curiously inaccessible, but humanity as a whole. Medieval men were often urged to love their neighbors, not for the fact of their humanity but for their virtues or potential virtues. When they loved them otherwise, they did so usually with an awareness that what they actually had in mind was not the benefit of the others but their own satisfactions. Chaucer's contemporaries were for the most part completely unsentimental, and when sentimental attributes appear, as they do for example in the picture of the Prioress in the Prologue to *The Canterbury Tales*, they are made the object of satire. Society did not then systematically protect itself from contact with disease, death, and bloodshed. Hence these things caused relatively little anguish and provoked little sentimentality.[17]

A belief in Providence added a dimension to medieval law that we have now lost. Law was not a matter of simple social utility but a reflection of Divine Law applied in an effort to restore the Natural Law that prevailed before the Fall. Absolute justice, not the convenience of the moment, was its aim. As Keen puts it, this situation implies that "there can be no ultimate conflict between social utility and private right." Justice, that is, is not divided

---

[16] Cf. Werner Hofmann, *The Earthly Paradise* (New York, 1961), pp. 161, 167, 329–330.

[17] For modern contrasts, see J. H. van den Berg, "Garder le lit," *Situation*, I (1954), 79.

and cannot be compromised. Because of the premise of an ineluctible Providential Order, there was "no room . . . for any ultimate miscarriage of justice."[18] This fact explains why Englishmen in the fourteenth century could readily resort to war, which was sanctioned by every law so long as it was "just," or based on reason rather than on selfish passion, or to judicial combat. In either instance what they were doing was simply putting their dispute before God, who cannot be corrupted and whose justice will, in any event, prevail.

These ideas and attitudes were not the province of any special class or "degree" in Chaucer's England. That is, they were not peculiarly "religious" and confined to ecclesiastics. The laws of war, for example, were administered by chivalric officials, not by priests. Two of the most "moral" treatises produced in fourteenth-century England, the *Livre de seyntz medicines* of Henry Duke of Lancaster and *The Two Ways* of Sir John Clanvowe, were written by distinguished warriors.[19] The latter was a friend of the poet Chaucer, who translated Boethius and was revered by his contemporaries for his *sentence*, or doctrine. We should not divide the medieval world into "religious" and "secular" realms. As R. G. Collingwood put it, with reference to art, "All art was religious art, or, what comes to the same thing, all art was secular art; there was no special kind of art for religious purposes, because there was no feeling that these purposes stood by themselves."[20] Ecclesiastics and laymen in the fourteenth century shared the same basic attitudes. English bishops were frequently royal administrators, sometimes of noble birth. And noblemen could be among the most devout members of society. But they also shared the same vices. The tendency of modern historians to condemn the bishops generally as "Caesarian clergy," echoing the sour line of Wyclif, overlooks the fact that it was customary during the later Middle Ages for ecclesiastics, from the humblest country vicar to the most distinguished bishop or abbot, to participate in the daily pursuits and ordinary affairs of the com-

---

[18] *The Laws of War*, pp. 224–225.
[19] The *Livre de seyntz medicines* has been published by the Anglo-Norman Text Society. *The Two Ways* has been edited by V. J. Scattergood, *English Philological Studies*, X (1967), 33–56.
[20] *Speculum mentis* (Oxford, 1924), p. 28.

munity. And to speak of the noblemen as "passionate and lustful men" is to forget that passion and lust know no social rank and that the "virtuous poor" are largely an eighteenth-century fiction. Christian ideas and ideals, as they were then understood, provided the ordinary assumptions and shaped the thinking of men in all walks of life, no matter how virtuous or vicious they might be. But they were not regarded as a bar to the enjoyment of life. Paganism had no exotic charms for men who thought of their city as being more ancient than Rome in foundation and Trojan in custom.

When we approach medieval London, we shall find ourselves in a strange land. Surface peculiarities strike us first. The city is much more colorful than any modern city. Bright colors fleck the churches, the exteriors and interiors of houses, and the costumes of the men and women in the streets. But these and other external peculiarities are not so strange as the inner natures of the people themselves. The changes that have taken place in the "universe of discourse" or the ordinary conceptual framework of thought and language since the fourteenth century are even more profound than the changes in costume, architecture, and technology. The better prepared we are to appreciate these differences, and the less inclined we are to think of medieval men sentimentally as being "human like ourselves," the more fruitful will be our study of the medieval city and its people.

TWO

A Visit to the City

Fire and enemy action, ancient destroyers of London, abetted by industrial progress, have left us very little of the city Chaucer knew. We cannot visit much of it, or examine it in old photographs; the best we can do is to construct it once more in the mind's eye. For this purpose we shall undertake, in this chapter, an informal tour on a summer day in the late fourteenth century. Our day will be a subterfuge, compounded of the memories of many summer days, and we shall frequently find it necessary to substitute history for description. Nevertheless, our tour should serve to create an impression, however artificial, of what London and its citizens looked like when Chaucer could see them.

Let us begin our tour at the town house or "inn" of the Bishop of Ely in Farringdon on the north side of Holborn Street, the scene of John of Gaunt's last interview with the king in Shakespeare's *King Richard II*.[1] This was one of many large houses scattered throughout the London area in the fourteenth century. By 1400 the two archbishops, sixteen bishops, twenty abbots, and six priors owned such houses in the city;[2] and there were many others belonging to noblemen and wealthy merchants. Sir Simon Burley, for example, owned two at the time of his execution. There were, in addition to these private inns, one hundred and

---

[1] For descriptions, see Margaret Aston, *Thomas Arundel* (Oxford, 1967), pp. 272–273; and H. M. Colvin in *Mediaeval England,* ed. A. L. Poole (Oxford, 1958), I, 75.

[2] Marjorie B. Honeybourne, "The Reconstructed Map of London under Richard II," *London Topographical Record,* XXII (1965), 33.

ninety-seven commercial inns in 1394, of which ninety-five were in Farringdon Without, near the Bishop of Ely's residence.[3] The area between London Wall and Westminster was thickly populated by royal clerks, lawyers, and apprentices at law; and the frequent meetings of Parliament at Westminster during the later part of the century made extensive accommodations for transients necessary. Moreover, men came from all parts of the realm to buy goods, wholesale and retail, from London merchants.

The London town house was essentially an adaptation of the "hall house" familiar in the countryside. Its principal room was the hall, which served as a social center and dining room. In winter it was heated by a fire, traditionally in the middle of the floor, although fireplaces with chimneys were common in the later fourteenth century. At one end of the hall was a screen that originally served to shelter the occupants from drafts from the outside entry, which was placed on one side near the end. The house grew, as it were, around the hall, but the screen with its passage tended to remain. The simplest elaboration consisted of a solar above a service room at the screen passage end of the hall. Blocks of two stories, or, in some instances, three, might appear at both ends, and further outbuildings were added, sometimes joined by walls, to form an enclosure around a courtyard. Near the screen end of the hall there might be a buttery, a pantry, and a kitchen. Private chambers, a parlor, and a counting room might appear at the other end. The house of an ecclesiastic or nobleman frequently included a chapel. Somewhere there

[3] A. H. Thomas, *Calendar of Select Pleas and Memoranda of the City of London 1381–1442* (Cambridge, 1932), pp. 78–79. There were 50 in Fleet Street, 13 in Langbourne, 9 in Castle Baynard, 7 each in Cripplegate Within and Cripplegate Without, 6 in Farringdon Within, 4 in Billingsgate, 3 each in Queenhithe and Tower, 2 each in Broad Street and Vintry, and 1 in Cordwainer Street. The general location of the wards is usually apparent on our map, but the boundaries are too complex to be conveniently indicated in a small map. Langbourne spread around Lombard Street, narrowed at the intersection of Gracechurch Street, and spread out again around Fenchurch Street. It has been held that a stream once ran along Fenchurch Street and spread in various branches down toward the river and that this stream is responsible for the name "Langbourne." However, the existence of the stream has been disputed.

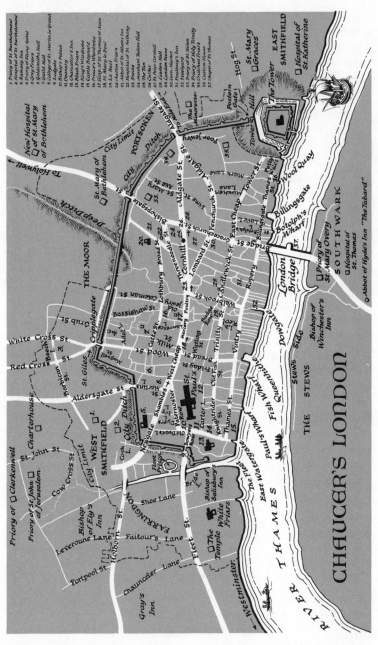

CHAUCER'S LONDON

would be also a vaulted cellar, useful especially to merchants for storage.[4] The courtyard might be paved, but if it were large enough it included a garden containing fruit trees, grapevines, vegetables, herbs, and flowers. At the entrance to the courtyard from the street there was often a large gateway. One enterprising citizen, Sir John Poultney, built the steeple of a small church over his entrance gate. In the busier sections of the city stalls and tenements might be built along the walls bordering the street.

To return to the Bishop of Ely's Inn, we may estimate its size by considering the measurements of the hall, which was roofed in lead, to have been about seventy-two by thirty-two feet. There were three principal chambers for the bishop, two smaller ones, and chambers for the chancellor, clerks, squires, the steward, and others. There was a bakehouse and a larder, and, at the rear, there were some stables and a grange. The garden in the front, famous in Shakespeare's time for strawberries and roses, produced, under the ministrations of Adam Vynour, the gardener, onions, leeks, cabbage, garlic, parsley, herbs, grapes, and other produce sufficient to gain a small annual income from sales.[5] A favorite herb in the area was lavender, a fact that would have pleased Sir Arthur Wing Pinero. The modern tourist can still visit the chapel, now St. Etheldreda's, and see the east window with its fourteenth-century tracery.[6]

This large establishment was necessary to accommodate the bishop's household. In 1387 Thomas Arundel had eleven clerks, seven squires, ten choristers, and an assortment of yeomen, grooms, pages, and specialized servants like Adam Vynour. Not all of them would be with him in London, but he might ride into

[4] See W. A. Pantin, "Some Medieval English Town Houses," in *Culture and Environment* (London, 1963), pp. 445–478; Sylvia Thrupp, *The Merchant Class of Medieval London* (Chicago, 1948), p. 133; H. M. Colvin in *Mediaeval England*, I, 75. The plan of a somewhat smaller merchant's house of the period that came to be called "Brown's Place," discussed below, was published by C. L. Kingsford, *Archaeologia*, LXXIV (1923–1924), 149. It is reprinted in *Archaeologia*, LXXXIII (1933), 310; Colvin in *Medieval England*, I, 73; Edith Rickert, *Chaucer's World* (New York, 1948), opp. p. 5.

[5] *Thomas Arundel*, pp. 272–274.

[6] See Walter H. Godfrey, *A History of Architecture in and Around London* (London, 1962), Pl. 15a.

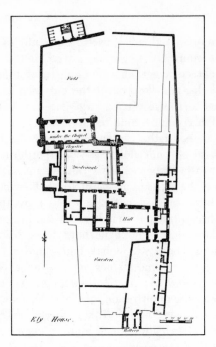

Plan of the Bishop of Ely's Inn.

London with forty or more horses in his train and a considerable retinue. The most lucrative post in his *familia* was held by one

View of the Bishop of Ely's Inn, early eighteenth century.

Walter Ash, the keeper of his wardrobe, who received £13 6s 8d a year for his services.[7] Altogether, the bishop might spend £1,000 annually on his household, much of which was devoted to entertaining. For example, during the later years of the century John of Gaunt, Duke of Lancaster, might be a guest at the inn. His own residence, the Savoy, located on the Strand toward the Thames between the inns of the Bishop of Worcester and the Bishop of Carlyle (off our map to the left toward Westminster), had been the most splendid house in the London area, if not in all England. It had been rebuilt by Duke Henry of Lancaster, the father of John's first wife, Blanche, whose virtues are memorialized in Chaucer's *Book of the Duchess*, at a cost of over £34,000. The magnificent buildings were surrounded by gardens and a waterside where the Duke kept his own barge. It was here that the captured King John spent most of his time in England after being brought to London by the Black Prince. His son, Duc de Berry, one of the most assiduous patrons of the arts during the later Middle Ages, was with him between 1360 and 1367.[8] The Savoy was not only a residence; it was also the administrative center of the Duchy of Lancaster.[9] The wardrobe was undoubtedly a prime source of trade for London merchants, and the administration brought many distinguished clerks and knights to London. When the Savoy was destroyed in 1381 by the rebels, it is likely that there were lost with it many fine tapestries, specimens of goldsmith's and jeweler's work, ivory carvings, and illuminated manuscripts, as well as splendid and historically important examples of fourteenth-century wall painting, stained glass, and architecture.

We can not know in detail what the interior of the bishop's inn was like. Perhaps a modern visitor would have been most forcibly impressed by the lack of furniture, especially chairs. Our ancestors seem to have spent most of their waking hours stand-

[7] *Thomas Arundel,* pp. 236–237, 234, 243.

[8] See C. L. Kingsford, "Historical Notes on Medieval London Houses," *London Topographical Record,* XII (1920), 16–20.

[9] T. F. Tout, *Chapters in Administrative History* (Manchester, 1923–1935), III, 195 ff.

ing rather than sitting. By far the most elaborate furnishings in the house were the beds. The bishop's bed and the beds provided for distinguished guests were equipped with testers, curtains, and drapes in bright colors ornamented with embroidered decorations. Earl Richard had left his son Thomas a set of drapes for a bed in embroidered green taffeta.[10] Such drapes appear frequently in the wills of the more wealthy men of the century and might be quite expensive. Robert de Vere, Duke of Ireland, had a set embroidered in gold valued at £68 13s 4d.[11] A good bed had deep feather mattresses and bolsters, white sheets, and blankets. Its occupants wore nightgowns and caps and could achieve a certain privacy by pulling the curtains. In the houses of ordinary citizens the beds were much simpler and there was no privacy. The bedchambers contained ambries, or standing closets, and chests for clothes and ordinary necessities, including, in more wealthy households, comb and brush sets in ivory or silver. The walls of the chamber were painted or whitewashed and decorated with hangings, either of tapestry work or of simpler embroidered material, the favorite colors being red, purple, orange, and green.[12] A few cushions might be arranged on the floor if the room were a large one.

A dais or raised platform for the main dining table stood at the end of the hall. Near the entry large water pitchers and washbowls were placed on stands so those about to dine might wash their hands. In most instances the dining table consisted of boards that could be set up on trestles and taken down after meals. Chaucer's Franklin, whose "portrait" is a caricature of Epicurean extravagance, had a "table dormant in his halle alway" that was "redy covered al the longe day," but the bishop would not have gone so far. When the table was set up, it was covered with a white cloth reaching to the floor and set out with silver spoons, knives, sauce dishes, and elaborate saltcellars. Small painted side tables held the food to be carved or otherwise apportioned for the guests. Wine was served in a large cup passed around the table from one guest to another. A large cupboard

10 *Thomas Arundel*, p. 379.
11 M. V. Clarke, *Fourteenth Century Studies* (Oxford, 1937), p. 117.
12 Cf. Thrupp, *Merchant Class*, p. 140.

near the table probably contained a selection of these cups, which were among the bishop's most prized possessions, elaborately fashioned of enameled silver or silver gilt. A favorite type of cup in more modest households at the time was made from the shell of a coconut, polished and set in a silver base. There is at least one reference to a similar cup made from the egg of an ostrich. At dinner the bishop sat in a chair placed in the center of the table facing the hall, and his guests occupied benches covered with decorative drapes. Servants and persons of lower rank ate at tables set up near the screen end of the hall. Behind the bishop, as he sat at table, the wall was decorated with a large pictorial tapestry. Along the sidewalls, which were painted in white, blue, and gold, hung gleaming lances, shields, and swords. The typical sword of the day had a blade broad at the upper end, a long straight decorated hilt, and a round pommel. It weighed only about three and a half pounds unsheathed and was delicately balanced. At night, the hall was illuminated with candles and oil lamps.

The bishop's kitchen had a large fireplace, with spits, grates, tripods, hooks, tongs, and an assortment of brass pots and copper pans. Mortars and pestles were used for grinding spices, much relished by our medieval ancestors, who enjoyed highly seasoned food. Axes and hatchets for cutting wood were near at hand, and there were scrubbed wooden tables for cutting meat and trimming vegetables. An important instrument was the fleshhook, used for removing meat from the large pots in which it was boiled. The spits were used mostly for fowl, which might range in size from small birds like thrushes to large swans. Nearby were wooden tubs for water. These served as bathtubs as well as for kitchen uses. The traditional American bath in the kitchen washtub on Saturdays has its fourteenth-century antecedents, although the bishop probably had his tub brought to his bedside and filled with hot water from the kitchen.

Holborn Street outside the gate of the bishop's inn was thronged with people moving to and from the city in the early morning, seemingly in holiday costume. The custom of dressing men in black or somber colors did not arise until the fifteenth century, when it suited the more serious air of the Renaissance. Merchants might wear gowns of red, scarlet, or violet, trimmed

A bath (copyright British Museum).

with grey furs, and many men wore short, tight-fitting coats with flaring sleeves and elaborately decorated girdles low on the hips. Toward the end of the century, long full gowns called "houppelandes" became fashionable for outdoor wear. Women's dresses fitted tight above the waist, although some wore long loose gowns. Both men and women enjoyed bright colors. Some men wore caps, and others beaver hats. Holborn Street would be busy with carts moving toward Newgate, and there might be an occasional drover urging his animals toward Smithfield Market.

Across Holborn Street stood Thaves Inn, and beyond it the Inn of the Bishop of Bangor. On the left toward the city was Scrope's Inn. But most of the houses in London were not so large and elaborate as these inns. Some, indeed, were only ten or eleven feet wide and seventeen feet deep.[13] Others might be as much as fifty feet wide.[14] A small shopkeeper had his shop proper opening on the street. His hall was either behind it or above it, with a kitchen, pantry, and butlery nearby. Sleeping quarters were located above the shop, or above the hall, sometimes with a room for a servant or apprentice in the garret. Customarily, the entire family slept in the same bedroom.[15] A small garden was usually available at the rear of the house, or, when shops were built in rows, a common garden might serve the needs of all the tenants. A carpenter's contract from the early part of the century calls for

[13] For example, see H. M. Chew, *London Possessory Assizes* (London, 1965), p. 64.
[14] A. H. Thomas, *Calendar of Plea and Memoranda Rolls of the City of London 1361–1381* (Cambridge, 1929), p. 79.
[15] Thrupp, *Merchant Class*, pp. 130 ff.

a hall and a room with a chimney, larder in between, a solar over
the room and larder, and an "oriole," or enclosed porch at the
end of the hall one step up from the ground. Two cellars were to
be under the hall and an enclosure for a sewer with two pipes
leading to it. An old kitchen and an old chamber were on the
site, but the carpenter agreed to erect a stable between the house
and the kitchen, with a solar above, and a garret above the solar.
He was also to build a new kitchen with a chimney and an
"oriole" or sheltered passage between the house and the old
chamber. The proposed tenant, a pelterer, was to pay the carpenter £9 5s 4d for completing the work "down to the locks"
and to give him, in addition, half a hundred marten skins for a
woman's hood and fur for a robe of his own.[16] This was a dwelling of moderate size.

Across from Scrope's Inn on the corner of Shoe Lane stood the
church of St. Andrew de Holborn, which was distinguished by
two university-trained rectors in the latter fourteenth century:
Lawrence Redford, a fellow of University College, in 1374 and
1375; and Robert de Elteslee, a bachelor of canon law from Cambridge, between 1394 and 1396. Sir Robert went on to become
rector of St. Bartholomews the Less on the northern side of
Threeneedle Street in 1398. From the slope of Holborn the
visitors could see the city wall and, rising above it, the magnificent spire of St. Paul's. From a little distance the city must have
looked somewhat like a grove of trees with glimpses of tile roof-
tops and clay chimney pots pierced by a veritable forest of
steeples. A hundred and ten parish churches stood within the city,
of which ninety-nine were within the walls. Across Holborn
Bridge the Inn of the Master of Sempringham lay on the left. Beyond it, up Cow Lane, lay the open ground of Smithfield Market,
crowded with livestock brought in from the country to be purchased by London butchers. On occasions when tournaments
were held there, the market and the roads leading to it were
festooned with colorful banners and draperies. Down Holborn
toward Newgate was the entrance to Cock Lane on the left. On
the right side of this lane was the Abbot of Leicester's Inn, and

16 H. T. Riley, *Memorials of London and London Life in the XIII, XIV, and
XV Centuries* (London, 1861). pp. 65–66.

across the lane stood a row of small houses where the prostitutes of the city were required to live. Most of the women were Flemings. Edward III had invited Flemish weavers to London with the hope that their superior techniques would be helpful to English weavers. But the English hardly accepted their foreign competitors with open arms, and the Flemings became the easy victims of hostile propaganda. It is possible that discrimination was in part responsible for the fact that many of the ladies of Cock Lane and of the Stews across the river in Southwark were Flemish. The girls were not universally unpitied. One Katherine Estmare, who may have been of Flemish origin, left in her will (1351) "to every poor Flemish woman sixpence."[17]

Shops and taverns crowded the sides of Holborn Street on the approach to Newgate, and the unpleasant odor of the Shambles, a short distance within, began to permeate the air. Southward along the wall were two small towers or "tourelles." The second one formed a part of the Inn of Marie de St. Pol, Countess of Pembroke, who founded Pembroke College, Cambridge. At her death in 1377 the tourelle reverted to the city.[18] Various towers and gatehouses were leased by the city as residences. For example, in 1305 a tourelle near Bishopsgate "together with its appurtenances" was leased to Nicholas de Cockfeld, with the proviso that he keep it in good repair.[19] The "appurtenances" probably included outbuildings and, perhaps, a garden. At the request of the Black Prince, Cripplegate was granted in 1307 to Thomas de Kent on condition that he "behave himself" and keep the roof repaired.[20] It was rented again in 1375 to John Watlyngton, sergeant and common crier of the city.[21] He also obtained a garden in Tower Ward for 2s a year. A tourelle south of Aldgate was rented to one Walter Parmenter and his wife Johanna for 2s in 1353.[22] In 1374 Geoffrey Chaucer, Squire, was granted "the

[17] R. R. Sharpe, *Calendar of Wills Proved and Enrolled in the Court of Husting, London* (London, 1889), I, 642.

[18] Thomas, *Calendar of Plea and Memoranda Rolls*, p. 242.

[19] Riley, *Memorials*, p. 56.

[20] *Ibid.*, p. 59.

[21] R. R. Sharpe, *Calendar of Letter-Books Preserved among the Archives of the City of London* (London, 1899 ff.), *Letter-Book H*, p. 2.

[22] *Letter-Book G*, p. 24.

dwelling-house above the gate of Aldgate, with the rooms built over, and a cellar beneath" together with the "appurtenances."[23] The porter of the gate in 1375 was William Duerhirst, who must have been one of Chaucer's daily acquaintances. In 1375 Aldersgate was granted to Ralph Strode, the Common Pleader of the city, who was a friend of Chaucer's and an internationally famous logician.[24] But the buildings around Newgate and Ludgate were used as prisons. After 1383 prisoners for debt, trespass, account, and contempt were sent to Ludgate; and prisoners for felony and maiming were lodged in Newgate.[25]

Outside Newgate and around the whole length of the wall except where it bordered on the Fleet was a ditch twenty feet wide that had been completed in 1213. Periodic cleaning became a public necessity, although we should probably assume that medieval men were more sensitive to foul smells, which they associated with pestilence, than most city dwellers are today. In 1354 the ditch was cleaned to prevent overflow at the moat around the Tower. John Philpot had it cleaned again in 1379, assessing every household 5d, or the equivalent of a day's work, for the task. It was cleaned once more by Richard II in 1386.[26]

Inside the massive ironbound wooden gates at Newgate a broad market street merged into West Cheap. As was the custom in most medieval cities, London tradesmen tended to congregate in separate localities, but the great markets of Newgate, Cheap, the Stocks, Leaden Hall, and Gracechurch attracted a variety of tradesmen. The Ward of Cheap contained, in 1319, mercers, pepperers, fishmongers, cheesemongers, bakers, poulterers, and cordwainers.[27] But the market before Newgate was dominated by the Shambles, a long row of butcher's stalls extending toward Cheap. Between the gate and the Shambles the "foreign" or noncitizen

[23] Riley, *Memorials,* pp. 377–378; Martin M. Crow and Clair C. Olson, *Chaucer Life-Records* (Oxford, 1966), pp. 144–145.

[24] Riley, *Memorials,* p. 388. An ordinance was issued in 1386, *ibid.,* p. 489, that city gates should no longer be granted for private use. However, Richard Forster obtained Aldgate, vacated by Chaucer in that year. See *Letter-Book H,* p. 290.

[25] *Letter-Book H,* p. 213.

[26] J. Stow, *A Survey of London,* ed. C. L. Kingsford (London, 1908), I, 19.

[27] Hermione Hobhouse, *The Ward of Cheap* (London, 1964), p. 50. The candlemakers were forced to move out of Cheap Market in 1283.

cheesemongers sold their wares.[28] Between the Shambles and
Greyfriars stood the cornmongers from the west,[29] and near them
were some stalls occupied by blacksmiths.[30] Across the marketplace beyond the Earl of Warwick's Inn near the Church of St.
Audoen on the corner of Old Dean's Lane the foreign drapers
had a market after 1387.[31] The Shambles themselves presented a
perennial problem to the city. Originally animals were slaughtered there, and the entrails and waste were carried away in
carts to be disposed of in the Fleet. However, this practice
created a kind of stinking highway built up of drippings from
the carts, which offended the sensibilities of prominent residents,
including Marie of St. Pol. A series of royal proclamations and ad-
monitions between 1369 and 1381 demanding that animals be
slaughtered outside the city, preferably at Stratford or Knights-
bridge, indicates that the butchers were reluctant to inconvenience themselves in this matter.[32] Finally, a latrine was removed
from the bank of the Thames and a house built for butchers to
use as a slaughterhouse. The refuse was to be taken to the middle
of the river at ebbtide so as to avoid harming the fish. These
arrangements were made in 1393. Along the south side of the
Shambles stood a row of poulterer's stalls.

North of Newgate Market stood the Convent of the Grey
Friars, or Franciscans, who had not yet assumed brown habits. In
Chaucer's day it embodied a great hall church three hundred feet
long, ninety-nine feet wide, and sixty-four feet high.[33] Of the nine
Franciscans who landed at Dover in 1224, four went to London
as guests of the Dominicans, where they remained for fifteen
days. Then they hired a house in Cornhill which they divided

[28] Riley, *Memorials*, pp. 405–407.

[29] *Letter-Book H*, p. 133.

[30] Riley, *Memorials*, p. 361.

[31] *Letter-Book H*, p. 301.

[32] *Letter-Book G*, p. 43; *Letter-Book H*, p. 372; Riley, *Memorials*, pp. 339–
340, 356–358, etc.

[33] Descriptions appear in Stow, *Survey*, I, 317 ff., and C. L. Kingsford, *The
Grey Friars of London* (Aberdeen, 1915), and W. Page, *The Victoria History
of London*, I, 502 ff. For a ground plan, see Geoffrey Webb, *Architecture
in Britain: The Middle Ages* (Baltimore, 1956), p. 171.

into small cells. After a few months, a London mercer, John Iwyn, gave them some land and houses in Newgate bordering on Stinking Lane (Pentecost Lane in the later fourteenth century), where the unworldly friars would suffer the odor of the Shambles gladly. By 1243 there were some eighty friars whose good behavior had endeared them to the citizens. The brethren received considerable support from the nobility, and in 1306 the foundation stone for the new church was laid in the name of Queen Margaret. The building, which had marble columns and a marble floor, was completed in 1327. Work on the cloisters was proceeding in 1345 and was continued throughout the century. Choir stalls for the church were donated by Margaret Segrave, countess of Norfolk, in 1380. The friars continued to prosper, although a hundred of them are said to have died of the plague in 1369. Perhaps the most famous London Franciscan of the second part of the century was Roger Conway, who was especially successful as a spiritual adviser to the nobility. Queen Margaret, Queen Isobel, Joan, Queen of Scots, Isabel, daughter of Edward III, Roger Mortimer, and the unfortunate Chief Justice Tresilian were among those buried in the church. Before the church was a fountain, and behind it toward the wall was a large orchard.

Down Ivy Lane, on the east side of which was located the Inn of Robert de Holand (Lovell's Inn), rose an even more impressive building, St. Paul's Cathedral. It was five hundred and eighty-five feet long and one hundred feet wide, with a transept spreading to a width of two hundred and ninety feet. Its stone tower was two hundred and forty-five feet high and was tipped by a spire stretching another two hundred and four feet upward, taller than the great spire that was to rise at Coventry. Inside, the ridge of the choir vault was ninety-three feet from the pavement below. The building was located on a site once occupied by a Saxon cathedral, destroyed by fire in 1087. Progress on the new building, designed in imitation of Winchester, was slow. The choir was completed in 1148. Clerestories for the nave in the new Gothic style were begun in 1200. The tower and spire were finished in 1221, and in 1256 the remodeling of the east end was undertaken. The new choir was built over the largest crypt in England, part of which was used for the Church of St. Faith. A

new spire was erected in 1345.[34] When we think of medieval
structures of this kind, we should seek to forget the general impression left by the dark and rather forbidding buildings still
visible today. In the Middle Ages, the cathedrals gave the impression of being "white," and the decorative stonework and
statuary, both on the exterior and interior, were painted in bright
colors. Chaucer's contemporaries liked color in their clothing, in
the drapes and furnishings of their houses, and in the buildings
they erected. The complex of Newgate and Cheap, which formed
a great plaza, with Greyfriars on one side and St. Paul's on the
other, and the rows of churches and other buildings extending
eastward down toward the Stocks Market, must have been, on a
busy sunny day, spectacular in a way that is difficult for us to
imagine.

The busy life of Cheap and Newgate spilled over into the nave
of St. Paul's, which, like the naves of other English churches, was
thought of as "belonging to the people" and was used by them
fully on weekdays. At the west end sat twelve scribes, ready to
prepare documents for merchants, tradesmen, and officials. In the
afternoons sergeants of the law stood, like the worldly wise law-
man in Chaucer's *Canterbury Tales,* "at the Parvys" or in the
aisles of the nave, seeking clients and discussing matters of current moment with clerks from Farringdon and inquisitive merchants. At one pillar a group of servingmen stood seeking
employment. Bargains were sealed, papers drawn up, and transactions of all kinds undertaken and concluded under the great
vaults. It is possible that some tradesmen set up stalls within the
cathedral, for in 1385 Bishop Braybrook condemned the practice
of marketing within the church. There is nothing especially
shocking about all this. Actually, the situation persists in a somewhat more artificial form today, when the cathedrals are crowded
with tourists, and it is often possible to purchase mementos at
stalls in the naves. In the fourteenth century, when "religious"
and "secular" affairs were not carefully separated and assigned
their own peculiar solemnities, it was not shocking at all, although it may have incovenienced the clergy.

[34] For a history and description of old St. Paul's, see G. H. Cook, *Old St.
Paul's Cathedral* (London, 1955).

Exterior of Old St. Paul's. The steeple is somewhat shortened.

The cloister, some ninety-five feet square, with a chapter house in the center, was begun in 1332 by William de Ramseye, a citi-

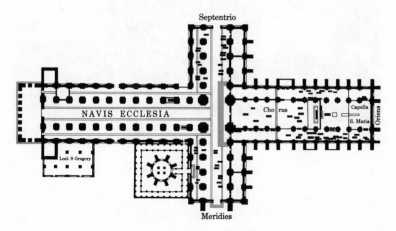

Plan of Old St. Paul's.

Interior view of Old St. Paul's.

zen of the Ward of Aldersgate, who has been called "one of the most significant architectural innovators of all time."[35] Ramseye

[35] John Harvey, *Gothic England* (London, 1948), p. 50.

was active in the completion of St. Stephen's Chapel, Westminster, one of the finest buildings in England, designed to rival the Ste. Chapelle in Paris. He also worked on the Tower, at Windsor, and elsewhere in England. His peculiar contribution was a modification of the decorated style in the direction of the perpendicular style, which began to flourish under his successor, Henry Yevele.

There were other buildings in the churchyard: the Chancellor's Inn in the southeast corner, the Old Palace south of the nave, the Deanery in the southwest corner, and the house of the minor canons on the north. The Church of St. Gregory, whose rector between 1392 and 1395 was an Oxford man, William de Gaynesburgh, stood against the southwest corner of the nave. A belfry and Paul's Cross stood in the churchyard proper on the northeast, and the whole was surrounded by a wall. About midway on the north side a gate led to the "Si quis" door on the north aisle of the nave, where notices were posted by clerks seeking benefices. A "Little Gate" led into the churchyard at the northeast corner from Cheap, and there were "Great Gates" on the south and west. Paul's Cross contained an elevated pulpit from which some of the most celebrated sermons of Chaucer's time were delivered, and the belfry contained, after 1344, one of King Edward's favorite new devices, a clock.[36]

If we were fourteenth-century visitors to the cathedral, we should probably wish to see the shrine of St. Erkenwald behind the high altar, erected in 1326. It gave the cathedral the status of

[36] Until the late seventies city ordinances usually refer to the time of day in accordance with the traditional medieval time scheme familiar in the works of Chaucer. That is, the day is divided into twelve hours from sunrise to sunset: *matins* or *lauds* usually indicates sunrise, *prime* is one sixth of the time between sunrise and midday, *tierce* is one half of the time between sunrise and midday, *sext* is midday, *nones* is one half of the time between midday and sunset, and *vespers* occurs at sunset. Curfew in London was usually set at sunset, or shortly thereafter. Under this system the daylight hours are short in winter and long in summer. Clocks began to be produced commercially in the early years of the century. See R. Allen Brown, "King Edward's Clocks," *Antiquaries Journal*, XXXIX (1959), 283–286. One of these, installed in the tower at Westminster, had a bell weighing 9,261 pounds. A mercer, Henry Deynes, bequeathed a clock to St. Pancras in 1368. See *Cal. Wills*, II, 112.

a pilgrimage church and might produce for it a substantial annual income. Outside, for the sake of London, we might wish to
say a prayer at the grave of the parents of St. Thomas Becket,
London's most distinguished citizen, which was visited cere-
moniously each year by the mayor, aldermen, sheriffs, and leading citizens. If our visit took place after 1398, we should also be
interested in the panel painting of St. Paul by Herebrecht of
Cologne south of the altar. If we were modern visitors, the funerary monuments inside might attract us, especially the tomb of
John of Gaunt and Blanche of Lancaster, Chaucer's "goode faire
White," between pillars just north of the altar. This monument
was designed and built by Henry Yevele, the most distinguished
mason of the later part of the century. Blanche died on September 12, 1369, a little less than a month after the death of Queen
Philippa. When her husband, who had been campaigning on the
Continent, returned to England, he ordered an alabaster tomb to
be erected in St. Paul's for Blanche and for himself, engaged two
chantry priests to sing there throughout the year, and arranged
for an annual memorial service to be held there on September
12.[37] It may have been at the service held in 1374, when the Duke
was able to attend for the first time, that Chaucer's poem, *The
Book of the Duchess* was "published," or read before an audience.
Although John of Gaunt formed an alliance of convenience with
Katherine Swynford, who had been caring for his children, and
married Constance of Castile, he was assiduous in his devotion to
Blanche. On his return from Scotland in 1381, he was grievously
insulted by Northumberland, and no doubt deeply disturbed by
the destruction of the Savoy. However, he was reconciled to
Northumberland, who had made a public apology, and, on
November 11, made his peace with the city. As the author of the
Anonimalle Chronicle tells it, he rode "to the City of London to
the cathedral Church of St. Paul with a great throng of people to
hear Mass and to make an offering for the former Duchess; and

[37] See S. Armitage-Smith, *John of Gaunt* (New York, 1964), pp. 75–78;
N. B. Lewis, "The Anniversary Service for Blanche, Duchess of Lancaster,
12 Sept., 1374," *Bulletin of the John Rylands Library*, XXI (1937), 176–192;
D. W. Robertson, Jr., "The Historical Setting of Chaucer's *Book of the
Duchess*," in *Mediaeval Studies in Honor of Urban Tigner Holmes, Jr.*,
(Chapel Hill, 1965), pp. 169–195.

the Mayor and Aldermen, with a great number of the City well mounted, met him and led him to the Church to make their devotion in honor of the lady aforesaid."[38] We can, unfortunately, no longer make our devotions before the monument of Blanche, who must have been a beautiful and gracious young woman and a genuine inspiration to English chivalry. But we can read Chaucer's poem.

Outside the south gate Carter Lane ran along the wall of the cathedral. It was lined with carts laden with fruit and vegetables from the gardens of the city's larger inns. A cart of Adam Vynour's produce may well have been there. Housewives and servants bargained there for figs, apples, pears, garlic, leeks, onions, cabbage, and herbs. Across from the gate St. Benet's Lane ran downhill past the bakehouse and brewhouse of the cathedral on the corner at the left, and the Church of St. Benet to the right on Thames Street, and thence between the riverside inns of Sir Simon Burley and Sir John Beauchamp to Paul's Wharf.

Westward on Carter Lane was the Inn of the Abbot of Peterborough, and beyond it the manor of the King's Great Wardrobe, located permanently on this site in 1361.[39] The wardrobe contained storehouses, workshops, and a dwelling suitable for royal visits to the city. In the workshops tailors prepared robes and other garments for distribution to members of the royal household, and, in general, goods such as drapes, cloths, furs, and other nonperishables were finished for royal use. The establishment of the wardrobe at this location was of enormous benefit to London dealers in durable goods and contributed to the growth of the city generally. Between 1390 and 1398 the Keeper of the Wardrobe was Richard Clifford, who may have been the son of Chaucer's friend Sir Lewis Clifford.[40] Richard was Keeper of the Privy Seal between 1379 and 1401, a canon of St. Paul's in 1397 and 1398, Bishop of Worcester between 1401 and 1407, and, from 1407 until his death in 1421, Bishop of London. Beyond the ward-

[38] Ed. V. H. Galbraith (Manchester, 1927), p. 156.
[39] Tout, *Chapters*, III, 179. On the economic impact of this establishment, cf. Elspeth M. Veale, *The English Fur Trade in the Later Middle Ages* (Oxford, 1966), pp. 52 ff.
[40] A. B. Emden, *A Biographical Register of the University of Oxford to A. D. 1500* (Oxford, 1957–1959), I, 440–441.

robe between Bowyers Row and the Inn of the Prior of Okeborne on the riverfront was the Convent of the Black or Preaching Friars (Dominicans).

When the Dominicans first came to England in 1221, they established a convent at Oxford. Within a few years Hubert de Burgh, Earl of Kent, gave them some land on the eastern side of Shoe Lane at the corner of Holborn Street for a London convent. By 1250 the friars had acquired sufficient land and erected adequate buildings to hold a general chapter of four hundred members there. In 1263, they housed seven hundred at a chapter meeting. But in 1276 Archbishop Robert Kilwardby, who had been a Dominican Provincial, obtained a site for the friars in the area of Montfichet's Tower, which, together with Castle Baynard, once formed a part of the western defenses of the city. Castle Baynard, erected by William the Conqueror, was destroyed by King John in 1212, when it was held by the rebel Robert Fitz-Walter.[41] A "second" Castle Baynard was later built on the riverfront to the east. Montfichet's Tower was dismantled by the Dominicans, who used it, in addition to some material from the end of London Wall, which originally extended straight down to the Thames from Ludgate, to build their new convent. The church was two hundred and twenty feet long and sixty-six feet wide. It became the final resting place of the heart of Queen Eleanor in 1290. There were two cloisters and a number of adjacent buildings.[42] Blackfriars frequently enjoyed close connections with the royal court and during the fourteenth century regularly supplied members of the royal family with confessors. The grounds constituted a sanctuary, and there was sufficient room to provide a convenient meeting place to discuss matters of current moment. For example, we read of the mayor and aldermen assembling there with members of the King's Council to discuss a rather delicate case involving the Prior of Christchurch and a horse.[43]

---

[41] See H. M. Colvin, ed., *The History of the King's Works* (London, 1963), I, 21.

[42] For a detailed early history of Blackfriars with maps and diagrams, see W. A. Hinnebusch, O. P., *The Early English Friars Preachers* (Rome, 1951), pp. 20–55.

[43] *Letter-Book H*, pp. 301–302.

Across the marketplace from St. Paul's, east of Greyfriars, was the College of St. Martin le Grand, said to have been founded in 700 by Wightred, King of Kent.[44] It was, in any event, a preconquest foundation that developed into a royal free chapel whose Dean and canons were usually clerks in royal service. Like Blackfriars, it was a sanctuary. The buildings fell into a state of decay in the mid-fourteenth century, and the canons thought seriously of abandoning them. But when William of Wykeham became Dean in 1360, he decided to rebuild the college with his own funds, restoring the church and cloister and adding a new chapter house.[45] The result won the unstinting admiration of his contemporaries, but we shall have to imagine as best we can a group of bright new buildings in the decorated manner on either side of St. Martin's Lane as it ran northward toward the Earl of Northumberland's Inn and Aldersgate. At the time of our visit, the Earl's inn belonged to Henry Percy, who held there an inn, twelve shops and solars, and a garden.[46]

In the midst of Cheap near the intersection of Paternoster Row, a wide thoroughfare probably named for the cluster of paternosterer's shops on its northern side, stood the Church of St. Michael le Quern. Pedestrians going to and from the Little Gate of St. Paul's customarily walked through the church. In 1378 the rector, who regarded this traffic as a nuisance, walled up the door. But the mayor and aldermen thought the ancient custom justified and ordered the passage restored.[47] Near the east end of this church stood an old cross, but it was removed in 1390 when St. Michael's was enlarged.[48]

St. Paul's was located near the summit of London's smaller hill. Looking down toward the Stocks, we should be able to see a throng of gaily dressed people, some on foot and others on horseback or driving carts and wagons. An occasional small dog would run to escape the horses and wheels.[49] On the left at the

---

[44] Dugdale, *Monasticon Anglicanum* (London, 1830), VIII, 1323.

[45] *Victoria History,* I, 555 ff.

[46] See Kingsford, "Historical Notes," *LTR,* XI, 57.

[47] Riley, *Memorials,* pp. 417–418

[48] Stow, *Survey,* I, 267–268.

[49] The Mayor issued a proclamation in 1387 against allowing any dogs except "chiens gentilz" to run free in the city. See *Letter-Book H,* p. 311.

entrance of Wood Street was the Church of St. Peter, and near it, in the middle of the plaza, stood London's Eleanor Cross, one of the monuments erected by King Edward I to mark places where the body of Eleanor of Castile rested on its journey from Lincoln to Westminster. Stow says that it was "like to those others which remain to this day," a statement that is not of much assistance to us,[50] although architectural historians inform us that some of the earliest examples of ogee arches in England appeared on these crosses. It has been suggested that the architectural decoration on the head of William of Wykeham's crozier at New College, Oxford, may embody an imitation of the Cross in Cheap.[51] In any event, it was a small, highly decorated stone tower containing sculptured scenes from the life of Christ set upon some stone steps. Stow does give us some account of its later history. It was "re-edified" in 1441 and occasionally new gilt. On June 21, 1581, some enterprising iconoclasts destroyed the lower figures on the cross and tore the Child from the arms of the stone image of Mary. In 1596 the steps were removed on one side, a "curious wrought tabernacle of grey marble" erected, and "in the same an Alabaster Image of *Diana,* and water conveyed from the Thames, prilling from her naked breast." In December, 1600, the Virgin was again attacked, stabbed in the breast, and otherwise abused.[52] Diana, evidently, remained chaste and unmolested. When Chaucer was living, the Cross was probably not only "new gilt" in appropriate places, but painted, and the Virgin left in rosy-cheeked tranquillity with her small Child, smiling vaguely at those who passed by, who, in turn, might pause occasionally to finger their paternosters with bowed heads, not in reverence for the stone image, but in memory of Queen Eleanor and veneration for the principle of justice tempered with mercy to the penitent.

The wealthy undoubtedly kept hunting dogs, but they were too valuable to be allowed to roam.

[50] Stow, *Survey,* I, 266. For an illustration of Gedding Cross, see Webb, *Architecture in Britain,* Pl. 118A. The crosses were not exactly alike.

[51] Illustrated in R. S. Loomis, *A Mirror of Chaucer's World* (Princeton, 1965), Fig. 37.

[52] *Survey,* I, 266–267.

On the south side of Cheap below Friday Street, where foreign tanners sold their leather, were the shops of the goldsmiths, in one of which Wykeham's crozier was probably fashioned. The craft maintained a hall across from the College of St. Martin le Grand below the large Church of St. John Zachary. A little farther down Cheap beyond Bread Street was a pump called the Standard, one terminus for the city water supply piped in during the thirteenth century from Tyburn.[53] Oddly, the source of this supply was near a gallows set up not far from the area now occupied by Marble Arch, and the Standard was a favorite place of execution within the city. In 1326 Walter Stapleton, Bishop of Exeter, was executed there, two fishmongers were beheaded there in 1351, and the redoubtable Wat Tyler beheaded Richard Lyons and others there in 1381. Another outlet for Tyburn water was the much more elaborate "Conduit" in the section of Cheap known as the Mercery near the Hospital of St. Thomas of Acon. This was an ironbound lead cistern in a building that contained various outlets for the convenience of the thirsty. Generally, London residents in Chaucer's day relied on water carriers, who regularly distributed sweet water to various parts of the city.

Below the Standard on the left was the Church of All Hallows Honey Lane, so designated for a small lane that curved beside and behind the churchyard. It is probable that the area behind this church stretching up toward Catte Street and the Guildhall was, in Chaucer's time, fairly open. Beyond All Hallows on the south of Cheap was one of London's most famous churches, St. Mary le Bow, on the site of which the ruin of Wren's substitute, severely damaged in 1941, still stands to attract the curious. Up against the north wall Edward III had built a stone shed to replace wooden scaffolds that collapsed there in September 1331. He and his entourage sat there to watch tournaments in Cheap. Standard lists were sixty paces long and forty paces wide with barriers seven feet high,[54] but narrower lists would have served for jousts in Cheap or on London Bridge. During the days of a tournament we can well imagine the whole length of Cheap

---

[53] See N. J. Barton, *The Lost Rivers of London* (London, 1962), pp. 69–70.
[54] Benjamin Williams, *Chronicque de la traison et mort de Richart Deux Roy Dengleterre* (London, 1846), p. 152, note.

richly decorated with bright drapes, banners, and, in proper season, flowers, and crowded with ladies and gentlemen and their
horses, suitably bedecked for the occasion. The wealthier would
wear furs trimmed with miniver and gris,[55] the best grades of
which came from squirrels caught in winter in the forests of
Russia, Poland, and the Baltic area. The skins were imported by
the Hanseatic merchants at the Steelyard. Others might wear
budge, black or white lambswool from North Africa or Spain.
The saddles of the horses would be newly painted with elaborate
designs, and the metalwork of their equipage would be highly
polished. But to leave the jousts and return to the church, St.
Mary le Bow was built over a great arched crypt, a stone from
which is now in Trinity Church, New York. The parish, like a
number of other parishes in the city, was a peculiar of Canterbury, subject to the jurisdiction of the Archbishop rather than the
Bishop of London.[56] The crypt contained a school and was also
the site of the Court of the Arches, one of the most important
ecclesiastical courts in England. Prominent young graduates in
canon law and more mature canonists of distinction acted as ad-
vocates there. For example, Henry Chichele was an advocate of
the court and Rector of St. Stephens, Walbrook, in 1396-1397. He
had two wealthy uncles, grocers of London, who undoubtedly
made his visit to the city more pleasant. Chichele eventually became Archbishop of Canterbury.[57]

On the west side of Lawrence Lane, which ran north toward
Guildhall, was Blossom Inn, described by Stow as a large hostelry

---

[55] Miniver was made from white bellies that might be either pure white or
white surrounded by gray. Gris was made from back skins of winter squirrels. For further information on these and other furs, see Veale, *The English
Fur Trade.*

[56] The following parishes were peculiars of Canterbury: Allhallows Bread
Street, Allhallows Lombard Street, St. Dionis de Backchurch, St. Dunstan
in the East, St. John the Evangelist (Watling Street), St. Leonard East-
cheap, St. Mary Aldermary, St. Mary le Bow, St. Mary Bothaw, St. Michael
Crookedlane, St. Michael de Paternosterchurch in the Ryole, St. Pancras
Soper Lane, St. Vedast Fosterlane. Other parishes were administered by
the Dean and Chapter of St. Paul's: St. Giles Cripplegate, St. Gregory
by St. Paul's, St. Helen's Bishopsgate. See Richard Newcourt, *Repertorium
ecclesiasticum parochiale Londinense* (London, 1708–1710), I, 57.

[57] Emden, *Biographical Register of Oxford,* I, 410–411.

for the convenience of travelers.[58] There were probably a number
of taverns nearby, since food and drink were not customarily
served at inns. The taverns here and elsewhere were marked by
long alestakes projecting from their facades. Evidently some
tavern keepers felt that longer stakes attracted more customers,
for a regulation was passed in 1375 limiting their length to seven
feet. Longer stakes were obstructing roadways and damaging
buildings.[59] The best ale served in the taverns was slightly sweet,
with a bouquet of ripe grain, for our medieval ancestors were not
fond of bitter food and drink. The average citizen who did not
regularly drink wine normally consumed a gallon of ale during
the course of the day. On our summer day, each private home
along the lane and elsewhere had a large vat of water standing
before it and nearby a ladder and some long crooks.[60] These were
precautions against fire in the dry season. If our visit were very
early, we might see the sweepers collecting the refuse placed in
kennels to be carried away in carts. Throwing waste water or
other refuse from windows was strictly forbidden, and efforts
were made to prevent residents from disposing of refuse in the
Fleet or in the Thames.

The problem of water pollution was recognized as a national
issue and became the subject of a statute in 1388:

For that so much dung and filth of the garbage and intrails as well
as of beasts killed, as of other corruption, be cast and put in ditches,
rivers, and other waters, and also in many other places, within, about,
and nigh unto divers cities, boroughs, and towns of the realm, and
the suburbs of them, that the air there is greatly corrupt and infect,
and many maladies and other intolerable diseases do daily happen . . .
it is accorded and consented that proclamation be made as well in
the city of London as in other cities, boroughs, and towns through the
realm of England . . . that all they which do cast and lay all such
annoyances . . . in ditches, waters, and other places aforesaid, shall
cause them utterly to be removed and carried away before this and
the Feast of St. Michael next ensuing . . . every one upon pain to lose
and to forfeit to our lord the King £20.

[58] *Survey,* I, 270–271.
[59] Riley, *Memorials,* p. 386.
[60] For example, see the regulation of 1375, *Plea and Memoranda Rolls,*
p. 199.

Offenders were to be called before the Chancellor.[61] Sanitary conditions in the city may have been temporarily ameliorated, but in the long run they deteriorated until the later eighteenth century.[62]

At the top of Lawrence Lane across Catte Street was the Church of St. Lawrence in the Old Jewry, described by Stow as being "fayre and large." It supported two fraternities: a Fraternity of the Holy Cross and a Fraternity of Our Lord Jesus Christ, His Blessed Mother, and St. Anne.[63] Almost everyone in London belonged to one or more fraternities. Beyond the church was the Guildhall, and to the east of it was Bakewell Hall. Guildhall, which was the center of the city administration, was rebuilt in 1411, so that we do not know anything about its appearance in Chaucer's time. However, we can imagine it as a set of buildings around a courtyard, including a chapel, much visited by merchants both local and foreign as well as by local and royal officials. Somewhere in the grounds was a cloth market, for a regulation stipulated that cloth made outside the city had to be sold either at the Guildhall or the Stocks Market.[64] Bakewell Hall was a large building erected before 1275 on the site of some houses formerly occupied by Jews. It belonged for a time to Sir Roger Clifford, who, in 1280, granted it to Sir John de Banquell (1293). Before 1395 it belonged to Robert de Bakewell, Rector of Allhallows, Bread Street, but in 1396 it became a market for woolen cloth. The site was later occupied by Gresham College, founded in 1579. Across Catte Street beyond Ironmonger Lane the Black Prince had his wardrobe, which served as a town house as well as a storehouse and workshop for goods to be used by his retinue.[65]

To return to Cheap, the area east of Ironmonger Lane was the

[61] *Statutes at Large*, I, 382; *Statutes of the Realm*, II, 59. For London specifically, see Riley, *Memorials*, pp. 67–68, 295–296, 298–299, 389; *Letter-Book G*, p. 300, etc. There were a number of local regulations in the seventies.

[62] It is probable that the poorer areas were even worse in the nineteenth century. See Barton, *Lost Rivers*, pp. 109 ff. In fourteenth-century London there were no "slums" in the modern sense.

[63] *Survey*, I, 275.

[64] *Letter-Book H*, p. 145.

[65] Cf. Tout, *Chapters*, III, 195 ff., V, 353.

Mercery, one of the wealthier sections of the city. On the south side of the street was the Great Seld, a covered market where many merchants had stalls. Near the Conduit, Bucklersbury curved down to the southeast. The air was redolent with spices, for Bucklersbury was a favorite haunt of grocers and apothecaries. On the north side of Bucklersbury there was a stone tower called Sernet's Tower or Servat's Tower. It belonged to Queen Philippa in 1338, and was later used as an exchange by Edward III. In 1358 he gave it to the Dean and canons of St. Stephen's, Westminster, and it came to be used as the meeting place of the grocers,[66] who had shops also in Sopers Lane. Between Sopers Lane and the Conduit a number of cordwainers had shops, although most of them were located on Cordwainer Street, running south between St. Mary le Bow and the Vintry.

Across Cheap in the Mercery stood one of the most celebrated religious institutions in London, the Hospital of St. Thomas of Acon (Thomas Becket). It stood on ground once owned by Gilbert Becket, and was established as the house of the Military Order of St. Thomas, Martyr, by Thomas Fitz Theobald de Helles and his wife Agnes, who was the sister of the Archbishop. In 1327 custody of the house was given to the Mayor and Commonality of London. It was rebuilt, beginning in 1383, with a large and impressive church consisting of a nave, choir, side aisles, and several chapels. Again, we shall be forced to imagine its appearance, probably in the early perpendicular style familiar in Yevele's nave at Canterbury Cathedral. In the latter fourteenth century the masters of the hospital were Thomas de Sallowe (1365), Richard Sewell (1371), and Richard Alred (1394).[67] Like the grave of Gilbert Becket and his wife at St. Paul's the hospital received frequent formal visits from the mayor, the aldermen, sheriffs, and great men of the city.

The Mercery became the Poultry east of the Old Jewry. We should imagine ourselves still in a wide street or plaza descending toward Walbrook and the Stocks Market, but now the air, full of the odor of spices and herbs near Bucklersbury, begins to smell a little like that near the Shambles once more, perhaps with

---

[66] Stow, *Survey*, I, 259–260; Kingsford, "Historical Notes," *LTR*, XII, 26–27.
[67] Stow, *Survey*, I, 269; Page, *Victoria History*, I, 491 ff.

an added whiff of fish wafting up from the Stocks. The dignified goldsmiths, mercers, and officials are now replaced by poulterers and their customers. "Poultry" during the later fourteenth century included suckling pigs and rabbits,[68] as well as swans, geese, ducks, and chickens. Game birds like woodcock, partridge, and pheasant were available, not to mention curlews, thrushes, herons, bitterns, egrets, pigeons, and other birds, although blackbirds did not become fashionable fare until the sixteenth century. Chaucer's monk, we remember, loved best a "fat swan," one of the most costly of all dishes in the fourteenth century, and the abstemious friar of the "Summoner's Tale" wanted the liver of a capon. Ordinary folk could find much less costly fare in the poultry markets, which extended across the Stocks Market and up Cornhill as far as the Tun. The Chapel of St. Mary Coneyhope stood on the north side of Poultry, and beyond it the rather wealthy Church of St. Mildred, which in 1366 produced for its rector, Robert de Chardelow, an income of twenty-five marks.[69]

At the foot of Poultry was a short section known as the Peltry, where Walbrook ran under Cheap, and from it, stretching down toward the Thames, ran Walbrook Street, the traditional home of the skinners of London, who settled there because of the convenience of the stream. They were restricted to Walbrook Street, Budge Row, and Cornhill by regulation in 1365.[70] The furrier's trade is an odorous one, and Chaucer, who was probably born in a house at the intersection of Walbrook and Thames Street and certainly spent his childhood there, was undoubtedly familiar both with smell and the work of the skinners. A visitor descending Walbrook Street would pass the Church of St. Stephen Walbrook on the right, whose chancel was washed by the stream. The rector here between 1391 and 1395 was John Brown de Hadlee, a lawyer trained at Cambridge who once served under Bishop Braybrook. Our visitor might pause and watch a skinner

---

[68] Rabbits spread northward from Spain during the early thirteenth century and were not cultivated in England until the middle of the century. They were still something of a delicacy in Chaucer's time. See Veale, *Fur Trade*, Appendix B.

[69] See R. C. Fowler and C. Jenkins, *Registrum Simonis de Sudbiria*, II, Canterbury and York Society, XXXVIII (1938), 162.

[70] Riley, *Memorials*, pp. 328–330.

at work in his shop. One feature of medieval life that is lost today was the ability of anyone to see exactly what anyone else
was doing. The tools of the skinner's trade were few: tables,
stools, tubs, shears, knives, thread and material for processing.
Probably near the rear of our skinner's shop an apprentice was
at work in the first step of tawing a pile of recently purchased
skins. Knife in hand, he scraped away the dry fat remaining on
the inside of a skin and threw the finished piece into a tub of
water to soak. The soaked furs were removed and stretched on
frames to dry in the rear of the shop. Meanwhile, another apprentice, more experienced, sat at a table "fleshing" the dried skins
with a knife, removing the inner layer. At intervals one or another
of the workmen would be at work tanning. The skins were rolled
up in a greasy preparation and placed in a large tub over five feet
deep. The workman stood inside the tub and rapidly kneaded the
skins with his bare feet, running in place and jumping inside the
tub. One such workman is said to have been able to jump out
of a tub of this kind, and to have been, in addition, an excellent
tennis player. The kneaded skins were stretched and hung to
dry, then cleaned with chalk. At the front of the shop sat the
master and mistress, shearing and trimming the skins and sewing
them together in strips. These strips were in turn sewn together
in rectangular furs of standard size. Master, mistress, and apprentices worked together, ate together, and slept under the same
roof, so that the busy shop had more the air of a family gathering
than that created by an owner with hired labor.[71]

A tourist from the country would wish to make at least a short
excursion down Candlewick Street, a center for chandlers,
weavers, and drapers, to see London Stone, an upright stone pillar of unknown purpose and origin that stood near St. Swithin's
Church on the north side of the street.[72] Local residents undoubtedly had a variety of legends concerning it to impart to the
inquisitive visitor. Below Budge Row on the west side of Walbrook Street stood the Church of St. John, Walbrook, the original
home of the Fraternity of Corpus Christi from which the guild

[71] The work of the skinners is vividly described in Veale, *The English Fur
Trade*, pp. 25–29.
[72] Stow, *Survey*, I, 224. For a photograph of the top of this stone, see R.
Merrified, *The Roman City of London* (London, 1965), Pl. 28.

of the skinners developed. And still farther down was the mansion called "The Copped Hall," which became the headquarters of the Skinner's Company. Walbrook itself was naturally subject to a great deal of pollution, "industrial" and domestic, although this was, in the Middle Ages, hardly a valid distinction.[73] It had to be cleansed from Moorfield to the Thames in 1288, but it was found stopped with filth and dung in 1383. Those having latrines over it were then obliged to pay 2s a year, a considerable sum, for the cleansing of the stream.[74]

Before the western course of the stream ran under Thames Street on its way beside Dowgate to the river, it formed, perhaps in a bend along the boundary of Vintry Ward, the northern limit of three tenements in Thames Street, one of which belonged to John Chaucer, Vintner, the father of Geoffrey Chaucer. John, who lived until 1366, was the son of Robert le Chaucer, Vintner, who came from a family in Ipswich. We know little about the property itself, except that it consisted of houses, solars, and two cellars said to be worth 13s 4d a year in 1395, when it passed in mortmain to the Prioress of Cheshunt.[75] However, we may well imagine Geoffrey as a small boy in the fifties thoroughly familiar with the neighborhood of Haywharf, the Steelyard, Dowgate, the Wine Wharf, and Queenhithe, which was full of foreign shipping and sailors. At the foot of La Reole on the west side stood the Church of St. Martin Vintry, rebuilt in 1399, where Chaucer's family probably attended services, and "over against it," as Stow says, or across the street, was the legendary house of Henry Picard, Vintner and Mayor of London in 1356–1357. Picard had inherited the house from John de Gisors, Vintner and Mayor of London in 1311–1312, whose granddaughter Margaret he married.

The house was "legendary" because of a widely circulated story to the effect that Picard had entertained five kings at dinner in 1357. Stow reduces this number to four in his *Survey*,[76]

[73] Riley, *Memorials*, p. 23.
[74] *Ibid.*, pp. 478–479.
[75] For details, see *Chaucer Life-Records*, pp. 1–2. The house was probably worth about £11.
[76] *Survey*, I, 239–240.

but C. L. Kingsford has shown that the feast, said to have included Pierre de Lusignan, King of Cyprus, cannot have taken
place in 1357 and that not more than three genuine kings could
have taken part in it.[77] Pierre de Lusignan's visit to England is
noteworthy, however, since Chaucer's Knight, a composite exemplar of fourteenth-century chivalry, fought in some of his
campaigns. After traveling about Europe in 1361 and 1362, seeking to inspire a new crusade, King Peter landed at Dover in
November 1363 with a pagan king and a great pagan lord in his
entourage. He was met by a number of eminent knights, including Chaucer's friend, Sir Richard Stury. King Edward greeted his
fellow king with great festivity, asserting, however, concerning
the crusade, "Certes, fair cousin, I have a great will to go on this
voyage, but I am too old, and I shall leave it to my sons." A
great tournament was held on St. Martin's Day. King Peter departed in December, suffering a robbery at the hands of some
brigands while passing through Kent. Whether he ever dined in
the Vintry we do not know, but Picard's house passed to Sir
John Stodie, Vintner and Mayor of London in 1357–1358, and
later, according to Stow, the vintners "builded for themselves a
faire hall, and also 13 Almes houses there, for 13 poore people."[78]

Up the street called La Reole on the corner across Knightrider
Street was the mansion from which the street took its name, in
turn probably named because wine merchants from La Reole in
Gascony once occupied it. The tenements there were granted to
Queen Philippa for her wardrobe in 1331. She undertook exten-
sive rebuilding in 1347. After her death in 1369 income from the
tenements was assigned to the Dean and chapter of St. Stephen's,
Westminster. Joan, Princess of Wales, was there in 1381, and
King Richard occupied the premises briefly in 1386.[79] In the
neighborhood on La Reole itself stood the principal mansion of
Sir Nicholas Brembre, Grocer, who married the daughter of John
Stodie and became one of London's wealthiest citizens. Nearby

[77] "The Feast of the Five Kings," *Archaeologia*, LXVII (1915–1916),
119–126.
[78] *Survey*, I, 240.
[79] See Kingsford's note to Stow, *Survey*, I, 243–244, and his "Historical
Notes," *LTR*, XII, 9–11.

on Knightrider Street was Ipris Inn, built in 1338. John of Gaunt
was dining there when the citizens rose against him and Henry
Percy in 1377 after the abortive trial of Wyclif at St. Paul's.

Westward on Thames Street was the city's garlic market, and
near the corner of Cordwainer Street stood the Church of St.
James Garlickhithe. Stow describes the church as "newly built"
in 1326 and calls attention to various famous men buried there,
including John de Gisors and Richard Lyons. Lyons' monument
showed him "with his haire rounded by his eares, and curled, a
little beard forked, a gowne girt to him downe to his feete, of
branched Damaske wrought with the likenes of flowers, a large
pursse on his right side, hanging in a belt from his left shoulder,
a plaine whoode about his necke, covering his shoulders and
hanging backe behinde him."[80] The rector of this church between
1359 and 1367 was Thomas de Aston, who had studied philosophy, medicine, and canon law at Oxford and received a degree
in canon law from Cambridge. He became a canon of St. Paul's
in 1374.[81] Thomas Cranely, future Archbishop of Dublin, was a
chantry chaplain in this church in 1381. He gave New College
a copy of St. Gregory's *Moralia*, a long series of homilies on the
Book of Job that had once attracted the interest of King Henry II
and was among John of Salisbury's favorite books.[82] The *Moralia*
was widely read in England during the fourteenth century and
should receive the sympathetic attention of all true Chaucerians.

The Steelyard, the name of which has nothing to do with steel,
located a short distance west of Haywharf, was the headquarters
of the Hanseatic merchants in England. Raw furs, timber, wax,
ashes, iron, and fish were brought there from ports in the Baltic
and Germany. Just north of the Steelyard was Northampton's
Inn, which became the property of the Earl of Nottingham in
1384. Farther west was Dowgate, a port anciently favored by
merchants from Normandy. At the foot of Vintries Lane, where
Chaucer's father must have done a great deal of business, was the
Winewharf, frequented especially by merchants from Gascony,
and a little farther west was the busy port of Queenhithe, where

[80] *Survey*, I, 249.
[81] Emden, *Biographical Register of Oxford*, I, 69; *A Biographical Register
of the University of Cambridge to 1500* (Cambridge, 1963), p. 21.
[82] *Biographical Register of Oxford*, I, 510–511.

the docks were laden with salt from southern France and other goods. All these ports were, so to speak, almost in Chaucer's front yard. Thames Street was noted for its cookshops, where hot food could be obtained at almost any time. A menu might contain items like the following:

Roast Pig	8d
Roast Hen	4d
5 Larks	1½ d
Hen in Pasty	5d

Oysters and mussels could be had for about 4d a bushel.

West of Queenhithe was Timberhithe, where flat-bottomed "shouts" or freight boats belonging to woodmongers landed their cargoes. Farther west lay Fishwharf, which served the fishmongers on Old Fish Street, Paul's Wharf, a free entry, and the Woodwharf. Among these ports were a number of great inns along the riverside: The Duke of Norfolk's Inn, the Abbot of Chertsey's Inn, the inns of Sir John Beauchamp and Sir Simon Burley, mentioned above, the Earl of Salisbury's Inn, Castle Baynard, the House of Lord Ros, and, bordering on the Fleet, the Inn of the Prior of Okebourne. On the north side of Thames Street was another series of inns, including those of the Bishop of Hereford and the Abbot of Reading. Still other inns lay between Dowgate and London Bridge, for the river offered considerable advantage as a highway to those who held property along its banks. The most famous of these inns was Cold Harbor south of the section of Thames Street called The Ropery, which was populated chiefly by corders and rope-makers belonging to the Grocer's Company.

The first man of prominence to be associated with Cold Harbor in our period was Sir John Poultney (or Pountney), Draper, who was Mayor of London in 1330, 1331, 1333, and 1336. He is remembered for having founded a college of chaplains on St. Lawrence Lane, a House of Carmelites in Coventry, and for having built All Hallows the Less before his messuage in Thames Street, with the steeple over his gatehouse. On February 14, 1347, Sir John granted his tenement "Cold Harbor," with its wharf and other buildings, to Humphrey de Bohun for life, for which he

was to pay "a rose at Midsummer."[83] The tenement passed next
to Nicholas de Loveyne, who married Sir John's widow, was
knighted, and became Governor of Ponthieu. Soon after 1375
Cold Harbor was granted to Alice Perrers. This famous lady
rebuilt much of the mansion and probably erected what came
to be known as "The Tower." In 1378 the mansion was granted
to John of Gaunt, but he surrendered it a year later, when it
passed to Edmund Langley, Duke of York. John Holland acquired "The Tower" and other portions of the property in 1390.
He is said to have entertained King Richard and some of his
council there in July 1397. After dinner the King rode out to
arrest his troublesome uncle, the Duke of Gloucester.

Poultney's other great mansion, which came to be called "The
Rose," was memorialized in the words of the Surveyor to the
Duke of Buckingham in Shakespeare's *Henry VIII:*

> Not long before your highness sped to France,
> The duke being at the Rose, within the parish
> Saint Laurence Poultney, did of me demand
> What was the speech among the Londoners
> Concerning the French journey.

The house, distinguished by a high and massive stone tower,
stood north of Cold Harbor and the Ropery on St. Laurence Hill,
to the southwest of the Church of St. Laurence on St. Lawrence
Lane, the yard of which served as a meeting place for the Flemish weavers of London. Sir John received license to crenellate his
dwelling in 1341. Meanwhile, in 1332 he founded a chantry in
the Church of St. Laurence, which developed into a college consisting of a master, thirteen priests, and four choristers. After Sir
John's death in 1349 the house passed to the Black Prince. It was
granted to Richard, Earl of Arundel in 1385, and, after his execution in 1397, it was granted to Edmund Langley.[84] Poultney
was obviously a very worthy man, who worked hard to establish
walls and customs in his city.

[83] *Letter-Book F*, p. 158; cf. Kingsford, "Historical Notes," *LTR*, X, pp.
94–100; Honeybourne, "Reconstructed Map," p. 49.
[84] Kingsford, "Historical Notes," *LTR*, XI, 74–78; Philip Norman, "Sir
John Pulteney and his two Residences in London," *Archaeologia*, LVII
(Part II) (1901), 257–284.

To return to the top of Walbrook Street at the Peltry, eastward toward the Stocks was St. Mary Woolchurch, in the yard of which was what Stow called "a great beam" for weighing wool, or "tronage." The rector between 1360 and 1385 was the prominent London physician William Tanterville, who officially assisted in the infirmary at Westminster. Beyond the church, the great market of Cheap ended in a plaza at the intersection of Threeneedle Street, Cornhill, and Lombard Street. It contained a large enclosed market with stalls around the sides shared by butchers and fishmongers. London consumed an enormous amount of fish in great variety. Both freshwater and saltwater fish were available, as well as salted fish. Rich and poor alike enjoyed it, so that this square in the heart of the city must have been the common resort of housewives and servants from London and the immediate suburbs. Fish could also be purchased in Old Fish Street and in Bridge Street. To one side stood the stocks and thews (stocks for women) where petty offenders were exhibited to the public gaze. The purpose of the stocks was not to punish the offenders physically, but to warn the community as a whole that the men and women confined there were not to be trusted. Frequently, the nature of the offense was indicated. A butcher who sold putrid meat might have his smelly commodity piled before him and burned under his nose, and a liar or deceiver of any kind wore a whetstone hanging from his neck to show that he had been deceitful "like a sharp razor":

Why dost thou glory in malice, thou that art mighty in iniquity?
All day long thy tongue hath devised injustice: as a sharp razor thou hast wrought deceit.

.   .   .   .

The just shall see and fear, and shall laugh at him, and say:
Behold the man that made not God his helper,
But trusted in the abundance of his riches . . . .

The slight indirection involved in the use of a whetstone rather than a razor to recall the fifty-first Psalm (Vulgate) is typical of medieval taste, and the laughter of the just, which seems inhumane to us, is typical of medieval humor.

Beyond the market rose London's larger hill, from the valley of Walbrook to Leaden Hall at the highest point in the city. In Chaucer's time Cornhill would have been busy with carts and packhorses proceeding to and from Aldgate and the countryside beyond. The eastern half of the city, especially toward the north, was less populous than the western half, but Cornhill was a principal highway. Near the intersection was the Cardinal's Hat, which contained, among other things, a grammar school in the late fourteenth century. Up Cornhill on the right was a large messuage that had once been the House of the Bardi in London. After King Edward repudiated the Bardi, the tenement passed to William de la Pole and to his son Michael, who became Earl of Suffolk. In the midst of Cornhill toward the upper end stood the Tun, a round stone building constructed as a reservoir for water in 1282 by Henry le Waleys, Vintner, who was several times Mayor of London, once Mayor of Bordeaux, and a distinguished royal servant under Edward I. In Chaucer's time the Tun served as a prison for "nightwalkers," prostitutes, adulterers, and, in spite of London's archdeacons, adulterous priests. Near the Tun was a group of blacksmith's shops.

The traveler on Cornhill leaving the city after a successful morning at the market might pause briefly at a haberdasher's shop to buy a gift for his wife or daughter. Such a shop would resemble a modern shop or American store more than any other establishment in medieval London. We may imagine a narrow tenement hardly more than nine feet wide with a staircase at the rear. Here our tradesman has for sale laces, points, bows, caps, light coats, purses, hats, spurs, gaming-tables, paternosters, pencases, boxwood combs, pepper mills, thread, girdles, paper, and parchment.[85] The items for sale are not expensive and if our traveler decided that he wanted a paternoster somewhat more elaborate than those offered by the haberdasher, he might pause at the next jeweler's stall, where he could probably find an amber paternoster or an *ave* in jet with silver-gilt gauds for a shilling. A paternoster in coral, like that worn by Chaucer's rather vain Prioress, might cost a little over twice as much, but, on the other hand, would undoubtedly be appreciated by the lady of the

---

[85] The contents of a shop of this kind are listed in Riley, *Memorials*, pp. 422–423.

house. He might also wish to pause at the shop of a turner. Here the master would be at work turning and finishing candlesticks, bowls, and mazers or cups, for most people could not afford the silver-gilt and enameled ware cherished by Thomas Arundel. The better mazers were set in silver stands and trimmed with silver along the rim, but it would be necessary to visit a goldsmith for one of these.

On the right near the intersection of Cornhill and Gracechurch Street, beyond some poulterer's stalls stood two very old churches, St. Michael's and St. Peter's. The rector of St. Michael's between 1393 and 1400 was John Haseley, an Oxford man, who became Dean of Chichester in 1407.[86] St. Peter's stood on the corner of Gracechurch Street, a north-south highway that led, with various changes in name, from Holywell Priory across London and London Bridge into Southwark and beyond. The intersection was known as "Carfukes" (Carfax), or "four corners." Across this street stood Leaden Hall, an ancient tenement used as a market. In the mid-century foreign poulterers had been confined to Leaden Hall Market, but after 1370 they were permitted to sell in Cheap before Greyfriars as well. To the west were two other large tenements, Green Gate and Zouche's Inn, and on the left beyond St. Mary Axe Street was the Church of St. Andrew "atte Knappe," or "on the hill," which became known later as St. Andrew Undershaft. Stow, whose monument was placed in the sixteenth-century church on this site, records that every year a Maypole was set up higher than the steeple before the south door,[87] but this custom was probably the product of the superstitious malaise of the Renaissance. The church represented a wealthy parish, worth in 1366 £10 annually to its rector, one Robert de Wissynden, who also held a chantry in St. Paul's worth £6.[88]

Up St. Mary Axe Street were the houses of well-to-do merchants, among which, on the eastern side of the street, was the tenement of Thomas Mocking, Fishmonger, remembered because the records of the city contain an inventory of his household

[86] Emden, *Biographical Register of Oxford,* II, 884.
[87] *Survey,* I, 143–145.
[88] *Registrum Simonis de Sudbiria,* II, 155–156.

goods made in 1373.[89] His house consisted of a hall, chamber, parlor, a small chamber next to the parlor, a servant's room, a solar above the servant's room for an apprentice, a storehouse, and a kitchen. The hall contained three dorsers (drapes) and three bankers (bench covers), six cushions, a dining board and two trestles, an iron fireplace with tongs, five basins, seven wash-bowls, four candelabra, and three checkerboards. The most valu-able articles here were the dorsers, bankers, and cushions, said to be worth £4 15s 8d. The chamber contained a new bed worth 42s, another bed, a girdle worth 20s, pillows, mattresses, and so on. Evidently, the master's robes had been removed, since these were likely to be, next to his bed and his silver, his most valued possessions. Thomas had, among the goods in his storehouse, six silver cups and twenty-four silver spoons worth altogether £10 6s 3d. There were also three coconut cups set in silver worth 40s. The only chairs in the inventory were in the chamber next to the parlor. Our ancestors had few luxuries beyond the work of the goldsmiths, robes, drapes, furs, and the delicacies of the poulter-ers and pepperers (or grocers) upon which to spend their money.

On the east side of St. Mary Axe Street, St. Helen's Lane ran through the Priory of St. Helen to Bishopsgate Street. The priory was a house of Black (Benedictine) Nuns, founded, according to Newcourt,[90] in 1212, by William le Goldsmith, and supported from time to time by other London merchants. Adam Fraunceys, Mercer, who was Mayor of London in 1352–1353 and 1353–1354, left the priory a large sum at his death in 1375. A small scandal was created in 1388 when one of the nuns ran away to marry.[91] This kind of rebellion was not so common in the Middle Ages as we might expect. North of the priory on the same side was the church from which the lane derived its name, St. Mary Axe, and behind it stood the Earl of Oxford's Inn. At the end of the lane against the wall was the little church of St. Augustine Pappey (Pavia), belonging to the Augustinian canons of Holy Trinity (Christ Church).

[89] *Plea and Memoranda Rolls,* pp. 154–156; Rickert, *Chaucer's World,* pp. 59–62.

[90] *Repertorium,* I, 363–364.

[91] Page, *Victoria History,* I, 457–458.

Cornhill became the northern branch of Aldgate Street beyond St. Mary Axe Lane. This street had two branches, one merging into Cornhill and the other merging into Fenchurch Street. Eastward beyond St. Andrew's on the lower side of the northern branch of Aldgate Street was the Abbot of Evesham's Inn, and beyond it on the north was St. Katherine Creechurch, which was, in Stow's time, in the graveyard of the Priory of Holy Trinity. This priory had a unique place in city life because the prior, whoever he might be, was an alderman of the city who sat in the Mayor's Court and rode with him in aldermanic livery.[92] This situation arose because the ancient Cnihtengild had granted the soke of Portsoken to the priory. The priory itself was founded in 1107 or 1108 by Queen Maud. Its grant included the gate of Aldgate, the Church of St. Augustine Pappey, the Church of St. Edmund in Lombard Street at the corner of Birchen Lane, and Allhallows in the Wall, above the Convent of the Austin Friars. Like St. Paul's and St. Martin le Grand, the priory maintained a school. It became customary for the mayor and aldermen to assemble at the priory in time of war to consider the defenses of the city. The church was rebuilt beginning in 1339. The priors in our period were Nicholas de London (1340–1377), William de Rysyng (1377–1391), and Robert of Exeter (1394–1408). As a resident of Aldgate, Chaucer must have known the first two of these men very well.

London trades, especially the minor ones, were well represented in Aldgate Ward, although there were some goldsmiths, vintners, and fishmongers there. In addition, there were many bell-founders, who produced pails, pots, and buckles as well as bells. As Chaucer walked down the southern branch of Aldgate Street toward the Custom House in the morning, he would pass the Church of St. Katherine Coleman on the left, representing a modest parish, which in 1366 produced for its rector, John Noble, four marks a year.[93] Chaucer probably turned to his left toward the river on Mark Lane, just beyond the manor of Blanche Appleton. Beyond the houses on the east side of this street was the Inn of Sir Robert Knolles and on the west, off Minchen Lane, was the Abbot of Colchester's Inn. The area around Minchen Lane was

[92] Stow, *Survey*, I, 120 ff. The custom is said to have lasted until 1531.
[93] *Reg. Sim. Sudbiria*, II, 169.

much frequented by Portuguese galleymen, who came to London in their long low ships in great numbers. Mark Lane became Sporrers Lane in its steep descent to the river beyond Tower Street, and when Chaucer reached Thames Street, the Custom House was before him. The entire walk would require only a few minutes, provided, of course, that our young controller did not pause to engage in too many casual conversations along the way. London was a city in which everyone knew everyone else; the impersonal atmosphere of our large metropolitan centers and the faceless masses that inhabit them had not yet come into being.

The customs had been collected on the Woolwharf, across the Water Gate from Asselyn's Wharf, or the tenement known later as "Brown's Place," since 1275.[94] The tronage or weighing for the ancient custom on wool had been established there in 1318. In 1364 the petty customs were also located on the wharf. Before 1378 there were two houses adjacent to the wharf proper, one for wool customs and the other for petty customs. The houses contained "trones" for weighing merchandise, balances, chests, and canvas with thread for sacking. There was also an exchequer in a counting house for balancing indebtedness and payment, an occupation that must have consumed long hours of Chaucer's time.[95] During Chaucer's tenure of office the houses were being rebuilt by John Chircheman, and, in 1390, Chaucer himself supervised their repair as Clerk of the King's Works.[96] His duty as Controller was to check the accounts of the Keepers of the Customs, among whom were, during Chaucer's tenure, Nicholas Brembre, William Walworth, and John Philpot.

"Asselyn's Place" or "Brown's House" across the Water Gate from the fourteenth-century Custom House and more or less on the site of the present one, belonged, after 1375, to Simon Sudbury, Archbishop of Canterbury (1375–1381), and to his brother John Cherteseye, a prosperous London draper. The house had a hall measuring forty by twenty-four feet and a garden sixty-nine

---

[94] See footnote 4 above.

[95] For a convenient description of an exchequer, see S. B. Chrimes, *An Introduction to the Administrative History of Mediaeval England*, Third Edition (Oxford, 1966), pp. 62–63.

[96] See Mabel H. Mills, "The London Customs House During the Middle Ages," *Archaeologia*, LXXXIII (1933), 307–325.

by forty-four feet. It is not unlikely that Chaucer had more than
a passing acquaintance with Sudbury, and he may well have
occasionally shared a cup of wine with Sudbury, Cherteseye, and
one of his more distinguished supervisors at the Custom House.
"Asselyn's Place" was granted in 1384 to a tallow-chandler,
Richard Willysdon, who rebuilt it.[97]

Eastward from the Custom House a short distance was the
Tower, and on the way there, on the north side of Tower Street,
was one of London's more famous churches, All Hallows Barking.
It stood, according to Stow, in a large cemetery toward the end
of the street. On the north side of the church was a chapel, said
to have been founded by Richard I, containing a famous image
of the Blessed Virgin erected by Edward I. King Edward is said
to have believed that if he visited it five times a year and kept the
chapel repaired he would be victorious over all nations.[98] The
chapel became the resort of pilgrims, and the church, although
not wealthy,[99] received rather frequent formal visits from persons
of rank.

The Tower was built on a small rise beyond the lower end of
Thames Street near the eastern end of the old Roman Wall, part
of which was destroyed to make room for it. It was designed by
Gundulf (b. ca. 1024), who entered Bec when Lanfranc was
prior and followed him to England. He became Bishop of
Rochester in 1077 and began the rebuilding of the cathedral
there. He also designed a castle for William II. His work on the
Tower included the original design and the supervision of the
initial construction. Basically, the Tower is a three-story rectangular keep whose walls are fifteen feet thick at the base.[100]
Various additions were made more or less continuously up until
and during Chaucer's lifetime. The original keep contained, and
still does contain, the beautiful Norman Chapel of St. John measuring only about sixty by thirty-five feet but conveying neverthe-

[97] C. L. Kingsford, "A London Merchant's House and its Owners, 1360–
1614," Archaeologia, LXXIV (1923–1924), 137–158.

[98] Newcourt, Repertorium, I, 238.

[99] The rector in 1366, Thomas Broke, received 8 marks for his benefice
there. He also served at the free chapel in the Tower. See Reg. Sim. Sudbiria II, 152.

[100] For details, see Colvin, The History of the King's Works, I, 28 ff.

The Tower and London Bridge, fifteenth century (copyright British Museum).

less an impression of the massive solidity characteristic of its style. During the fourteenth century the Tower was used as a royal residence and as a privy wardrobe largely devoted to arms, saddles, and weapons of all kinds. In the later part of the period cannon and gunpowder were manufactured there.

From a turret of the Tower a visitor would be able to see a great deal of the eastern half of the city as well as some important structures outside the walls. East of the Tower was the Hospital of St. Katherine, founded in 1148 by Queen Matilda for a master, bretheren, sisters, and thirteen poor persons. Custody of the house was granted to the Priory of Holy Trinity, but the Queen reserved the right to appoint the master. Queen Eleanor refounded the establishment in 1273, so that it contained a master, three priests, some sisters, and twenty-four poor persons, of

whom six were to be poor scholars. The right of appointing
masters and filling vacancies among the brethren and sisters was
reserved to the queens of England. Philippa took a great deal of
interest in the hospital and drew up a set of regulations for it.
For example, she decreed that each sister should have two kinds
of meat daily, or fish, to the value of 1½d, as well as one white
and one brown loaf. The Church of St. Katherine's was rebuilt in
1343, and both King Edward and King Richard made substantial
grants to the foundation.[101]

North and east of St. Katherine's on some marshy waste ground
was the Cistercian Abbey of St. Mary Graces, founded by Ed-
ward III in 1350 in honor of the Blessed Virgin, to whom the
King attributed his victories by land and by sea. Geoffrey of
Monmouth's King Arthur had carried an image of the Virgin on
his shield and had proclaimed her name as he rode into battle.[102]
The obvious devotion of Edward I, Edward III, and Richard II
to the Virgin was a manifestation of one of the basic features of
English chivalry. Mary was, in the words of the *Pearl* poet, the
"Quene of cortaysye," the highest inspiration to chivalric virtue
and enterprise. Edward III made generous bequests to his new
abbey, as did Richard II and Henry IV. The cloisters were built
between 1368 and 1379, and the house became the usual meeting
place of the chapter-general in England.[103]

North of the Tower was the House of the Minoresses, or Sisters
of St. Clare (Franciscan), founded in 1293 by Edmund Earl of
Lancaster and occupied originally by French nuns. The house
became a favorite object of charitable donations among the
nobility. Queen Isabella, Elizabeth de Burgh, and other ladies
contributed to its welfare. In 1397 John of Gaunt bequeathed
£100 to be distributed among the sisters. The Duke of Gloucester and his family had especially close connections with the
Minoresses. The Duchess died there, and her daughter Isabel

[101] Page, *Victoria History*, I, 525 ff.

[102] Ed. Griscom, pp. 438–439.

[103] Page, *Victoria History*, I, 461 ff. There is a detailed description with a
map in Marjorie B. Honeybourne, "The Abbey of St. Mary Graces, Tower
Hill, "*Transactions of the London and Middlesex Archaeological Society*, n.s.
XI (1951), 16–26.

grew up in the convent, chose to remain, and eventually became abbess.[104] Within London Wall south and west of the Minoresses was the Convent of the Crutched (Crossed) Friars, established in 1298. The order itself was a small one, but the London house was well supported by London citizens during the second part of the century.

Thames Street west of the Custom House would have been full of carts, horses, and porters, and the air near Billingsgate would have been permeated, as it still is, with the odor of fish. North of Thames Street near the intersection of St. Dunstan's Lane was the Church of St. Dunstan in the East, where today a rather depressing ruin of Wren's rebuilding remains. In Stow's time the church was "fayre and large" and stood in a large churchyard.[105] The parish, he says, contained many rich merchants, especially salters and fishmongers. Its rector between 1395 and 1397 was John de Maydenhithe, who was also a canon of St. Martin le Grand and may have held a law degree from Oxford. From Porter's Lane westward Thames Street was called Billingsgate, after the ancient port on the river which was then, as now, largely devoted to fish. West of the port was St. Botolph's Lane, and on the southwest corner of its intersection with Thames Street stood one of four London churches named for St. Botolph, an obscure British abbot of the seventh century. The other three stood just without Aldersgate, Bishopsgate, and Aldgate. The lane ran down to the river and Botolph's Wharf. Boats from Gravesend brought passengers to dock here, each of whom was allowed to transport free any box or trunk he could carry. The wharf was also used to bring in small sacks of grain (one to three bushels), lambs, and "small victual" from the east.[106] The boats probably carried passengers and this light cargo together, pausing frequently at small landings along the river in their journeys up and down.

On the corner near the end of London Bridge, now relocated west of the old site, stood the Church of St. Magnus, in Stow's words a "fayre Parish Church." The monument of Henry Yevele was still visible there in Stow's time.[107] The rectors in the late

[104] Page, *Victoria History*, I, 516 ff.
[105] *Survey*, I, 134–135.
[106] *Letter-Book G*, p. 225.
[107] *Survey*, I, 212.

fourteenth century were relatively distinguished, including Richard de Medford (1381–1383), who had been a Fellow of King's Hall, Cambridge. He became a royal secretary in about 1385. His successor at St. Magnus, Nicholas Stoket, was an Oxford man who acted as Envoy to Prussia in 1388.[108] One resident of the neighborhood, Gilbert Maghfeld, had a large household including a butler, cook, two maids, a clerk, three valets, some bailiffs who supervised his country holdings, and a number of other servants. He imported iron, wax, ginger, woad, Spanish asses, herring, beaver, wine, and other commodities, and shipped out grain and cloth. In his later years he engaged in moneylending. Among his clients were John of Gaunt, Henry Yevele, and Geoffrey Chaucer.[109]

London Bridge in the fourteenth century was a village in itself, partly in the parish of St. Magnus and partly in the parish of St. Olave in Southwark. There was a tavern at each end, and, in 1358, there were one hundred and thirty-eight shops along its length. In the middle was a chapel dedicated to St. Thomas Becket, which was sumptuously rebuilt in the new perpendicular manner by Henry Yevele between 1384 and 1386. Between the sixth and seventh piers from the southern side was a drawbridge necessary to allow shipping to proceed up the river, and beyond it on the north was a large stone gate, which served as one of the gates of the city. The gate was occasionally adorned with the heads of the great, set up on poles, including those of William Wallace and Simon Sudbury. It is said that in 1390 a joust was held on the bridge between Sir David Lindsay and Lord Wells.[110]

The bridge made a good vantage point for watching shipping in the Port of London. The river was crowded with small boats, some crossing between London and Southwark, some carrying passengers between London and Westminster, or between London and Gravesend, or to other points downriver. A few repre-

---

[108] Emden, *Biographical Register of Cambridge,* pp. 398–399; *Biographical Register of Oxford,* III, 1786.

[109] See Margery K. James, "A London Merchant of the Fourteenth Century," *Economic History Review,* VIII (1955–1956), 364–376; *Chaucer Life-Records,* pp. 393, 500–503, and the references there.

[110] Cf. John Hearsey, *Bridge, Church, and Palace in Old London* (London, 1961).

sented private fishing expeditions, for fishing was a sport that many Londoners enjoyed. Among larger craft were "shouts" carrying timber or other freight, vessels of London fishmongers, and the gaily decorated barges of the noblemen moving to and from their inns along the shore. Ships moving to and from foreign ports had, in the fourteenth century, only one mast, but they might displace as much as a hundred tons and carry crews of sixty to seventy men. These merchantmen could readily be converted into warships simply by erecting towers fore and aft. Here and there the visitor might see a Portuguese galley. Some of these had as many as three hundred oars.

At the south end of the bridge lay Southwark, which was not a part of London in the fourteenth century. To the west at the end of the bridge was the Priory of St. Mary Overy ("Over the River"), where Chaucer's friend and fellow poet, "moral" Gower, lived. Richard Arundel had the right in mid-century to use rooms in the priory as a residence. The priory itself was severely damaged by fire and was largely rebuilt beginning in 1390. Beyond the priory to the west was the Bishop of Winchester's Inn, along the river on Stewes Side were the houses of the prostitutes of Southwark. For a time these were the property of the See of Winchester. Rowing across the river to and from these houses after sunset was discouraged by the London authorities, and it was generally felt that a professional woman should keep her visitor all night. South of the priory and across the road was the Hospital of St. Thomas, a building erected by Peter des Roches, Bishop of Winchester (1215), to replace one said to have been established by Thomas Becket within the priory. This establishment was severely disrupted by the Black Death, so that it contained in 1392 a master and only four brethren.[111] Southward on the same side of the street was the Abbot of Hyde's Inn, a part of which was used as a commercial inn, the Tabard. It was here that the Chaucer of *The Canterbury Tales* met his fellow pilgrims on the way to the Shrine of St. Thomas.

To return to London, Thames Street just west of the bridge was called Oyster Hill and westward toward the Ropery became "Stockfishmonger's Row." The Stockfishmongers held a hall below

[111] Page, *Victoria History,* I, 538 ff.

St. Michael's Lane, and to the west of it was the Inn of Sir William Walworth, one of London's most eminent fishmongers. In 1380 Sir William united a number of chantries in the Church of St. Michael, which stood on the east side of St. Michael's Lane near Candlewick Street, and founded a college for a master and nine priests. According to Stow, [112] St. Michael's Church was built by Walworth's old master, John Lovekyn.

The neighborhood of Bridge Street was generally dominated by the fishing industry. East Cheap contained some butcher's stalls, the shops of turners and basketmakers, and some cookshops. As Bridge Street rose toward Lombard Street its character changed, and at the intersection was London's largest grain market. Cornmongers from Cambridge, Huntington, Bedford, and Ware stood by the wall of Allhallows Church, built well back from the intersection on the northwest corner. Citizen cornmongers were instructed to stand by themselves and not to mingle with the strangers.[113] The authorities wanted no connivance that might raise prices.

Between Cornhill and Threeneedle Street near the northern corner of Fynkes Lane was a large tenement once owned by Sir Oliver de Ingham, Seneschal of Aquitaine. It passed through various hands until 1347, when it became the holding of the Merchant Tailors of London. Across the street to the north was the Hospital of St. Anthony, established in the thirteenth century by the Brothers of St. Anthony of Vienne for two priests, a schoolmaster, and twelve poor men. It was the custom in London to tie a bell around the neck of any pig too poor for slaughter. These belled pigs were the property of St. Anthony's Hospital, so that it was an act of charity to feed them. The brethren could thus claim many well-fattened pigs as free gifts of the citizens. Pigs other than belled pigs were not, however, allowed to roam the streets. North of the hospital was the Inn of the Abbot of St. Albans, who, in our period, was Thomas de la Mare. Abbot Thomas was one of the great men of the realm, a Privy Councillor to Edward III, and a close friend of the Black Prince and of King John of France. He was an austere man, tall and lean, who al-

[112] *Survey*, I, 219.
[113] *Letter-Book H*, pp. 133, 138.

Canons (copyright British Museum).

lowed himself only one meal a day and constantly wore a hair
shirt under his robes.-Although he was feeble and ill during the
last few years of his life, he lived to what was, at that time, the
unusual age of eighty-seven.[114]

Within the curve of Broad Street to the north stood the Convent of the Austin (Augustinian) Friars, founded by Humphrey
de Bohun V, Earl of Hereford and Essex, in 1253. The church,
a rectangular hall like Greyfriars, was rebuilt by Humphrey IX
in 1354.[115] Humphrey X (seventh Earl of Hereford), whose
daughter Mary married Henry of Lancaster (later Henry IV),
continued to assist the foundation. He is remembered as one of
the great patrons of manuscript illumination in the fourteenth
century, and a series of Psalters, probably illuminated in London,
is associated with his name. The Augustinians were noted for
their humanistic learning in the later Middle Ages. The areas
west of Austin Friars was marshy in the fourteenth century and
not heavily populated. Near Cripplegate was a hospital founded

[114] For an account of Thomas de la Mare, see David Knowles, *The Religious
Orders in England* (Cambridge, 1955), II, 41 ff.
[115] For a plan, see Godfrey, *Architecture in and Around London*, p. 72.

in 1337 by William de Elsing, Mercer, intended to house one
hundred persons. Blind or paralyzed priests were to be favored.
After 1340 the house was ruled by five Austin canons. It was
generously supported by London citizens in the later fourteenth
century. A large endowment was left to it, for example, by John
of Northampton, the famous reforming mayor.[116]

Our visit to the city should include a number of establishments
outside the walls in addition to those seen from the Tower. For
this purpose, if we were actual visitors, we should need horses.
First, outside Bishopsgate, the hinges of which were maintained
for many years by the Bishop of London in exchange for one
stick of wood from every cart carrying wood into the city, beyond the Church of St. Botolph, whose rector between 1395 and
1398 was a Mertonian, John Campden, stood the Hospital of
St. Mary of Bethlehem. Land for the hospital was donated in
1247 by Simon FitzMary, who had extensive holdings in London,[117] to Godfrey, Bishop of Bethlehem, to found a priory of
the order of St. Mary of Bethelehem. The house was taken under
the protection of the city in 1346. In 1403 there were three sick
persons and six lunatics there.[118] Farther out Bishopsgate Street
on the east side was the Hospital of St. Mary Without Bishopsgate, founded by a London citizen, Walter Brown, and his wife in
1197. The house consisted of Austin canons and lay brothers and
sisters. In 1235 it was refounded and the church moved eastward,
but during the fourteenth century it was much impoverished and
suffered from annual floods. It gained a certain distinction after
1391, however, when annual sermons were delivered there. A
learned preacher, Stow tells us, was appointed to preach on the
Passion at Paul's Cross on Good Friday. On Monday, Tuesday,
and Wednesday afternoons following, there were at the hospital
sermons of the Resurrection. Finally, a summary sermon was
preached on Low Sunday at St. Paul's. These sermons were attended by the mayor and aldermen in livery.[119]

---

[116] *Cal. Wills*, I, 562–563, Newcourt, *Repertorium*, I, 347; Page, *Victoria History*, I, 535.

[117] For Simon, see Gwyn A. Williams, *Medieval London from Commune to Capital* (London, 1963), pp. 203–207.

[118] Page, *Victoria History*, I, 495 ff.

[119] *Survey*, I, 167–168.

Outside Cripplegate a little to the west was the famous Church of St. Giles. In Chaucer's time, Cripplegate Ward was the "artist's quarter" of London, although the artists were men like Gilbert Prince, King's Painter, who were by no means "alienated" from the rest of London society.[120] Gilbert is said to have ornamented a set of curtains for King Edward's bed, to have painted banners for the trumpets of the minstrels, and generally to have contributed to the colorful decor of funerals, festivities, and maskings in Richard's time. He was buried at St. Giles. A will of the period mentions an altar of St. Mary "de pictoribus" in the church.[121] After the death of King Richard a "fraternity or chantry of the Blessed Mary and St. Giles" was established there for his soul.[122] The altar of this fraternity may perhaps provide a further conjectural location for the Wilton Diptych, now thought to have been of English origin.

Outside Aldersgate to the northwest were the Hospital and Priory of St. Bartholomew. As legend has it, Rahere, minstrel to King Henry I, after a "pleasant and witty" youth, went to Rome and repented. But he fell ill and during his illness vowed to build a hospital for the poor. On his way home he had a vision in which a monster with four feet and two wings carried him to a high precipice, below which was a bottomless pit. As he was about to fall, a handsome man appeared and offered to save him. When Rahere asked what the man would have him do, since he was ready to do anything, the man replied that he was St. Bartholomew. He told the frightened minstrel to go to Smithfield and build a church in his name without worrying about the cost. Rahere returned home and obtained a grant of land in Smithfield from the King. He went out into his new domain and played the fool, clearing the ground. Many, attracted by his antics, came to help him. With their aid he built a hospital and a church and a priory.[123] The priory was a house of Austin canons that became separate from the hospital in the thirteenth century. Meanwhile, the hospital had financial and other difficulties in the fourteenth

[120] Harvey, *Gothic England*, pp. 61–62.

[121] *Cal. Wills*, I, 640.

[122] *Ibid.*, II, 435.

[123] Newcourt, *Repertorium*, I, 293. For a ground plan, see G. H. Cook, *English Monasteries in the Middle Ages* (London, 1961), p. 182.

century. Its master, Richard de Sutton, admitted incontinence with one of the sisters in 1375, but he remained in office until 1386. The prior and convent had the right to hold a fair at Smithfield once a year between August 23 and August 25. In the fourteenth century, however, this was a cloth fair, not characterized by indecorous behavior.[124]

North of the Priory of St. Bartholomew was Charterhouse, founded in 1371. During the plague of 1349, when there was insufficient space for burial, Sir Walter Manny rented thirteen acres from St. Bartholomew's for a cemetery and built a chapel on the site. Manny had intended to establish a college of canons and secular priests, but a hermitage was formed instead. Bishop Michael de Northburgh proposed to establish a house of Carthusians on the site and left £2000 for the purpose in his will.[125] Finally, John Luscote, Prior of Hinton, successfully revived the project, and in 1371 Henry Yevele began work on the cloister. The cells were donated by individual benefactors, and by 1400 there were eighteen of them, each with its little garden. Among the donors were Sir William Walworth and Sir Robert Knolles.[126] Northwest of Charterhouse stood the Priory of St. John of Jerusalem, burned by the rebels in 1381, and farther north was the Priory of St. Mary Clerkenwell.

Outside Ludgate, which had been decorated with statues in the late thirteenth century, between the Wall and the Fleet stood Fleet Prison surrounded by a ditch ten feet wide. In 1355 the ditch was found to be stopped up. There were three tanneries on it, and eleven latrines, but the city was evidently successful in finding remedies for these encumbrances.[127] Another difficulty appeared some years later, for in 1377 a petition in Parliament alleged that the debtors in Fleet Prison were being allowed to go about their business by day and by night. It demanded that they be confined until their debts were settled.[128] Finally, in 1381, Wat Tyler burned the prison.

[124] See *Letter-Book G,* pp. 310–311.
[125] *Cal. Wills,* II, 611.
[126] For a full account, see D. Knowles and W. F. Grimes, *Charterhouse* (London, 1954).
[127] Riley, *Memorials,* 279–280.
[128] *Rotuli Parliamentorum,* III, 25.

Across Fleet Bridge beyond the Bishop of Salisbury's Inn was the Convent of the White Friars (Carmelites), founded by Sir Richard Gray in 1241. After the fall of the Temple in 1308, White-friars became closely associated with the royal administration, so that during the reigns of Edward II and Edward III both royal and ecclesiastical councils were held there. The priory was rebuilt in 1350 by Hugh Courtenay, Earl of Devon; and after 1396 the church was rebuilt with assistance from Sir Robert Knolles. The Carmelites maintained a theological school and were famous for their learning and skill as confessors.

Farther west on the north side of Fleet Street was the Church of St. Dunstan in the West, and north of it, on Chauncelor Lane, stood the "Domus Conversorum," established by Henry III in 1232 as a house for converted Jews. Enlargements were made of the house in 1265 and of the chapel in 1275, but, in the fourteenth century, there were no converts. The building was granted in 1377 to the Keeper of the Rolls of Chancery for his records.[129] Farther north on the corner of Holborn Street was the Bishop of Lincoln's Inn near the site of the Old Temple. Nearby the Knights Templars first settled in London, probably in 1128. But they moved to the riverside in 1161.

By 1185 both the Templars and the Hospitallers of the Priory of St. John had completed their churches with round naves fashioned in imitation of the Church of the Holy Sepulchre. They were dedicated in that year by Heraclius, Patriarch of Jerusalem. The New Temple had close connections with the royal administration, which used it as a bank. In 1308, however, the Templars were finally suppressed through Papal action. They had been accused, no doubt falsely, of blasphemy, idolatry, and heresy, and of such outrages as tramping on the Cross and worshiping images of cats. After some complications, the property of the London Templars passed to the Knights of St. John, who did not need the entire manor and began to rent it, after 1347, to lawyers.[130] It has been suggested that Chaucer may have studied for a time at the Temple.

[129] Newcourt, *Repertorium*, I, 337–338; Colvin, *History of the King's Works*, I, 158.
[130] See W. H. Godfrey, "Recent Discoveries at the Temple," *Archaeologia*, XCV (1953), 124–140; Page, *Victoria History*, I, 485 ff.

Beyond Temple Bar, Fleet Street became the Strand, the highway to Westminster. Between the Strand and the river was a
series of great inns. Toward Westminster stood Charing Cross, a
companion monument to the High Cross in Cheap, erected in
memory of Queen Eleanor. On a fourteenth-century afternoon
the highway would be crowded with judges, lawyers, clerks,
noblemen, prelates, and more substantial London merchants. A
few less attractive persons inhabited the lanes on the sides. Rob-
beries and assaults along the road were not unknown. On the left
near the Cross was the Hospital of the Blessed Lady of Rounci-
valle whence came that "gentle" scoundrel the Pardoner of *The
Canterbury Tales*. Riding into Westminster from London, the
visitor would find the town dominated by the spires of the Abbey.
During the fourteenth century there were about forty-four monks
there. In a tenement in the garden of the Lady Chapel, Chaucer
spent the last months of his life. Perhaps he visited the Abbot
from time to time in his large house with a courtyard off the nave,
completed in 1386. The house was used frequently for royal
guests for whom there was not sufficient room at the Palace.

On the bank of the river near the Abbey was St. Stephen's, a
two-storied chapel ninety feet long and thirty feet wide begun by
Edward I and, as we have seen, completed by William Rameseye
of London. Glazing and painting were begun in 1349 and continued for ten years. Every inch of the interior was painted,
gilded, diapered, or stenciled in brilliant colors, and there were
wall paintings under the windows.[131]

The Royal Palace was primarily a residence, but it also served
for administrative and judicial functions. By the time of Henry II
it became normal for the biennial sessions of the Exchequer to be
held there. In the thirteenth century the Court of Common Pleas
held its sessions in the Great Hall, and in the fourteenth century
the King's Bench settled down there also. Perhaps the most
spectacular room in the Palace was the Painted Chamber, joined
to St. Stephen's by a gallery. Two friars who visited London in
1322 wrote, "Near the Abbey stands the celebrated palace of the
Kings of England, in which is that famous chamber on whose

[131] For a full account, see Maurice Hastings, *St. Stephen's Chapel* (Cambridge, 1955); and Colvin, *The King's Works*, I, 510 ff.

walls all the warlike scenes in the Bible are painted with wonderful skill, and explained by a complete series of texts beautifully written in French, to the great admiration of the beholder."[132] These paintings were kept in repair throughout the fourteenth and fifteenth centuries, but were whitewashed in the sixteenth century. The chamber was located in a building eighty and a half feet long, twenty-six feet wide, and thirty-one feet nine inches high. A small chapel projected from the north side. There was a fireplace on the north wall and a small window opening into the chapel so that the King could hear Mass from his bed. The floor was of glazed tile, and the ceiling was boarded and studded with flat bosses. On the west wall by the entrance were the words KE NE DUNE KE NE TINE NE PRENT KE DE-SIRE, "He who does not give of what he has does not take what he desires," an admirable injunction to feudal largess, but perhaps a little heady for the young King Richard. The paintings included the four Evangelists and scenes from the story of Joseph and the Books of Maccabeus.

North of the chamber stood Westminster Hall, built by William Rufus in 1099. At the time it was probably the largest hall in Europe, two hundred and forty feet long and sixty-seven and a half feet wide. Richard II had the roof rebuilt, beginning in 1394, probably under the supervision of William Hurley, Master Carpenter, and Henry Yevele. The magnificent hammerbeam roof thus produced survives as one of the finest monuments of medieval carpentry. A visitor to the Hall before work on the new roof was begun might well have found Parliament in session with the lords spiritual and temporal on either side of the King attended by sumptuously gowned officials. Chaucer, who occupied an office in the Palace grounds when he was Clerk of the Works, attended Parliament in 1386 as a member from Kent. Most of those present at a session in Westminister would return in the evening down the Strand to London where innkeepers awaited them, or where their own servants were preparing for their return to inns like that of the Bishop of Ely in Farringdon.

---

[132] Quoted from Colvin, *The King's Works,* I, 499. This work includes an excellent map of the medieval palace and a full description.

THREE

City Customs

"Certainly, if the land does not bountifully render its fruits," warned Bishop Brinton of Rochester in a sermon delivered in January 1375, "and, even worse, if misfortune, pestilence, and war beset England, these things should largely be attributed to our sloth."[1] The bishop was not complaining about simple laziness or lack of industry of the kind that might have incurred the censure of Benjamin Franklin. He meant instead neglect of duty to God. Sloth was neither that monastic *acedia* that was later to attract the interest of those suffering from *ennui*, nor a simple failure to get up early and go to Matins. It was the beginning of disobedience. From "man's first disobedience" came all the world's ills, for if man did not obey God, then those things subject to man would not obey man. As the bishop went on to explain, "Since earth should be inferior to man that it may serve him, and man should be inferior to God that he may serve God, an harmonious proportion is established, so that just as man serves God, his superior, the earth and the elements ought to serve man, their superior. . . . But men, and especially idle youth, withdraw their just service to God. Thus God justly permits the earth and other elements to be not profitable but injurious to man." This attitude explains in part medieval reactions to floods, pestilences, tempests, and other natural disasters. But it has its human or "social" implications as well. Sloth, as Chaucer's Second Nun puts it, is

[1] *Sermons*, No. 48, p. 216, ed. Sister Mary Aquinas Devlin, O. P. (London, 1954).

The ministre and the norice unto vices,
Which that men clepe in Englissh ydelnesse,
That porter of the gate is of delices.

These "delices" are of the illicit variety. Thus, the bishop continues, "Where idleness exists, there also is every evil, like theft, rapine, gluttony, lechery, incest, and adultery."[2]

We should be careful not to dismiss the bishop's remarks as the empty moralizing of an ecclesiastic. They reflect, first of all, a strong sense of hierarchy. Clergymen and laymen alike in the later Middle Ages conceived of the world as a manifestation of an hierarchical structure that dominated nature, society, and the individual, not to mention celestial beings as well. Hence the bishop's conclusion that what we would call social problems are essentially moral would have startled no one. Immorality was for the bishop and his contemporaries not simply a personal matter; it might lead to the destruction of an entire community. If sloth was a prime disrupter of hierarchies, what constituted a good realm?

In a sermon delivered at Paul's Cross in the same year, on May 13, the bishop explained that the honor of a king, hence of a kingdom, rests on military power, clerical wisdom, and the just regimen of the people. With reference to the first point, he reminded his listeners that England was once the kingdom of kingdoms because it enjoyed so many victories, captured so many kings, and occupied so many dominions. But, he said, "God, who was once an Englishman, abandons us." Success in warfare, which, we should remember, was chivalric warfare when the bishop spoke, was a mark of God's favor, since its outcome was Providential. Failure in warfare was attributed to moral weakness. Here the bishop was most concerned about idleness and lust among noblemen, and especially about adultery, which alone might bring about the destruction of the realm. With regard to the second point, the bishop was careful to distinguish between

[2] The history of the concept of sloth has recently been treated by Siegfried Wenzel, *The Sin of Sloth* (Chapel Hill, 1967). However, the broader implications of the idea of sloth are often neglected. There is, for example, a real sense in which Shakespeare's *Hamlet* is a study in sloth, which was conventionally associated with melancholy.

"clerical wisdom" and worldly wisdom, or what we might call long-range policy based on self-interest. Finally, his conception of a just "regimen of the people" was especially relevant to the citizens of London in his audience. If the merchants have their reward within the realm, the bishop explained, and security in transacting their affairs outside the realm for the benefit of the public welfare, and the cities have just officers and rulers, then the whole realm loves and honors the king. But if the merchants have no profit, but foreigners do, and the people are subject to extortionate action from their rulers, then they speak evil of their king, to the peril of their souls.[3]

We might find it strange to hear a bishop advocating victory in war, true wisdom as distinct from worldly strategies in the conduct of affairs, and the prosperity of merchants. There is nothing revolutionary, or even "social," in what the bishop has to say. He did not mention the masses for the simple reason that the masses did not then exist. On the other hand, it is clear that the bishop had a great deal of confidence in the order of the universe and also in the order of his society. The decay he complains about has nothing to do with faulty organization or poor planning. It is, on the other hand, purely and simply a matter of individual morality directed toward the maintenance of an hierarchical structure. It is in the light of ideas such as these that we should seek to understand the structure of London's government, its laws, and its customs in the later fourteenth century.

London was divided into twenty-four wards, twelve on each side of Walbrook, until 1394 when Farrigdon Without, because of its growing population, became a ward in its own right, bringing the total to twenty-five.[4] Each ward was governed by an alderman, who, together with his officials, a beadle and a staff of sergeants and constables, was responsible for defense, police, sanitation, and routine administration within the ward. Aldermen were required to hold biennial "wardmotes," or meetings of the residents under their jurisdiction. All residents and hired servants

---

[3] *Sermons*, No. 12, p. 47.
[4] R. R. Sharpe, *Calendar of Letter-Books Preserved among the Archives of the City of London* (London, 1899 *et. seq.*), *Letter-Book H*, pp. 407–408; *Statutes at Large*, I, 414; *Statutes of the Realm*, II, 91–92.

A beadle (copyright British Museum).

over the age of fifteen, except knights, squires, females, apprentices at law, and clerks, were required to attend on pain of a fine of 4d. Usually, such meetings were held in the principal church of the ward. The beadle called the roll, keeping the names of freemen and nonfreemen separate. At these meetings beadles, aleconners, scavengers, and other officials were elected. Bakers registered their stamps, weights and measures were set, and inquiries were made concerning any matters pertaining to the city.[5] The alderman heard any complaints about irregularities that might arise and sought to correct them, unless they were of sufficient importance to be referred to the mayor.

[5] *Liber Albus: The White Book of the City of London,* ed. H. T. Riley (London, 1861), pp. 32 ff.

Everyone present at a wardmote was required to take an oath of frankpledge as follows:

You shall swear, that you shall be good and true unto the King of England and to his heirs, Kings, and the King's peace shall you keep; and to the officers of the City you shall be obedient, and at all times that shall be needful, you shall be ready to help the officers in arresting misdoers, and those disobedient to the King's peace, as well denizens as strangers. And you shall be ready, at the warnings of the Constables and Bedels, to make the watches and other charges for the safeguard of the peace, and all the points in this Wardmote shewn, according to your power, you shall well and lawfully keep. And if you know any evil covin within the Ward of the City, you shall withstand the same, or unto your Alderman make it known. So God you help, and the Saints.[6]

In this manner all male permanent residents not otherwise obligated to lords lay or spiritual were formally introduced to a certain civic responsibility as a part of their allegiance to the Crown. In a society still largely dependent on verbal contracts, such oaths were probably taken somewhat more seriously than they might be today, when practically all contractual agreements are written. Temporary visitors to the city were not, of course, bound by any such obligations. But efforts were made to see to it that innkeepers were responsible for the behavior of their guests. Thus in 1384 all innkeepers were sworn not to harbor anyone for more than one day and one night "unless they were willing to answer for them and their acts." They were not to receive travelers without surety for their good behavior and were liable to a fine of £100 if a guest caused serious trouble.[7]

Aldermen were originally elected at the wardmote, but aldermanic elections, like those of the sheriffs, were later held at the Guildhall by representatives selected from the wards. After 1376 the mayor was elected by the aldermen and by the "commons," that is, by the "more wealthy and more respectable commoners of the city" especially summoned as a council for the purpose. During the second half of the century the mayor automatically assumed the office of Royal Escheator for London, so that the

[6] *Liber Albus,* p. 273.
[7] A. H. Thomas, *Calendar of Select Pleas and Memoranda of the City of London* (Cambridge, 1932), pp. 78–79.

office had a formal link with the Crown. On various occasions the council of the city was elected by the misteries rather than by the wards. Thus in 1351 the Drapers, Goldsmiths, Woolmongers, Vintners, Skinners, Tailors, Cordwainers, and Butchers each elected four members and the Ironmongers two members.[8] Such an arrangement was possible because the "more wealthy and respectable" men of the wards were, in effect, the "more wealthy and respectable" men of these misteries, and the misteries themselves were sufficiently well organized to act as responsible units of civic government. When a similar experiment was tried between 1377 and 1384, some fifty-one crafts were represented, a fact that bears witness to the growing number of misteries with responsible organizations as well as to the widening of representation in civic affairs. The new "Common Council," as it was called, was responsible for the election of the mayor and sheriffs. The latter, sheriffs of London and Middlesex, were by this time primarily city officers in London, the "eyes of the Mayor."

In January 1384 the election of the council was returned to the wards. The aldermen were instructed to assemble their wards within fifteen days after their election on the Feast of St. Gregory (March 12) to elect four qualified persons from each ward for the council. However, the mayor was not to accept more than eight persons from the same mistery. If more were nominated, the mayor and aldermen were to select four of the best and instruct the wards to elect replacements for the others. The effort here was obviously to avoid the domination of the council by a small group of misteries. As we shall see, the crafts were by no means of equal importance and power, so that the wealthier misteries could undoubtedly arrange to dominate the city government under the old system. It was further suggested that the wards should elect councillors roughly in accordance with population:

6 from Farringdon, Cripplegate, Cordwainer, Cheap, and Bridge

4 from Vintry, Dowgate, Walbrook, Candlewick Street, Billingsgate, Tower, Cornhill, Queenhithe, Langbourne, Bishopsgate, Aldersgate, Castle Baynard, Broad Street, and Bread Street

[8] G. Unwin, *The Gilds and Companies of London*, 4th ed. (London, 1963), p. 77.

2 from Bassishaw, Coleman Street, Lime Street, Portsoken, and
   Aldgate.

This made a total of ninety-six, the equivalent of four from each
ward. The problem envisaged was probably the fact that a small
ward like Lime Street might not be able to supply four "good
and sufficient" men if only eight men could be elected from a
single mistery. The council was to meet once a quarter, on pain
of 40d for absence. The mayor, at least fifteen of the aldermen,
and the council were to meet every year on St. Matthew's Day
(September 21) "with other more sufficient men" to elect
sheriffs.[9] The "other more sufficient men" were undoubtedly summoned by the mayor, who seems always to have been allowed
considerable leeway in influencing city elections.

It is fairly obvious that the elections thus held were not in our
sense "democratic" and that the "commons" of the council did
not represent a cross section of London citizens. The underlying
rationale of the city government was still feudal. That is, feudal
custom demanded that a man be judged by his peers, or by those
in an equivalent degree. In the same way, men were elected by
their peers, and, if necessary, modifications in an election were
made by superiors. Once elected, moreover, a man ranked a very
definite step higher than his former peers and expected to be
treated accordingly. The mayor of London ranked as an earl "as
well in the King's presence as elsewhere."[10] Severe penalties
were exacted for striking or insulting an alderman. Respect for
authority was not only inculcated upon every young man as a
part of his moral education but was rigidly enforced.

An incident that occurred in 1340 while the King was abroad
vividly illustrates the kind of respect demanded by London officials and by an efficient king. Some skinners and fishmongers
engaged in a street brawl. A few were arrested, and their fellows
tried to rescue them. What happened is revealed in a letter King
Edward wrote to the mayor:

And . . . one Thomas, son of John Haunsard, fishmonger, with his
sword drawn, seized you, the aforesaid mayor [Andrew Aubrey], by

9 *Letter-Book H,* pp. 227 ff.
10 *Liber Albus,* p. 12.

the throat, and would have struck you on the neck, if he had been able; and one John le Brewere, a porter, wounded one of our serjeants of the said city, so greatly that his life was despaired of; in contempt of us, and in great affray of the good folks of our said city; by reason whereof, the aforesaid Thomas and John were forthwith taken and brought to the Guildhall, and there before you of their violence and excess were arraigned, and thereof by their own admission convicted; and by your award were condemned to death, and beheaded in Chepe. Wherefore we do signify unto you, that upon what has been done to the said misdoers, to the punishment of the bad, and the comforting of the good, we do greatly congratulate you; and your doing therein do accept, and, so much as in us lies, do ratify the same. And we do let you know for certain, that contempts and outrages so committed against our servants, we do hold as being committed against ourselves; and if you had not acted in such manner therein, we should have taken the same so grievously as toward yourselves and the franchise of our said city, that it would have been for an example to you, and to all your successors in time to come.[11]

The hierarchy of the mayor, sheriffs, aldermen, and commons of London was an integral part of the hierarchy of the kingdom. The reference to the King and to the King's peace in the oath of frank-pledge was not empty rhetoric. King Edward took it very seriously indeed, and the extent to which he was able to maintain his officials as extensions of his person determined his greatness as a king. King Richard, for reasons not altogether of his own making, was, in spite of his "tyranny," far less able than King Edward to control and protect his men.

The city sent four representatives to Parliament, none of whom, after 1373, could be a sheriff. Again, however, Parliament was not a "democratic" institution in the Middle Ages. It was an outgrowth of the King's Council that first began to include "peers of the land" under Edward II. Its chief function was to submit petitions to the king for decision. If the petitions were successful, they resulted in statutes. During the thirteenth century petitions were submitted by the barons on behalf of the community at large. After 1327 petitions were submitted by the commons, and the peers of the realm became judges and justices. From that time

[11] H. T. Riley, *Memorials of London and London Life in the XIII, XIV, and XV Centuries* (London, 1861), pp. 210–211.

forward the commons formulated the grievances of the people and requested remedies, but during the fourteenth century their petitions were often suggested to them by the lords. The commons also submitted private petitions for judgment during the later years of the century. But the commons were not agents of revolution, did not have much influence on decisions concerning war and peace, and were not "common people." Moreover, few had any ambitions to serve in Parliament, since attendance there was onerous and relatively unrewarding.[12] Personal relations between the mayor and the Crown, or between the mayor and the Duke of Lancaster or other magnates, were far more important to the city than its representation in Parliament.

The hierarchy of the city government was formally displayed in a number of processionals. Our information about these comes from the *Liber Albus,* but it probably represents late fourteenth-century practice without much modification. Election Day for the mayor occurred each year on the Feasts of St. Simon and St. Jude (October 28.). On the weekday thereafter the mayor, the new mayor (when the old one was not reelected), the aldermen, sheriffs, the members of the new mayor's mistery, and the more substantial members of the other misteries assembled at the Guildhall at nine o'clock. They rode along Cheap, out Newgate, down to Fleet Street, and along the Strand to Westminster, where they dismounted. The Londoners proceeded first to the Exchequer, where the recorder announced the new mayor. The latter repeated his oath of office, assumed his office as Escheator, and appointed an attorney for the city. Then the mayor and his followers proceeded to the Common Bench to appoint an attorney, and to the King's Bench, where they appointed two attorneys. The new mayor, led by sergeants at arms, mace-bearers, and and his sword-bearer and flanked by sheriffs carrying white wands, proceeded back to London and through Cheap, followed in procession by the recorder, aldermen, and the men of the misteries in their liveries. After dinner, the mayor and aldermen assembled at the Church of St. Thomas of Acon. Thence they marched to St. Paul's, pausing in the nave to pray for Bishop

[12] See H. G. Richardson, "The Commons and Medieval Politics," *Transactions of the Royal Historical Society,* XXVIII (1946), 21–45.

William, who is said to have "obtained from his Lordship William the Conqueror great liberties for the City of London." The procession then moved to the churchyard to play at the grave of the parents of St. Thomas Becket. Afterward they returned to the Hospital of St. Thomas of Acon, where the mayor and aldermen each offered a penny. If the Exchequer was not sitting at Westminster, the procession would go to the Constable of the Tower instead.[13]

Another procession followed on All Saints Day (November 1), when the mayor and his household, the aldermen, and the more substantial men of the misteries went after dinner to the Church of St. Thomas of Acon dressed in their liveries, and proceeded thence through Cheap to St. Paul's to hear Vespers. Similar ceremonies were held on Christmas, on St. Stephen's Day, and on the day of St. John the Evangelist (May 6). On the Feast of the Innocents (December 28) the mayor, sheriffs, and aldermen heard Vespers at the Church of St. Thomas and went to Mass and Vespers there on the following day. Similar ceremonies occurred on the Circumcision (January 1), Epiphany (January 6), and the Purification (February 2). On Monday of Pentecost, the mayor, sheriffs, aldermen, and those of the livery of the mayor and sheriffs met at the Church of St. Peter on Cornhill. The rectors of London, the sheriffs and their liverymen, those of the mayor's livery, the mayor, the recorder, and the aldermen marched through Cheap to St. Paul's. They met the clergy of Paul's at the north door, proceeded out the south door, and thence to the great western door of the nave, where they made their offerings. A similar procession took place on Tuesday beginning at St. Bartholomew's, except that it was led by the commons of Middlesex. On Wednesday, the mayor, sheriffs, aldermen, and others met at the Church of St. Thomas of Acon and were led to St. Paul's by the commons of Essex.[14]

These processionals were at once a display of the municipal hierarchy in relation to the Crown, the ecclesiastical hierarchy, and the adjacent counties, and a visible expression of city *pietas*. The prayers and religious observances that accompanied them

[13] *Liber Albus*, pp. 24–26.
[14] *Ibid.*, pp. 26–27.

should not be taken as dry formalities, old customs, without content. They represent, to use the language of Bishop Brinton, a kind of formal defiance of sloth. Insofar as the city is concerned specifically, the strong emphasis placed on the memory of St. Thomas Becket, London's chief citizen, is especially significant. Most citizens witnessing these ceremonies or taking part in them must have done so with considerable feeling for their city and its traditions. But who were the citizens of London?

In the first place, a man born in the city whose father was a citizen might acquire citizenship by taking an oath at the Guildhall when he became of age. However, London had a "floating" population. There was a steady stream of newcomers to the city, and, at the same time, a large number of persons who had acquired wealth in the city returned to their ancestral neighborhoods. In the second part of the fourteenth century especially it was unusual for a family to remain in London for more than two or three generations. If a man were not the son of a citizen, he had to demonstrate his moral and economic qualifications. That is, he was required to show that he was of good reputation, loyal to the king and to the officers of the city, and capable of earning his livelihood.[15] Specifically, the two means open to him were apprenticeship and redemption. If the first course were chosen, the young man, about fifteen, would find a master who would accept him as an apprentice, and then pay a series of fees—one for his teaching, one for the mistery he wished to enter, and one for the city. It was generally recognized that an apprentice was being prepared not only for the exercise of his mistery, but also for a position in the city government. Terms of apprenticeship varied between seven and nineteen years.[16] Those who obtained citizenship by redemption were usually well-established merchants from other locations. The fee required was adjusted to the means of the applicant, to whom citizenship was desirable because it meant freedom from tolls throughout the kingdom.[17]

Once a citizen, a man had the status of tenant in chief of the

[15] Sylvia L. Thrupp, *The Merchant Class of Medieval London* (Chicago, 1948), p. 16.
[16] A. H. Thomas, *Calendar of Plea and Memoranda Rolls of the City of London, 1361–1381* (Cambridge, 1929), pp. xxx–xxxii.
[17] *Ibid.*, pp. xlvii ff.

Crown. During the later thirteenth century this status was taken quite seriously, and citizens demanded to be treated as barons, or noblemen, whose peers were the counts and barons of England. During the fourteenth century, the social status of citizenship may have deteriorated somewhat, but there are still definite traces of the old attitude. In 1308 a London citizen who had been alderman and sheriff returned to his native village, where he was arrested as a villein by the bailiff with a demand that he serve as reeve. The Court of Common Pleas freed him, however, and granted him damages of £100.[18] To avoid instances of this kind, it was decreed by the Common Council in 1387 that anyone who became alderman, sheriff, or mayor and had been born a villein who had not previously notified the mayor of his servile condition should lose the freedom of the city.[19] Generally, it was not likely that many villeins would become citizens. About a third of the daughters of fourteenth-century aldermen who married entered gentle families, and it was not uncommon for widows of aldermen to marry noblemen.[20] For example, John Montague, later Earl of Salisbury and something of a poet, married the daughter of Adam Fraunceys, Draper.

A large proportion of the population of the city at any given time was "foreign," or noncitizen. There were, of course, actual foreigners there, Flemish and Brabant weavers, merchants from Germany, France, or Italy, sailors from foreign ports, and so on. In addition, there was a large noncitizen clerical population, there were numerous royal servants, apprentices at law, and servants and retainers of the noblemen and prelates who maintained residences in the city. There were common laborers, porters, small tradesmen from the country at the markets, and even a few noncitizen shopkeepers. Moreover, as we have seen, London's commercial inns were often busy. The commercial life of the city tended to maintain its total population and even to increase it. Other cities and towns in England and Europe did not recover from the ravages of the Black Death, but London continued to grow and to prosper, especially during the last two decades of the century.

18 *Ibid.*, p. xxv.
19 *Ibid.*, p. xxvi.
20 Thrupp, *Merchant Class*, p. 266.

Apprentices afforded the most important source of new citizens, many of them fresh from the countryside. An apprentice could expect to live with his master, share his meals, and generally regard his master and mistress as father and mother. The master supplied board, lodging, clothing, and instruction, both technical and moral. If the apprentice misbehaved seriously, the master could take him before the mayor for correction. On the other hand, an apprentice could plead before the mayor if he thought his master was treating him improperly or failing to train him. Legally, the master owned the term of an apprentice's service. With the consent of the apprentice, any portion of that term could be sold or willed to a beneficiary. Frequently a merchant left the remaining terms of his apprentices to his wife. When the term of an apprentice was completed, he might remain with his master as a "servant." In a will of 1349 a tradesman provided a bequest to his servant, formerly his apprentice, that included the remaining terms of his two apprentices. Relationships between masters and apprentices varied, as might be expected. There are records of runaway apprentices, but, on the other hand, there are instances like that of John de Croydon, Fishmonger, who left a chantry for the soul of his late master and other bequests to his own apprentices.[21] The great merchant William Walworth left a chantry for the souls of John Lovekyn, his late master, and his wife. It is not difficult to understand that the relationship between master and apprentice in the fourteenth century was most conveniently thought of in moral terms.

In the Prologue to *The Canterbury Tales* Chaucer introduces us to a number of London tradesmen:

> An haberdasshere and a carpenter,
> A Webbe, a Dyere, and a Tapycer—
> And they were clothed alle in o lyveree
> Of a solempne and a greet fraternitee.
> Ful fressh and newe hir geere apiked was:
> Hir knyves were chaped noght with bras
> But al with silver; wroght ful clene and weel
> Hir girdles and hir pouches everydeel.

[21] R. R. Sharpe, *Calendar of Wills Proved and Enrolled in the Court of Husting, London* (London, 1889), I, 519, 502.

Wel semed ech of hem a fair burgeys
To sitten in a yeldehalle on a deys.
Everich, for the wisdom that he kan,
Was shaply for to been an alderman;
For catel hadde they ynogh and rente,
And eek hir wyves wolde it wel assente,
And elles certeyn were they to blame.
It is ful fair to been ycleped "madame,"
And goon to vigilies al bifore,
And have a mantel roialliche ybore.

Frequently it is said that these figures are typical of London tradesmen in the later fourteenth century. They are depicted not in the livery of a mistery, but in that of a parish fraternity, all with expensive knives, girdles, and pouches. Each, Chaucer says, was wise enough to sit on the dais as an alderman, for all had sufficient property and income, not to mention encouragement from their wives, who enjoyed the prospect of precedence at vigils and rich mantles royally carried. But in late fourteenth-century London the possibility of any of these gentlemen becoming an alderman was remote. Among identifiable aldermen between 1377 and 1394, the misteries represented are as follows.

Grocers	108
Mercers	85
Fishmongers	58
Goldsmiths	44
Drapers	35
Vintners	28
Skinners	24
Waxchandlers	9
Woolmongers	5
Ironmongers	3
Armorers	2
Broderers	2[22]

Haberdashers were mostly small tradesmen, carpenters ordinarily possessed only their skills and a few tools, and the rest were not

[22] See A. B. Beaven, *The Aldermen of the City of London* (London, 1908–1913), I, 360 and *passim*.

of much importance after the middle of the century. It is fairly obvious that Chaucer was, as usual, writing with a smile, and that his tradesmen with their somewhat gaudy holiday attire, wisdom based on property and income, and ambitious wives, were intended as amusing exemplars of persons seeking to rise above their station. They are neither "types" of London craftsmen nor "realistic" characters; they are instead exemplifications of a common weakness of the small businessman.

Chaucer was himself quite well acquainted with such prominent merchants as William Walworth, Nicholas Brembre, and John Philpot, not to mention John Chaucer. He knew very well what such men were like but showed no interest in leaving us accurate portrayals of them. The Merchant of the General Prologue has a forked beard, like that of Richard Lyons as Stow described it on his monument or like that worn by Chaucer himself in the portraits that survive. But this merchant seems to talk a great deal about "th'encrees of his wynnyng" while remaining in debt. That is, he, like his fellows the tradesmen, pretends to be something he is not.

The various misteries were not, then, of equal importance. In the course of the fourteenth century more and more of them acquired official recognition. As we have seen, in 1377 fifty-one were recognized as being capable of furnishing members for the city council. By the mid-fifteenth century twice that number enjoyed a corporate organization. The guilds of medieval London played an important part in civic affairs, but the parish fraternities, although they had considerable social importance, had no civic significance.

The origin of the guilds is obscure and may, indeed, not be a proper subject for discussion. That is, some organizations of tradesmen are very old, and some are clearly outgrowths of parish fraternities. When new guilds were established, they tended to imitate the structure of those already in existence, and that structure might be rather different at different periods. During the second half of the fourteenth century guilds and fraternities multiplied rapidly, and the various misteries acquired charters and officially recognized regulations. The problem of disentangling the situation historically has been complicated by the effort to apply modern categories, like "religious," "secular," "democratic," "free," and so on, to situations where they have little or no meaning. The misteries were hardly uniform institutions. Some were made up mostly of artisans, men whose chief assets were a knowledge of traditional techniques and manual skill. Others were made up of men engaged mainly in international trade. Organizations of the first type might be relatively poor, but even this category falls down when we come to consider the goldsmiths, some of whom were artisans of very great skill. International trade had been a feature of medieval life for centuries. In the fourteenth century its basic conventions were still feudal, and it helps little to call men engaged in it "capitalists." The situation puzzled authorities in the fourteenth century itself. Thus in a declaration concerning franchise in 1369 we find it said that "it seems right that everyone who is enfranchised ought to buy and sell wholesale, within the City and without, any manner of merchandise on which he can make a profit; but he may keep a shop and sell at retail only those goods that belong to his own particular mistery, which he ought to support whenever necessary."[23] Vintners were encouraged to buy cloth and fish for export "to keep their money in the country," and, in general, we should expect to find "the more substantial men of the misteries" engaged in enterprises that had little to do with their guild membership.

There is a sense in which the traditional basis for a guild is a fraternity, although not all guilds originated as fraternities, and at least one guild abolished its fraternity in the fourteenth century. Unwin observes that "society in the fourteenth and fifteenth centuries was literally honeycombed with fraternities . . . . Kings and princes, barons and knights, cathedral canons, rectors of churches, curates, parish clerks, lawyers, wealthy merchants, comfortable shopkeepers, poor journeymen, peasants, and football players were bound together for the pursuit of their special class interests under similar social and religious forms and sanctions."[24] It is true that persons of all kinds belonged to fraternities, but the idea that the fraternity represented "class interests" needs modification. Men of very diverse degree might belong to the

[23] *Letter-Book G,* p. 179.
[24] *The Gilds and Companies of London,* p. 98.

same fraternity. There was obviously no "fraternity of kings" in England, and the same might be said of the other "classes" mentioned by Unwin, with some exceptions. But even these exceptions do not represent real "classes" in the modern sense.

The most numerous fraternities in the fourteenth century were those attached to parish churches, of which we have evidence of over seventy in London. Historians of early European fraternities have discovered that the common element in all of them is a regular "feast," so that there has been some tendency to look upon these organizations as being, in effect, drinking clubs. However, in fourteenth-century London a parish fraternity in the Church of St. Sepulchre without Newgate maintained a chaplain to celebrate continually and a light before the image of St. Stephen. Every member expected to attend Mass on St. Stephen's Day and to offer at least a farthing. On the following Sunday the members dined together, all wearing cowls of the same color. On the death of a member, tapers were provided for the funeral Mass and provisions were made for three trentals. The fraternity contributed 14d weeky to the upkeep of impoverished members. These activities were fairly typical.[25] The wardens of such fraternities were expected to help settle differences among members and, sometimes, to oversee their moral conduct. Thus the Fraternity of St. Anne in the Church of St. Lawrence in the Old Jewry threatened to expel any member "who lay in bed too long, who haunted taverns, or who ran about to wrestling matches."[26] Fourteenth-century wills contain numerous bequests to fraternities. For example, in 1373, Agnes Pickerell, the widow of a saddler, left bequests to the Fraternity of the Holy Cross in the Church of St. Vedast, to the Fraternity of St. Katherine in the Church of St. Matthew in Friday Street, and to the Fraternity of St. John of the Tailors of London.[27] Women seem to have been especially attracted to fraternal activities.

In addition to parish fraternities, there were "confraternities," or lay organizations associated with religious groups of various

[25] W. Page, The Victoria History of London, I, 213–214.
[26] Thrupp, Merchant Class, p. 38.
[27] Cal. Wills, II, 154. For typical bequests to fraternities, see I, 504. 541, 547, 564, 565, 576, 647, 648, etc.

kinds. Chaucer's wife, for example, belonged to the confraternity of the canons of Lincoln Cathedral, which numbered among its members Henry of Lancaster, John of Gaunt, Henry Earl of Derby, John Beaufort, and other persons connected with the family.[28] In Chaucer's "Summoner's Tale," the friar assures his intended victim Thomas that he is a brother.

"I took oure dame oure lettre with oure seel."

In other words, Thomas has become a member of one of the penitential confraternities fostered by the fraternal orders.[29] The difference between a fraternity and a confraternity is not, however, a rigorous one.

The manner in which a fraternity might take on the features of a guild may be illustrated in the history of the organization formed by the Skinners of London. As we have seen, the skinners originally settled along Walbrook below Cheap, where there was a plentiful water supply useful for cleaning and soaking furs. Apparently, most skinners attended the Church of St. John, Walbrook, and there some of them formed a Fraternity of Corpus Christi in the church. The fraternity secured a royal charter in 1327, which specified the standards for finished furs, allowed the skinners of the fraternity to appoint "good and trusty men" to inspect furs in the city and its suburbs, and to report defective furs to the mayor, who could seize the false goods and punish the offending tradesmen.[30] Perhaps it is useful to regard the trade regulations as an extension of the moral supervision conventionally exercised by fraternities. In 1393 the Fraternity of Corpus Christi became a livery company and shortly thereafter obtained the "Copped Hall" in Dowgate for its headquarters. Meanwhile, the journeymen skinners had belonged to two other fraternities. These merged into a Fraternity of Our Lady's Assumption in St. John's Walbrook after 1397. Like the Fraternity of Corpus

---

[28] Martin M. Crow and Clair C. Olson, *Chaucer Life-Records* (Oxford, 1966), pp. 91–93.

[29] See John V. Fleming, "The Summoner's Prologue: An Iconographic Adjustment," *The Chaucer Review*, II (1967), 95–107. Fleming supplies extensive bibliographical information.

[30] Riley, *Memorials*, pp. 153–154.

Christi, this one enrolled members who were not skinners, but who were not so distinguished as the members of the Livery Company who were not skinners. The Fraternity of Corpus Christi enrolled noblemen as members and enjoyed the patronage of Edward III, Queen Philippa, the Black Prince, Queen Anne, and Richard II. It went on solemn procession through the city on the Feast of Corpus Christi, accompanied by the mayor and aldermen. The move to the "Copped Hall" was probably the result of enlarged membership, prosperity, and similar factors and had nothing to do with "secularization."[31]

In much the same way the Salter's Company was originally a fraternity, also of Corpus Christi, in All Hallows Bread Street. It began to elect wardens in 1394.[32] The Grocers of Sopers Lane were originally organized as a Fraternity of St. Antonin whose members dined at the Inn of the Abbot of Bury on June 12 and supported a priest at 15d weekly.[33] The Whittawyers kept a wax candle burning in the Church of All Hallows London Wall and maintained a poor box there for widows and infirm whittawyers, who could draw 7d a day.[34] The Brewers maintained a fraternity in the same church, but they did not become officially organized until after our period. It might be said that in the fourteenth century a guild is an organization consisting chiefly of men associated at least in part with a given trade, which may or may not either be a fraternity or contain one or more fraternities and which has some sort of regulatory authority over the trade. But it is better, perhaps, to avoid definitions and simply to remember that guilds were not all alike and that they acquired civic as well as social importance when they were granted official recognition as regulatory bodies.

In some instances, like that of the skinners, separate fraternities existed for the masters and journeymen of the trade. The valet-tailors had a fraternity of their own, but the young men who belonged to it misbehaved, and in 1415 they were told to

---

[31] Elspeth M. Veale, *The English Fur Trade in the Later Middle Ages* (Oxford, 1966), pp. 44–46, 105–111; Thrupp, *Merchant Class*, p. 30.
[32] J. Stevens Watson, *A History of the Salter's Company* (Oxford, 1963), pp. 6–8.
[33] Unwin, *Gilds and Companies*, pp. 103–104.
[34] Riley, *Memorials*, pp. 222-223.

subject themselves to the rules of the Fraternity of Tailors.[35] The regulations of the saddlers (1362) and the fullers (1363) specifically forbade the formulation of servants' associations "for the obtaining from their masters a higher wage than they are worth in their mistery to the damage of the people."[36] In spite of this regulation, the journeymen saddlers congregated at St. Mary le Bow in 1380 without the assent of their masters. They were strictly forbidren by the city to repeat the performance.[37] Similarly, the servingmen cordwainers assembled at Blackfriars in 1387 under the inspiration of a Dominican to form their own fraternity "to the prejudice of the trade." They assaulted a cordwainer for disagreeing with them. The city authorities regarded their action as a violation of a royal proclamation of 1383 against congregations and conspiracies.[38] In 1386, the cordwainers, still torn by dissension, dissolved their Fraternity of St. Mary in the Church of the Carmelites as a source of trouble, saying that the more "able" of their members would wear the livery and help the poor.[39] This does not mean, however, that the cordwainers were more "secular," "free," or "enlightened" than their fellows in other misteries. It probably means that they had difficulties in self-government brought on in part by the friars. London shoemakers were not Harbingers of the Modern World.

A municipal effort to organize the misteries was instituted in 1364:

Also it is ordained that all the misteries of the City be lawfully ruled and governed, each in its kind, so that no deceit or false work be found therein by good men elected and sworn from each mistery.[40]

In this year the weavers, butchers, smiths, and glassmakers were organized, and the fishmongers were granted a new charter. They were followed in succeeding years by the founders, skinners, drapers, tapicers, vintners, haberdashers, and smiths. Like the

[35] *Cal. Wills,* II, 403, note.
[36] *Letter-Book G,* pp. 143, 160.
[37] *Plea and Memoranda Rolls,* p. 264.
[38] Riley, *Memorials,* p. 495.
[39] *Letter-Book H,* p. 432.
[40] *Letter-Book G,* p. 174.

skinners, the fishmongers had more than one fraternity, but they maintained an especially strong and efficient organization. Generally, the charters and regulations of the misteries are designed to prevent "false work" as the city suggested. They contain items concerning the terms of apprentices, the quality of the goods produced, proper weights and measures, working at night (forbidden to the blacksmiths because of noise,[41] and to others because poor light impaired the quality of the work), and so on. Neither the city nor the king was interested in "secularizing" fraternities, in establishing medieval equivalents of trade unions, or in furthering "freedom" for craftsmen. They wanted more efficient administration along lines already established. The guilds for their part seem to have taken a genuine interest in maintaining their reputations by producing goods of standard quality. They were not, strictly speaking, "middle-class" organizations. Noblemen might belong to their fraternities, and they were governed for the most part by their more substantial members, who, as we have seen, constituted a city equivalent of the feudal aristocracy. No one wished to have his organization in the position of the poulterers before 1366, who were then supervised by men not of their trade appointed by the mayor.[42] The extension of this system would have created an expensive bureaucracy and destroyed the community life of the misteries. "Guilds" or fraternities devoted largely to the interests of a special group were not confined to tradesmen. London rectors, for example, formed a guild that held regular quarterly meetings, elected wardens to assist poor members, settled disputes, drew up regulations, and assisted with funerals for its members.[43]

An organization of special interest to literary students that had certain characteristics of a guild or fraternity was the Pui. It must have been an institution of some distinction in London, for Henry le Waleys, Vintner and Mayor of London in 1273-1274, 1281-1284, and 1298-1299 and an important royal servant, gave

[41] See the delightful little poem "The Blacksmiths" in R. H. Robbins, *Secular Lyrics of the XIV and XV Centuries* (Oxford, 1952), No. 118, p. 106.
[42] P. E. Jones, *The Worshipful Company of Poulterers of the City of London*, 2nd ed. (London, 1965), pp. 4–6.
[43] Unwin, *Gilds and Companies*, pp. 100–101.

the brethren five marks a year toward the support of their chaplain at the chapel of the Guildhall.[44] There were chapters of the Pui in a number of European cities, and we have five songs by Jean Froissart said to have been "crowned" by the Pui, but not in London. The regulations of the London chapter survive,[45] informing us that the brethren met

In honor of God, Our Lady Saint Mary, and all saints, both male and female; and in honor of our lord the King and all the Barons of the country; and for the increasing of loyal love. And to the end that the City of London may be renowned for all good things in all places; and to the end that mirthfulness, peace, honesty, joyousness, gaiety, and good love without end may be maintained. And to the end that all blessings may be set before us, and all evils cast behind.

With these worthy motives, the Pui held a festival once a year to select a new Prince. Each new member was to pay 6d on entrance, and all members either paid 12d or submitted a song on the day of the festival. A new song from among songs submitted by the members was selected and "crowned." Generally, the songs celebrated "the becoming pleasaunce of virtuous ladies," although no ladies were allowed at meetings. The brethren, it was said, ought to "cherish and commend all ladies, at all times and in all places, as much in their absence as in their presence." All this clearly has nothing to do with what has been misleadingly called "courtly love," which demands concentration on a single object of desire. It is, rather, a manifestation of the kind of disinterested concern for ladies that was a feature of chivalric ideology, exemplified, for example, in the conduct of Hector toward Criseyde in Chaucer's *Troilus*. Unfortunately, we do not know how long the London Pui survived, and it is doubtful that it still existed in the more somber years of the later fourteenth century. However, it is not difficult to imagine poems like Chaucer's "Womanly Noblesse" being sung or recited before somewhat similar gatherings.

[44] Riley, *Memorials*, p. 42. For an account of Henry's career, see Gwyn A. Williams, *Medieval London from Commune to Capital* (London, 1963), pp. 333–335.
[45] They have been printed by Riley in the *Liber Customarum* (London, 1860).

The proliferation of officially recognized guilds during the second half of the century afforded the city government a means of delegating responsibility, and, at the same time, provided new and more diverse sources for membership in the Common Council, even after elections to the council had been transferred back to the wards. In fact, the movement may well have been stimulated by problems arising from a growing population. Exact figures for the population of the city are impossible to obtain,[46] but we should probably not go far astray if we set an average of around fifty thousand for the second half of the century, remembering that the city lost about a third of its inhabitants in 1348-1349 as the result of the Black Death and received another severe blow from the same source in 1369. That recovery from losses due to pestilence was relatively rapid is attested by the formation of Farringdon Without as a separate ward, and it is possible that the population in 1400 may have been near sixty thousand. The number of hired workmen living outside the houses of their masters probably increased sharply toward the end of the century, giving rise to new economic, administrative, and social problems. Many Continental cities, and not a few towns in England, tended to stagnate or decay under the impact of pestilence. Oxford, for example, became a depressed town with a population of about five thousand. But the increasing importance of London as an administrative and commercial center endowed it with a unique prosperity and, at the same time, helped to maintain the essentially hierarchical structure of its society. Bristol, a clothmaking center, was also prosperous in the later fourteenth century. But the difference between the two cities is well indicated by the fact that Bristol became a center of Lollardy, whereas in London the new movement, with its appeal to persons who felt alienated from the prevailing social structure, never became popular. At the same time, however, London was only about a fourth as large as Paris, and its atmosphere did not produce the kind of longing for simple rural life apparent in Petrarch's *De vita solitaria*.

In spite of the increasingly disastrous state of the royal finances during the second half of the century, general economic condi-

[46] See the discussion with bibliography in Williams, *Medieval London*, Appendix A.

tions tended to favor the prosperity of the city. The early fourteenth century had been a period of expansion for the great
estates of the nobility, and there was no general or lasting decline in their incomes after the Black Death, even though the
population dropped about one third. Decreased population meant
less demand for food and a drop in agricultural prices. To meet
this contingency, noblemen resorted to the device of leasing their
lands in order to maintain their incomes. Leased lands became
very common toward the close of the century, and there was a
corresponding decline in villein tenements.[47] Some of the new
peasantry, working leased lands, became relatively prosperous,
whereas others were still subject to the customary services of
villein tenure. At the same time, the statute *Quia emptores* of
1290 had discouraged subinfeudation and had taken the flexi-
bility out of the feudal hierarchy. Feudal lords were coming to
depend more and more on monetary contracts with their in-
feriors.[48] In London, the agricultural depression helped to stabil-
ize food prices, while the continued prosperity of the greater
nobility and their reliance on monetary contracts assured demand
for the goods London could supply. Although precise measurements are impossible, real wages seem to have risen in London
during the second half of the century. They fell in the fifteenth
century and showed no firm upward trend until after the process
of industrialization, which began in the second half of the eighteenth century, was well under way.

The purchasing power of noble households was considerable.
John of Gaunt had over £12,000 a year from his English lands.
His wealth was exceptional, but it is probable that a number of
earls had incomes of £3,000, and, as we have seen, the Bishop of
Ely could spend £1000 a year on his household. London mer-
chants could sometimes assemble considerable sums. In the
seventies Richard Lyons advanced 20,000 marks to the king.
Nicholas Brembre, William Walworth, John Philpot, and John
Haddeley lent the king £10,000, but most of this sum was prob-
ably made up of contributions from their friends. Philpot was

---

[47] See G. A. Holmes, *The Estates of the Higher Nobility in the Fourteenth
Century* (Cambridge, 1957), pp. 113 ff.
[48] *Ibid.*, pp. 83–84.

able, in 1378, to outfit a fleet in London and put down some
pirates who had been attacking English shipping. In general,
however, the households of the higher nobility were incom-
parably larger than those of wealthy Londoners, and their incomes were greater. The royal households of the century indulged
in expenditures far beyond their means.

There was no annual budget in the fourteenth century, merely
an effort to keep strict account of current obligations to the
Crown and current debts. The reign of Edward I closed with an
indebtedness of around £68,000. Edward III was, until 1369,
successful in war, a deceptively attractive pursuit financially that
enabled him to collect £268,000 in ransoms between 1360 and
1370.[49] But wars were nevertheless expensive and left a large
indebtedness that had to be met by taxation. Many persons still
had faith in the feudal dictum that "the King should live of his
own," but when John Barnet made an estimate of income and expenditures in 1362-1363, he found that the Exchequer could not
possibly balance its books, even including the ransom paid for
King John of France. The result was, in part, a continuous series
of requests for subsidies in Parliament, culminating in the famous
poll tax that precipitated the revolt of 1381.[50] When King Richard
declared his maturity on May 3, 1389, he probably said in effect,

You know well that for the twelve years of my reign, I and my
realm have been ruled by others, and my people oppressed year by
year with grievous taxes. Henceforth, with God's help, I shall labor
assiduously to bring my realm to greater peace and prosperity.[51]

Wykeham was made Chancellor, and, in the general spirit of reform, Chaucer was made Clerk of the Works in the following
year. King Richard probably took comfort in the prosperity of
London in the early nineties. But he quite naturally wished to
live like a king and to fulfill the ideal of feudal largess, so that
the finances of the kingdom made no spectacular recovery, and
Richard acquired a reputation for extravagance.

---

[49] Denys Hays, "The Division of the Spoils of War in England," *Transactions
of the Royal Historical Society,* IV (1954), p. 93.
[50] T. F. Tout, *Chapters in Administrative History* (Manchester, 1923–1935),
III, 241 ff.
[51] *Ibid.,* III, 454 ff.

Meanwhile, the Exchequer had long resorted to the device of anticipating revenues by issuing "tallies"—sticks cut with notches, dated, and split down the middle so that the Exchequer could keep half. The recipient was forced to seek out a sheriff who could cash the tally and use it as a part of his biennial accounting at the Exchequer. A system of "wardrobe debentures" was also devised for small creditors.[52] These were short-term expedients and a great source of annoyance to those who had dealings with the government, although it is perhaps fortunate that the Exchequer did not think of the Florentine (and modern) expedient of the funded debt. S. B. Chrimes sums up the situation by saying that "The financial history of the period was on the whole one of failing resources, greater resort than ever to declining credit, of attempts, not very successful, to procure a general survey of assets and liabilities, of growing deficits . . . ."[53] The resultant taxes produced social unrest and probably helped to spread Lollardy. Thus in 1382 John Aston preached that "if the King confiscated the wealth of the church, taxes would no longer be necessary."[54] But the insistence of the king on the maintenance of a royal household in royal style, leaving the financial consequences for others to worry about was of great benefit to the city of London, which supplied the necessary materials and services.

Although the general financial situation described by Chrimes may sound familiar to Englishmen today, its causes were then very different, and there is little basis on which to compare medieval and modern economies. Fourteenth-century prices, for example, are difficult to compare with modern prices, partly because the latter are subject to rapid inflation and partly because the structure of fourteenth-century society was not at all like ours. Before considering prices, we may find it helpful to know something about wages and ordinary expenses. The wage regulations of 1350 designed to prevent inordinate charges following the Black Death stipulate that masons, carpenters, plasterers, and sawyers were to receive 6d a day during the "long" days be-

[52] See S. B. Chrimes, *Introduction to the Administrative History of Medieval England*, 3rd ed. (Oxford, 1966), pp. 141–142.

[53] *Ibid.*, p. 211.

[54] Joseph Dahmus, *William Courtenay* (University Park and London, 1966), p. 96.

tween Easter and Michaelmas (September 29) and 5d a day
during the "short" days of winter. Ordinary unskilled workers
were to receive 3½d and 3d.[55] It is doubtful that these schedules
were long maintained. The ordinary pay scale for military men
under Edward III was as follows:

An Earl	6s 8d
A Banneret	4s
A Knight	2s
A Man at Arms	1s
A Mounted Archer	6d
A Foot Archer	3d
A Welsh Lancer	2d[56]

A royal squire not on campaign ordinarily received 1s a day,
which was a comfortable income. It was said that it cost 8d a
week to board a girl in 1380 and that her total expenses might
amount to about £3 a year.[57] A boy could be maintained and
sent to Oxford in 1374 for £9 1s 8d a year.[58] A poor parson of
London might have only about £4 a year, but a more fortunate
one might have £10 or more. It might be said that a single person could live humbly in London for around £4, although he
would neither drink wine nor ride horses. An income of £10
would be fairly comfortable. One might ride occasionally and
enjoy a varied diet. It should be remembered that a great many
persons in London enjoyed some sort of largess from their
superiors in addition to their monetary incomes, a complicating
factor that is difficult to assess.

Since the government had no funded debt and did not engage
in social welfare expenditures, inflation had no special attractions
as a method of hidden taxation. Ale, the daily beverage of persons
of modest means, was graded as either "best," "medium," or
"common." The "best" ale cost 1d a gallon in 1305 and 1½d a
gallon in 1377. "Common" ale could be purchased for 3 farthings

[55] Riley, *Memorials*, pp. 253–258.
[56] H. J. Hewitt, *The Organization of War under Edward III* (Manchester,
1966), p. 36.
[57] Riley, *Memorials*, p. 447.
[58] *Ibid.*, p. 379.

a gallon at either time.[59] Ordinary bread was made in either large loaves or small loaves. Four small loaves or two large ones could be purchased for 1d in 1305 and for 1d in 1388.[60] Fishmongers were almost continuously under suspicion for charging too much throughout the second part of the century. However, in 1368 red herring sold at 8 for 1d and white herring at 6 for 1d. In 1382, when the fishmongers were under special pressure, it was ordered that no one sell herring at more than 9 for 1d.[61] It was possible to purchase herring wholesale at Billingsgate in that year at 22 for 1d.[62] One person who did so and resold them at the Stocks at 6 for 1d was given an hour on the pillory with some of his fish hanging about his neck. The price of wine, which was a luxury, rose during the period. Gascon sold for 4d a gallon in 1342, 6d in 1362, and 10d in 1380. Poultry, which was relatively expensive, tended to remain fairly stable throughout the period. It is clear from the spread of the poultry markets that it was popular in London, and that a great deal of it was consumed. P. E. Jones has constructed a table of prices in 1378, ca. 1380, 1388, and 1393.[63] Taking the two extremes of this period, swans declined from 4s to 40d, suckling pigs from 7d to 6d, capons from 6d to 5d, teal from 2d to 1½d, wild mallard from 4d to 3d, tame mallard from 3d to 2d, pheasant from 12d to 8d, heron from 16d to 14d. No prices of 1393 are higher than those of 1378. In 1363 Parliament set the price of capons at 4d, hens at 2d, pullets at 1d, and geese at 4d, but slightly higher prices were allowed in the city. Lambs sold from 6d to 10d each.

A few miscellaneous prices may be helpful to create a general impression, which is all that the present discussion intends to convey. The regulations of 1350 specified that a cart from Aldgate to the Conduit in Cheap should cost 3d. The same fee applied to a cart from Cripplegate to Cheap. A cart from Dowgate to Cheap cost ½d, and from the Woolwharf to Cheap 4d. A gown garnished

[59] Riley, *Memorials*, p. 57; *Letter-Book F*, pp. 27–28. Hostelers were allowed to sell "best" ale at 2d a gallon during a session of Parliament in 1371. See Riley, *Memorials*, pp. 347–348.

[60] Riley, *Memorials*, p. 57; *Letter-Book H*, p. 337.

[61] *Letter-Book G*, p. 221; *Letter-Book H*, p. 196.

[62] *Letter-Book H*, p. 202.

[63] *The Worshipful Company of Poulterers*, pp. 132–133.

with serge and sendal cost 18d, and one with linen and buckram 14d. A coat and hood cost 4d, cordovan shoes 6d, spurs 6 to 12d, shoes for a courser 2½d. In 1375 a night's supply of hay for a horse cost 2d and a bushel of oats 6d. In 1381 the Bishop of Ely's agent bought a "charet," the late medieval equivalent of a limousine, for £4 16s 8d and a cart for 7s 2d. A falcon and a tercel cost 17 marks. An embroidered cope might cost between £30 and £40. An illuminated missal representing the labor of two years cost £34 13s 7d. One might rent a large house for 22 marks, a market stall for prices ranging from 8s to £2, a small shop for 30s, or a large one in a good location on Paternoster Row for £4. Chaucer's income would have enabled him to enjoy a good diet of fish, meat, and the less expensive kinds of poultry, to share a cup of wine with Philippa at dinner, and generally to feel comfortable among the more substantial citizens of London. He could afford to hire horses, and his house probably contained luxuries like cups, silver saltcellars, and good draperies, some of which were gifts from noble friends or wealthy associates among London citizens. His admiration for persons content with a "suffisaunce" probably kept his economic expectations modest and left him, except for occasions when his remuneration from the government was slow, without serious economic worries.

It has been customary to describe medieval London as a violent city, full of picturesque and uninhibited passionate action. To a certain extent this description is just, but the violence was for the most part personal, unlike the casual, impersonal, and obscurely motivated violence of a large American city today. There were occasional riots. The city lapsed into more or less indiscriminate looting and brawling in 1326, some Lombards were attacked in a "violent affray" in 1359, there were occasional outbreaks between guilds, like that between the skinners and fishmongers referred to earlier, or later outbreaks between the followers of Northampton and those of Brembre, and, finally, law and order broke down completely during the revolt of 1381. The fact that King Edward fell into a good-natured but irresponsible dotage in his later years and died leaving a boy king who was never able to get a very firm hold on his realm probably contributed to a general unrest in the country. The prestige of England declined steadily after 1369. Success in war was largely a thing of the past,

A fight with knives (copyright British Museum).

taxation was onerous, the growing importance of money in the economy led to a weakening of old personal ties, and the mischievous, the malcontent, and the returned soldier banded together to enjoy rape and robbery. In 1378 there were complaints in Parliament about confederacies of outlaws, from Chester and Lancaster especially, committing robbery and rape among the people. The King sent out commissioners to investigate.[64] However, in the following year it was revealed that the commissioners had imprisoned a number of innocent men, so that they were withdrawn and their prisoners released. A further complaint concerning outlaws from Chester was registered in 1382.[65] Such bands seem to have disturbed London only once, in December 1393.[66]

Violent or "unnatural" deaths in the city were recorded on the Coroner's Rolls, but these are unfortunately fragmentary today, so that it is difficult to find evidence for the second part of the century. In 1339 some twenty-seven persons were murdered or killed in quarrels, and there were ten accidental deaths. Most

[64] *Rot. Parl.*, IV, 42–43, 62; *Statutes of the Realm*, II, 9–10.
[65] *Rot. Parl.*, III, 139–140.
[66] *Letter-Book H*, p. 405.

commonly, the killings were effected with knives. Two of the accidental deaths were those of drunks who fell into the Thames and were drowned, and one man was struck by a cart while relieving himself in a ditch. Whether murders and killings continued at this rate during the remainder of the period we do not know. A murderer could find sanctuary in a church, or at Blackfriars or St. Martin le Grand. Since these places were seldom watched carefully, he might escape by night, as five of the felons did in 1339. Alternatively, he might abjure the realm and be allowed to proceed to the nearest point of departure. In 1351 a royal proclamation forbade the wearing of arms, including long daggers, within the city and suburbs.[67] An innkeeper was imprisoned in 1372 for failing to warn a lodger to leave his knife indoors, and in 1373 some skinners and tailors playing football in Sopers Lane and Cheap were detained for carrying knives.[68] How effective the city's effort to suppress knives was in preventing violent deaths we do not know. A man who murdered his wife in the early part of the century was condemned to prison, "there in penance to remain until he should be dead."[69] The goods of felons escheated to the Crown, as did ladders, carts, knives, and other articles involved in fatal accidents, so that the mayor, as Escheator, had to be especially careful to inquire into fatalities. The sentence "Chattels he had none" ending an official account of the apprehension of a felon or of a fatality simply means that the mayor and sheriffs could find nothing for the Crown. It should not be regarded sentimentally.

Theft, especially the robbery of homes or shops, was regarded with great seriousness, and in general thieves found in possession of stolen goods were hanged. This drastic treatment seems to have been an effective deterrent, for between 1378 and 1384 only four thieves were hanged in the city.[70] A man found to have stolen a leg of mutton in 1391, however, was merely put in the stocks for half an hour with the leg around his neck.[71] Generally, there seems to have been a tendency toward lighter penalties as

[67] Riley, *Memorials,* pp. 268–269.
[68] *Plea and Memoranda Rolls,* pp. 146, 152.
[69] Riley, *Memorials,* p. 199.
[70] See *Letter-Book F,* pp. 249 ff.
[71] Riley, *Memorials,* pp. 530–531.

A thief (copyright British Museum).

the century progressed, although attacks on the city's officials were taken very seriously. In 1390 a ward constable making his quarterly collection for "rakery," a tax to pay for cleaning refuse from the streets, was assaulted by a tailor. The tailor was sentenced to Newgate for forty days and fined 100s.[72]

Ancient feudal custom demanded a very severe penalty for rape, now generally treated rather lightly when we have acquired an enlightened respect for individual integrity, especially that of the rapist. The ancient penalty was blinding and the loss of the testicles, although if the felon had a wife she could come forward before the passing of judgment and claim the testicles as her own.[73] During the later Middle Ages this harsh penalty was seldom applied. For example, in 1370, a certain Walter Baker, Chaplain, was accused of ravishing the wife of Walter Croxton at Colchester and taking goods and chattels belonging to Croxton. The jury decided that he had not taken any goods and chattels, but had indeed "ravished Margaret, wife of Walter Croxton and with force of arms detained her." He was made to pay Croxton

[72] *Ibid.*, p. 522.
[73] J. M. Kaye, *Placita corone* (London, 1966), pp. xvi-xvii, 9.

£20.[74] The Parliamentary complaint of 1382 concerning outlaws in Chester called attention to the frequent rape of "femmes, dames, damoiseles, et files," but indicated that many of the women consented after the fact. It was decided that the husbands and fathers of such women should pursue the ravishers and attain them of life and member, even if the victims consented. In such cases, apprehended felons were not allowed to claim wager of battle, but were forced to submit to an inquest.[75]

Rape is seldom mentioned in the London records. In 1368 John Fish, Diker, alleged that his journeyman, John Halliwell, had run off with his wife taking goods and chattels worth £200. Halliwell confessed that he had lain with Elizabeth Fish, but denied stealing anything. He was fined forty marks and sent to prison. Again, in 1382, Thomas Norwich, Chaplain, was accused by Henry de Wilton of carrying away his wife, woolen cloths, silver, plate, dishes, pewter saltcellars, and iron and brass pots and pans. A jury decided that Henry's wife was "nothing but a common strumpet," so that no damage was committed in that respect. Goods valued at 60s had, however, been taken, and Thomas had either to repay that sum or go to prison.[76] These and other cases in the fourteenth century suggest that women did not take lightly what they regarded as insufficient sexual attention. False accusation of rape was a not infrequent means of inconveniencing a legal adversary. Thus in 1362 a man who had been disseised of lands held by right of his wife brought a writ of novel disseisin against the offenders. But they arranged to have him accused of rape and during his imprisonment had his wife brought to court to make a fine with regard to the property. The fine was paid unjustly, but the only means of recovery would have been a petition in Parliament.[77]

Chaucer's experience with Cecily Champain was probably an effort to forestall an action of this kind. He took Cecily before the Chancellor in Westminster Hall on May 1, 1380, to swear that

[74] G. O. Sayles, *Select Cases in the Court of the King's Bench,* VI (London, 1965), pp. 136–139.
[75] *Rot. Parl.,* III, 139–140. On the subject of appeals and wager of battle, see Kaye, *Placita corone.*
[76] *Select Pleas,* pp. 18–19.
[77] Sayles, *Select Cases,* V, xciii.

she had no charge of rape or any other action whatsoever to bring against him. The witnesses included three distinguished knights, Sir William Beauchamp, Sir William Neville, and Sir John Clanvowe, and two merchants, John Philpot and Richard Morel, Grocer of Aldgate, the first of whom was a very distinguished citizen indeed. Clanvowe was a man of deep moral sensibility, so that we may be well assured that Chaucer did not rape or otherwise molest Cecily and then force her to make a false statement. The fact that the statement was filed with the Chancellor is an indication that it did not fall under the ordinary jurisdiction of the regular courts. Another action in what is apparently the same process appears in the records of the Mayor's Court on June 28. Its appearance here is an indication that the transaction involved was basically financial. Richard Goodchild, Cutler, and John Grove, Armorer, here release Chaucer from all legal action against him evidently at Chaucer's behest. On the same day Cecily filed a quitclaim of all action against Goodchild and Grove, probably at their request. But on July 2 Grove acknowledged that he owed Cecily £10 payable at Michaelmas. The record indicates that the sum was paid. It is possible to construct various series of events to account for these records, but it seems most probable that what was involved was a sum of money and that Cecily was an agent for Goodchild and Grove. It is also likely that the action originated because of some transaction at the Custom House, where Philpot had been, until May 1, a collector of petty customs. The "sex" element in the case was probably legal. It is unlikely also that the sum of money involved any indebtedness on Chaucer's part. The records specifically state that Chaucer did not rape or otherwise give Cecily cause for any action, and they contain no indication of an indebtedness on his part. These facts have not, of course, prevented modern scholars, both literary and legal, from weaving fanciful conjectures about Chaucer's probable indiscretions.[78] They would like very much

---

[78] Plucknett's suggestion in *Law Quarterly Review*, LXIII (1947), 491–515, that Chaucer may have seduced Cecily is sheer fiction. There are various possible interpretations of the evidence, but it nowhere suggests this enticing bit of romantic foolery, which would not, in any event, be a matter to concern Clanvowe, Philpot, and the Chancellor.

to make him a "good fellow," but we shall return to this concept later.

Slander was much more seriously regarded by London citizens than it is by modern Chaucerians. In 1364 Simon de Worstede, Alderman, arrested one Beatrice Langbourne for throwing filth in the street. This was a ward matter, and nothing more. But when she called him a "false thief" and a "broken-down old yokel," he turned her over to the sheriffs.[79] In the same year, John de Hakford accused Richard Hay, Fuller, of forming a covin to overthrow the best citizens of London. But Richard's neighbors in Cornhill said that the accusation was false. John was condemned to Newgate for a year and a day and made to spend one day each quarter in the pillory with a whetstone around his neck marked with the words A FALSE LIAR.[80] Slandering members of the higher nobility was especially dangerous. One Thomas Knapet, Clerk in the Church of St. Peter the Less near Paul's Wharf, spoke "disrespectful and disorderly words" concerning John of Gaunt. When his action was revealed, he was sent to Newgate, there to remain until he could obtain pardon from the Duke. Fortunately, the clerk had a wife, who went before the Duke and asked mercy. Conservative feudal tradition, about which the Duke was very sensitive, demanded mercy for distressed ladies, so that the Duke, recognizing the clerk's acknowledgement of the error of his words, asked that he be released on condition that he did not seek to discover the person or persons who had reported his indiscretion. He sent his squire, Henry Ward, to Mayor John Philpot (1378–1379) with a message to this effect. Philpot released Thomas when he had obtained six mainpernors liable for £20 each to see that he met the Duke's condition.[81]

London, as we have seen, had its prostitutes. On the Continent some successful efforts were made by ecclesiastical organizations to reform prostitutes and to find husbands for them. But in London they were controlled in various ways by the city authorities, who sought to confine them to Cock Lane and to see to it that

[79] *Plea and Memoranda Rolls*, p. 15.
[80] Riley, *Memorials*, pp. 315–316.
[81] *Ibid.*, p. 425.

they did not dress too well so as to counterfeit erring ladies of respectable households. The presence of clergymen in the city from all over England temporarily "on their own affairs" or seeking chantries complicated the problem of sexual offenses somewhat, since such clergymen felt that the crowded conditions of the city and the absence of their immediate superiors permitted them a certain amount of latitude. Traditionally, clergymen caught in adultery were, like prostitutes, put in the Tun on Cornhill, in spite of the objections of the archdeacons. When John of Northampton was mayor (1381–1382, 1382–1383), he sought to regularize city practice concerning these and related matters. Walsingham accused him of being a "Wyclifite," but he was actually doing nothing more than refurbishing some traditional customs. His formulations remained influential, for they found their way into the *Liber Albus.*

It was decreed that each alderman should receive complaints in his wardmote concerning common whoremongers, common adulterers, common bawds, common courtesans, common adulteresses, common female bawds, and common scolds. The names of such offenders were to be submitted to the Mayor's Court within two days.[82] It is of some interest that "scolds," who might be either male or female, were included among whoremongers, bawds, and prostitutes. Further, it was decreed that if any man were convicted in the Mayor's Court of being a common whoremonger, his head and beard were to be shaved except for a fringe two inches wide around the head, and he was to be put in the pillory for a period to be determined by the mayor and aldermen. For a second offense, he was to have the pillory and ten days in prison. If he offended a third time, he was to be made to abjure the city. If a woman was found to be a bawd, she was to be taken from Newgate to the thews at the Stocks Market with minstrels. Her hair was to be cut around her head, and she was to remain at the discretion of the mayor and aldermen. A second offense would send her to prison, and a third would remove her from the city.

If any woman proved to be a common courtesan, she was paraded from Newgate to Aldgate in a hood of striped cloth carry-

[82] For this and the regulations following, see *Letter-Book H*, p. 189; *Liber Albus*, pp. 394–396.

ing a white wand.[83] From Aldgate she was returned to the thews, where her cause was proclaimed. Then she was taken through Cheap and out Newgate to Cock Lane and told to reside there. Upon a third offense, she was to have her hair cut, be placed in the thews, and then made to abjure the city. Brawlers (male scolds) and scolds were to be taken in procession to the thews, holding a distaff with flax on it in the right hand. The distaff must have been peculiarly humiliating to brawlers, since it implied that they were effeminate in their lack of control over their emotions. If a priest were found with a woman, he and the woman were to be taken to the Tun in Cornhill with minstrelsy. A priest so found a third time was to be made to abjure the city. Adulterers and adulteresses were to be taken to Newgate, where the women were shaved, and then paraded through Cheap with minstrelsy to the Tun.

In 1385 Elizabeth, wife of Henry Moring, was brought before Mayor Brembre and the aldermen for pretending to maintain women in the craft of broidery in her house in Broad Street in the parish of All Hallows. She was actually hiring her women out to "friars, chaplains, and other men" as whores. The case arose because an "apprentice" was ordered to spend the night with a chaplain and bring back what she could. She stole a breviary. Elizabeth was placed in the thews for an hour and then made to abjure the city.[84] Renewed penalties for prostitution were imposed in 1393:

Whereas many and diverse affrays, broils, and dissensions, have arisen in times past, and many men have been slain and murdered, by reason of the frequent resort of, and consorting with, common harlots, at taverns, brewhouses of *huksters*, and other places of ill fame, within the said city, and the suburbs thereof; and more especially through Flemish women, who profess and follow such shameful and dolorous

[83] The white wand was a conventional sign of truce or safe-conduct, used by garrisons that had surrendered territory in return for permission to proceed to their own lands. See M. H. Keen, *The Laws of War in the Late Middle Ages* (London and Toronto, 1965), p. 110. Here the whores were in "enemy" territory on their way "home" to Cock Lane. However, prostitutes on the Continent were sometimes made to wear white badges or to carry white wands.
[84] Riley, *Memorials*, pp. 484–486.

life:—We do by our command forbid . . . that any such woman shall lodge or go about in the said city, or in the suburbs thereof, by night or by day; but they are to keep themselves to the places thereunto assigned, that is to say, the Stews on the other side of the Thames, and Cokkeslane; on pain of losing and forfeiting the upper garment she shall be wearing, together with her hood, every time that any one of them shall be found doing the contrary of this proclamation.[85]

This preamble, the fact that prostitutes were merely confined to certain areas, and Northampton's inclusion of scolds in his list of offenders all point to the fact that the city authorities were not so much concerned with personal morality as with keeping the peace.

Throughout the period, curfew was maintained in the city, roughly between dark and dawn. The gates were closed, and those wandering in the streets by night, unless they were well-known persons carrying torches, were arrested and placed in the Tun. Men in the habit of going out at night, frequenting taverns with harlots, and causing disturbances by brawling were called "rourers," "bruisers," or, more frequently, "common night-walkers." In 1373 one Roger de Ware, Cook, was accused by the jurors of Langbourne of being a "common nightwalker." He admitted the offense and placed himself at the mercy of the court.[86] In 1385 three servants were imprisoned "because they went wandering by night in the Ward of Billingsgate about the eleventh hour of the clock." Next day they were mainprized under the penalty of £20 each.[87] It was quite possible to offend the city authorities by engaging in disorderly conduct during the day. Thus in 1371 John Stacy, servant of William Talbot, Tailor, was committed to prison for irritating the skinners by walking through Walbrook contemptuously crying "Mew!"[88]

Various small transgressions might bring the offender to the stocks. John of Northampton was not the first mayor to punish scolds. Thus in 1375, after being indicted in the wardmote of Alderman John Haddeley of Tower, Alice Shether was brought before the mayor "for that all the neighbors, dwelling in the

---

[85] *Ibid.*, p. 535.
[86] *Plea and Memoranda Rolls,* p. 156.
[87] *Select Pleas,* pp. 1–2.
[88] *Plea and Memoranda Rolls,* p. 135.

vicinity, by her malicious words and abuse were so greatly molested and annoyed; she sowing envy among them, discord, and ill-will, and repeatedly defaming, molesting, and backbiting many of them, sparing neither rich nor poor . . . ." Alice was placed in the thews for an hour.[89] Another woman was sent there for an hour because she had kidnapped a baby to use when she went begging.[90] In 1382 a man stood in the pillory for an hour because he had pretended to locate thieves by sorcery, and there was a similar case in 1390.[91] Generally speaking, there were few complaints about sorcery until the later years of the century. By far the most numerous small offenses were those involving false measures, petty fraud of one kind or another, and fishnets in the Thames, which were regulated in such a way that small fish would not be caught.

A few examples will illustrate the city's treatment of fraudulent practice. In 1316 two bakers were found selling bread deficient in weight. Their punishment, which became more or less standard throughout the century, was to be drawn through the streets tied to a hurdle or wooden frame behind a horse and thus exhibited to the public at large. The bread was confiscated and sometimes given to the prisoners at Newgate.[92] Butchers who sold putrid meat were customarily placed in the stocks and their meat burned before them.[93] The same punishment might be used for other "false" goods. For example, in 1385 a man who had made defective bowstrings was placed in the stocks for an hour and his strings were burned beneath him.[94] In 1320 a man sold a garland in a tavern he said was worth 1 mark sterling. But since it was actually worth only 2d, he was placed in the pillory from Tierce to Vespers and made to abjure the city for a year and a day.[95] An ingenious fraud was perpetrated by some bakers and bakeresses in 1327. They had devised molding boards with trapdoors. When a customer brought in dough to be baked, a boy under the

[89] Riley, *Memorials,* pp. 385–386.
[90] *Ibid.,* p. 368.
[91] *Ibid.,* pp. 462–463, 518–519.
[92] *Ibid.,* pp. 119–120 and *passim.*
[93] *Ibid.,* pp. 132–133.
[94] *Ibid.,* p. 486.
[95] *Ibid.,* pp. 133–134.

table opened the little door and took some of the dough. The bakers who had dough from this source were placed in the stocks with dough around their necks, and the bakeresses, who were found to have husbands, were placed in Newgate for further action.[96] At various times persons were convicted of "enhancing" prices in the markets. Thus a man in 1347 who bid 1½d per bushel above the current selling price for his own wheat was imprisoned for forty days.[97] In 1364 a vintner who sold unsound wine was forced to drink some of his unpalatable beverage, and the remainder was poured over his head. He was made to forswear the calling of a vintner in the city.[98] Wine was not bottled in the fourteenth century and had to be handled with some care. Dicing was a favorite pastime among the less worthy, as Chaucer's Franklin indicates. In 1382 a man found to be using false dice was placed in the pillory with his dice around his neck.[99]

One of the most celebrated cases of the later part of the century, mentioned in the *Historia Anglicana* of Walsingham, who did not like London, was that of a false physician of 1382, who claimed to cure the sick with a parchment charm. It was decided that he "should be led through the middle of the City with trumpets and pipes, he riding on a horse without a saddle, the said parchment and a whetstone, for his lies, being hung about his neck, an urinal also being hung before him, and another urinal on his back."[100] Walsingham says that he rode backward with the tail of the horse in his hands. The elaborate iconography of this display is somewhat reminiscent of the grotesques that adorn some fourteenth-century manuscripts, and it appealed undoubtedly to the same taste for "moralized" humor.

Generally, the city, like England as a whole, seems to have been much less concerned about homicide than we should be today. Theft, on the other hand, was treated wth extreme severity. The attitude toward both murderers and thieves reveals far less sensitivity to the "sanctity of human life," which was not a medieval concept, than we have. The treatment of minor offenses,

96 *Ibid.*, pp. 162–165.
97 *Ibid.*, pp. 235–236.
98 *Ibid.*, p. 318.
99 *Ibid.*, p. 457.
100 *Ibid.*, pp. 464–466.

on the other hand, reveals a great deal of confidence in the efficacy of public shame. The scornful laughter of the community was something to be feared, and it is not at all surprising that it was a potent instrument in both literature and the visual arts. It is the basis for much of Chaucer's humor, which cannot be appreciated fully unless we are prepared to regard his underlying moral outlook with some sympathy. The face of a man in the stocks with a whetstone hanging from his neck was not soon forgotten, and he was likely to be regarded with a certain derisive mistrust in the community to which he belonged until he had demonstrated greater reliability. In general, the criminal was neither romanticized as a rebel against a "system," nor accorded any sympathy on "psychological" or "social" grounds. Craftsmen took pride in their work and in the standing of their misteries, merchants and noblemen were sensitive about their public reputations for integrity, and the city could depend on these feelings as deterrents. The noncitizen population, especially among laymen, was more of a problem, but even they had neighbors with whom it was advantageous to be on good terms.

Although the transgressions of ecclesiastics, except adultery, were usually reserved for the archdeacons, an occasional ecclesiastical case appeared in the Mayor's Court. In 1392 John Harmesthorpe, Master of the Hospital of St. Katherine, complained that a ward of his, a boy of about ten, who had been placed in school with Richard Exton near the Crutched Friars, had been approached by certain of the friars and asked to translate the following sentence into Latin: "Y oblisshe me to be a frere of the Croys." When the boy performed this exercise successfully, one of the friars kissed him and said that all the bishops in England could not absolve him from being a member of their order. They took him away to their convent and dressed him in their habit. Whatever the bishops might have done, the mayor was not so literal-minded, but sent the boy home to the Master of St. Katherine's.[101] It is possible that the Crutched Friars may have learned this device from the four major orders, who had been accused for many years by the followers of William of St. Amour of "seducing" boys into their convents.

[101] Select Pleas, p. 282.

City officials were not always completely honest or free from malice. A series of complaints was lodged against John Botele-sham, sergeant of the city and jailor of Ludgate in 1388. He had, it was alleged, kept a cordwainer away from his shop by force of arms for three months, "procured and abetted the beating of Joan Payne, wife of John Payne, Goldsmith, in bed and else-where" in Ludgate Prison, and finally driven her "naked except for a single gown" to Newgate, where he put her in a "piteous cell." He is said also have deprived William Walleys, Tailor, of his rights of Holy Church at Easter and at other times and to have prevented his being set free when 26s 8d was supplied for the purpose. He had also withheld alms submitted for prison-ers.[102] In 1394 it was alleged in Parliament that city officials at Smithfield, empowered to seize the third best beast of a herd for the City custom, had done so even when the "herd" amounted to only three beasts.[103] The mayor and aldermen were ordered to inquire into the truth of this allegation.

On the whole, the city seems to have been reasonably con-scientious. The mayor and aldermen wrote letters to foreign cities, in England and elsewhere, on behalf of London merchants, suggesting that justice be done if the recipients wished their own citizens to be treated with respect in London. The city govern-ment provided an office for recording debts and obligations, and sought to see to it that such debts were paid. It collected tolls and taxes for the maintenance of the streets, walls, and public facilities of the city, punished fraud, and exerted itself to keep the peace. Occasionally, cases arose that were not in the jurisdic-tion of the Mayor's Court and could not conveniently be brought before the Court of Common Pleas. In such instances, recourse might be had to the Chancellor. For example, in 1388 a London mercer complained before the Chancellor that one Thomas Hol-bein, together with twenty archers, impeded the conduct of his affairs in Kent.[104] Again, a Genoese merchant complained there that certain other Genoese merchants held his money so that he could not pay his creditors.[105] Another Genoese merchant in

[102] *Ibid.*, pp. 156–160.
[103] *Rot. Parl.*, III, 321.
[104] William Paley Baildon, *Select Cases in Chancery* (London, 1896), p. 8.
[105] *Ibid.*, p. 10.

1396 found himself hounded from court to court in England on false charges and complained to the Chancellor for a remedy "so as not to be destroyed and annihilated forever by so being annoyed, imprisoned, and put to costs without any cause."[106] In general, although human frailty intervened, the realm and the city did what they could to insure the prosperity of merchants and a due respect for the king. Long-range policies, either financial or political, were almost impossible under medieval conditions. Both the government and individuals adapted themselves to the exigencies of the moment as best as they could, but these adaptations were always made with a view toward maintaining a set of inherited ideals and traditional institutions. No one had any special desire to be dynamically progressive, for medieval men lacked that essential uneasiness and lack of confidence in the past and future that characterizes much of modern life.

The clerical population of the city was, if anything, more fluid than the merchant population, perhaps in part because clerical incomes on the lower level were meager and somewhat easier to bear in village surroundings. Thus the Church of St. Botolph's Bishopsgate had at least fifteen rectors between 1362 and 1404.[107] London benefices were exchanged frequently, to the distress of ecclesiastical authorities like Archbishop Courtenay, who wrote heatedly on the subject to Bishop Braybook of London in 1391. The straying clergymen in London were characterized as being "not rectors of churches but robbers unfortunately, not good shepherds who know their flock but rather hirelings who have no concern for the sheep . . . who without need or reason impudently spend their time in London, devouring the patrimony of Jesus Christ, and, to their own destruction, consuming in villainous ways the goods of the poor, the bread of the hungry, the clothing of the naked, and the ransom of captives."[108] Fraternities and chantries, moreover, offered opportunities for relatively easy positions together with the amenities of London life.

The restraint of Chaucer's Parson, who is actually a collection of the attributes of a good pastor, probably results from the poet's experience with unworthy clergymen of various kinds:

[106] *Ibid.*, pp. 20–21.
[107] Page, *Victoria History*, I, 217.
[108] Dahmus, *Courtenay*, p. 263.

> He sette nat his benefice to hyre
> And leet his sheep encombred in the myre,
> And ran to Londoun unto Seinte Poules
> To seken hym a chaunterie for soules,
> Or with a bretherhed to ben withholde;
> But dwelte at hoom, and kepte wel his folde,
> So that the wolf ne mad it nat myscarie.
> He was a shepherde, and noght a mercenarie.

The essential purpose of this statement is not to characterize an individual "personality," but to condemn, by contrast, the behavior of a large number of London clergymen. Chantries were not necessarily an evil in themselves. After 1215 there was an increased awareness throughout Western Christendom of the efficacy of the Mass. The chantry offered the founder an opportunity to name the saints in whose honor the Masses were to be celebrated and to select the prayers to be used. He could also fix the times of celebration, which were frequently arranged at daybreak, so that servants and laborers could participate.[109] However, the movement to establish chantries spread rapidly, and almost three new ones a year were established in late medieval London. It was difficult to control the priests, too many of whom probably resembled the lax "annueleer" of Chaucer's "Canon's Yeoman's Tale." Sir John Poultney's device of forming a college of a group of chantries was one solution to the problem.

By far the most important ecclesiastical center in London was the Cathedral of St. Paul. As in other cathedrals, the administrator was the Dean, who nominated the major and minor canons and presided over the chapter. There were thirty major canons at the cathedral, each of whom was allotted five Psalms to say daily, so that the entire Psalter was recited each day at the cathedral. Each canon served at the high altar in turn for one week, each had a prebend, a daily allowance of bread and ale, a pittance from the Chamber, and a portion of the offerings. The resident canons, both major and minor, participated in the services of the

---

[109] See K. L. Wood-Leigh, "Some Aspects of the History of Chantries in the Late Middle Ages," *TRHS*, XXVIII (1946), pp. 43–83. For details of late medieval ecclesiastical organization, see A. Hamilton Thompson, *The English Clergy* (Oxford, 1947).

canonical hours. It was sometimes difficult to maintain a full quota of resident canons to carry out the services. During his first year of residence, a new canon was expected to act as host for a number of the ministers of the church and to hold two feasts for the bishop, the major canons, the mayor, sheriffs, aldermen, justices, and great men of the court. Next day he entertained the lesser clergy. A minor canon had a prebend of 5d weekly, with an extra penny on feast days, and a daily allowance of bread and ale. There were twelve minor canons, all priests. The best musician among them was chosen subdean and had charge of the choir.

The archdeacons of London, Essex, Middlesex, and Colchester were at St. Paul's. The Chancellor was the master of the school at the cathedral and had charge of all London schools except those at St. Mary le Bow, which was under the jurisdiction of the archbishop, and St. Martin le Grand.[110] Paul's Cross in the churchyard was the scene of many notable sermons during the century. Bishop Brinton considered that it was one of the duties of a bishop to preach in London as well as in his own diocese "because of the greater devotion and intelligence of the people."[111]

It is likely that the discipline of the London schoolboy, at St. Paul's or elsewhere, was fairly rigorous, somewhat like that recommended for the boys of Westminster Abbey in the thirteenth century. When they rose in the morning, they recited the Creed, three Paternosters, and five Aves. After making their beds, they washed and went to church, without running, jumping, or talking and without carrying bows, staffs, or stones. On entering the church, they made the sign of the Cross and proceeded to the choir two by two. Bowing to the Cross, they took their seats, keeping their eyes toward the altar. They were not to smile, laugh, nor deride poor singers, nor poke one another, nor respond sharply if addressed. On leaving the choir, everyone was to bow toward the altar. Boys who knew Latin but spoke English or French were to receive a blow with a ruler, an instrument that was not spared for "rusticitas" of any kind. Anyone with dice

[110] See Page, *Victoria History*, I, 421–422.
[111] *Ibid.*, I, 211.

A schoolroom (copyright British Museum).

was to receive a blow for each spot. The boys were not to go to town on feast days, nor to visit the homes of rustics.[112] Undoubtedly boys did all the things they were not supposed to do, but, on the other hand, they were not treated as though children belonged to a world apart, and their misbehavior was not regarded with much tolerance. In general, schoolboys were taught from the Bible, from the Latin classics, and from medieval texts like the Elegies of Maximian. Most of the citizen population of London had probably been subjected to an elementary education, could read and write a little Latin, and could follow the church services. The ordinary language of city proclamations throughout the century was French, but sheriffs were allowed to hold court in English after 1356.[113] A substantial merchant of the city prob-

[112] Armitage Robinson and M. R. James, *The Manuscripts of Westminster Abbey* (Cambridge, 1909), pp. 67–68.
[113] *Letter-Book G,* p. 73. On the use of French as a written language, see Mrs. Helen Suggett, "The Use of French in England in the Late Middle Ages," *TRHS,* XXVIII (1946), 61–83.

ably had some familiarity with Latin, could read and write French, and was, at the same time, a native English speaker. The humbler residents of London probably knew no language but their own and could not manage that very well. Middle English, except in its sophisticated literary forms, was neither clear, accurate, nor capable of much subtlety.

We do not have any records of the courts of the archdeacons in London during the fourteenth century. An archdeacon, to use Newcourt's description, was "bound yearly to visit all his Archdeaconry throughout; there to inquire into all Crimes and Misgovernment of the People, as well the Clergy as the Laity, by churchwardens and others; and to reform whatsoever they found otherwise than well, either committed heinously against the Laws of God, or the ordinance of the Prince for a quiet Common-weal, dissonant to God's Laws, Man's Laws, and the Politick order of the World; to reform the same, either by Good Persuasion, or good Advice, or by Pains and Penalties, according to Humility and humble Subjection of the Offender, and Repentance of his Offense."[114] Some archdeacons, together with their officers the summoners, seem to have been more interested in fees than in the repentance of sinners. As Chaucer's Friar says, an archdeacon

> . . . dide execucioun
> In punysshynge of fornicacioun,
> Of wicchecraft, and eek of bawderye,
> Of diffamacioun, and avowtrye,
> Of chirche reves, and of testamentz,
> Of contractes, and of lakke of sacramentz,
> Of usure, and of symonye also.

Archdeacons had enjoyed an evil reputation ever since the twelfth century, and this reputation, as well as the corrupt practices that gave rise to it, was undoubtedly intensified in the fourteenth century when money became a much more powerful source of motivation in all ranks of society. The chief weapon of the archdeacon's court was excommunication, which was not very

---

[114] *Repertorium ecclesiasticum parochiale Londinense* (London, 1708–1710), I, 55. Late medievel archdeacons were frequently remiss in making their visitations.

An archdeacon (copyright British Museum).

efficacious unless the person excommunicated lived for a fairly long period in the court's jurisdiction. If an offender did not submit within forty days, the archdeacon could have the bishop, or, in London, the Dean of St. Paul's or the Dean of St. Martin le Grand, issue a "significance of excommunication" to the Chancellor, after which he could be imprisoned by the secular authorities.[115] As Chaucer says, in his description of the Summoner,

> Of cursyng oghte ech gilty man him drede,
> For curs wol slee right as assoillyng savith,
> And also war hym of a *Significavit.*

Chaucer's repulsive and unscrupulous Summoner, who is a "good fellow" beyond all others—"A bettre falawe sholde men noght fynde"—is, of course, not a "typical" man of his degree, but, rather, an exemplification of the evils that such men occasionally practiced. His "gerland" and "bokeleer" made "of a cake" give

[115] See H. E. Salter, *Snappe's Formulary* (Oxford, 1924), pp. 22, 29–32.

114

him the air of a grotesque and are, like the urinals and whet-stone of the false physician of 1382, iconographic attributes that no "real" summoner would wear if he could help it. Many arch-deacons were men of some learning and integrity who sought to make the best of their office.

A number of London's residents were contemplatives who lived in accordance with a rule. Each monastic order had its peculiar institutions, but in general the routine of daily life was similar in monasteries or nunneries of any kind. After 1311, all monks were required to take orders, so that monastic churches had to be well supplied with altars. The monastic day was divided into seven hours: Matins and Lauds, Prime, Tierce, Sext, Nones, Vespers, and Compline.[116] In addition, there were Masses cele-brated by individual priests and the Mass for the community. All brethren were expected to attend the offices unless they were ill or away from the monastery on official business. The monks arose early for Matins and Lauds and then, especially in the long days of summer, returned to the Dorter until Prime. After Prime, they went about their daily tasks, reading, meditating, or receiving instruction. Breakfast, or *mixtum*, followed, except on feast days and on the weekdays of Lent, when it was omitted. It consisted of bread and a little wine or ale. Tierce followed, and afterward the meeting of the chapter, which lasted about twenty minutes. Between the meeting of the chapter and High Mass, the abbot conferred with his officials in the cloister, holding what was tra-ditionally called a "Parliament." High Mass was celebrated, and then the monks went to dinner, usually about an hour before midday. The afternoon was spent in study, writing, or recreation. Supper followed Vespers, and the day closed with Compline.[117] Friars led a similar regular life, except that they had license to beg, preach, and hear confessions. The Dominicans gave a spe-cial emphasis to Compline, usually held when there was still sufficient daylight to read the service without candles. Their serv-ice, which closed with *Salve regina*, could be attended freely by laymen, who would not ordinarily be occupied with other matters at that hour. At dinner and at High Mass in a monastery a num-

[116] Cf. above, Chapter II footnote 36.
[117] For a fuller account, see G. H. Cook, *English Monasteries in the Middle Ages* (London, 1961), pp. 107 ff.

An abbot and his monks (copyright British Museum).

ber of persons other than the monks might be present. It was frequently possible, in the first place, to purchase a "corrody," or provision for board or lodging in a monastery or nunnery. Again, monks and nuns regularly extended hospitality to strangers in need. At times dinner, at which monks or nuns were silent, might be enlivened by reading. A clerk might read aloud from a work that could be thought of as being instructive for both the community and its guests.

Again, we should beware of taking Chaucer's Monk in the "General Prologue" to *The Canterbury Tales* as typical. He rides luxuriously and ostentatiously, is contemptuous of study, labor, and the life of the cloister, wears a habit trimmed expensively with gris,[118] and loves a "fat swan," which, as we have seen, might cost 40d, or enough to hire a mason or a carpenter for more than a week. The result is an exaggerated picture of the inconstancy to which some monks were subject, in one way or another, and a rather bitter comment on the extravagance that such inconstancy entailed. Although the Monk's weakness may appeal to the romantic imagination, because of its rather childish rebelliousness, and to the almost instinctive postromantic feeling that monastic discipline is repressive to the free development of the personality,

[118] See above, Chapter I, footnote 55.

we should remember that responsible medieval men generally respected monastic ideals and had no "personalities" to repress. Chaucer's picture reveals greed, gluttony, a suggestion of lust, and a disregard for monastic obligations both to God and to the poor, who were the beneficiaries of monastic hospitality and charity. Much the same kinds of things might be said for Chaucer's Prioress, with her silly affectation of "courtly" manners, stupid sentimental concern for her dogs, and careful attention to an *Amor* that clearly has nothing to do with the love of God and her neighbor. All this is not to say that Chaucer was being "Puritanical." His characters are not "persons" but exemplifications of the ideals and foibles of members of various "degrees" in his society.

To return to the life of the ordinary layman, various forms of recreation were available to London residents. In 1379 the first "Common Hunt" of the city, John Charney, was appointed.[119] His duties were "to do all things concerning hunting and fishing" for the citizens who set forth on the Thames to fish or sought game in the countryside around London. Football, handball, tennis, and cockfighting were popular sports that might attract men of all degrees, including bishops. The authorities made distinct efforts in 1363, 1365, and 1388 to encourage the practice of archery in preference to other sports.[120] Residents of the larger inns might find room to practice within the city, but fields and meadows were not far away in the fourteenth century. Wrestling matches were held at Clerkenwell, and in some years there were plays there. On the Feast of St. John (June 24) the city was decorated with flowers, boughs, drapes, and banners, and the residents went out into the streets for dancing, singing, and other merrymaking. The processions, celebrations, pageants of the greater fraternities, and occasional tournaments at London provided a fairly constant round of diversions. In general, the colorful dress, ebullient spirits, and comparatively unrestrained emotional expressiveness of medieval Londoners must have given the city an air of festivity that survives today only occassionally in the south of Europe.

[119] *Letter-Book H*, pp. 121–122.
[120] *Letter-Book G*, pp. 154, 194; *Statutes of the Realm*, II, 57.

London was not, by modern standards, a good city in which to bring up children. Infant mortality was high, and adults had a relatively short life expectancy, although it did not lengthen markedly until recent times. Women frequently married at about thirteen or fourteen, and men, who had to remain single during apprenticeship, at about twenty-five or twenty-six. Instances of widows remarrying, especially among the wealthier citizens, were fairly common. Marriages were generally "prudent," as they are among ordinary people in most Latin countries today. The city did not provide, as a modern city does, continuous stimulants to the lustful imagination, and there was little feeling of youthful desperation about sex. Adolescence, as we know it today, is a recent phenomenon, dating from a time after the eighteenth-century "discovery" of the child. In the fourteenth century a boy of fifteen was expected to be headstrong and impulsive, but generally capable of a man's work and a man's responsibilities. Sexual frustration among the young was probably quite rare. On the other hand, "love" or sexual infatuation was regarded as a nuisance. In the mid-fifteenth century a young man was actually haled into court because "he used the company of a woman which was to his grete loss and hinderying for asmoch as he was so affectionate he resorted daily unto her."[121] More casual affairs were less serious in the eyes of both secular and ecclesiastical authorities. It is probable that contraception, which had been condemned by ecclesiastical authorities since the early Middle Ages, was rather widely practiced. The use of dilute vinegar for this purpose seems to belong to the realm of general European folk medicine.

The genuineness of the civic spirit of Londoners is attested by their wills, which frequently contain bequests not only to the poor prisoners of Newgate and the Fleet, to the anchorites and hermits of London, to the orders of friars, to hospitals, fraternities, and churches, but also for the maintenance of roads or the repair of London Bridge. Sir John Philpot, who did much for the city during his lifetime, left "the reversion of all his lands and tenements not otherwise disposed of" to "the Mayor, Aldermen, and Commonality of the City of London to use and behoof of the

---

[121] Thrupp, *Merchant Class,* p. 169.

City as most needed, for the making of conduits, common latrines, and so on."[122] Sir John was not, in Bishop Brinton's terms, a slothful man.

Certain salient features of London life emerge from our brief survey of fourteenth-century city customs. London was, first of all, a city of merchants and craftsmen. They were the citizens who governed the city and assumed responsibility for its relations with the Crown. When a mistery received formal recognition, it became, in effect, a part of the city government, although its action was indirect. It supplied members of the city council, and, if it were wealthy enough, candidates for the offices of alderman and mayor. But a man might be a "burgess" and a knight at the same time, and his daughter or widow might marry a nobleman. There was no necessary conflict between the feudal nobility on the one hand and the city aristocracy on the other, and the line dividing them is not so sharp as we might like to have it for purposes of historical simplification. Our tendency to think of society as being sharply divided into classes—lower, middle, and upper—has little bearing on the actual situation in fourteenth-century London. The only character among Chaucer's pilgrims who has what was to become later a "middle-class" outlook is the Franklin, and he is neither a tradesman, a Londoner, nor a member of anything Chaucer might have thought of as a "middle" class.

Similarly, medieval institutions escape rigorous classification. The word *guild* is used for a variety of organizations, whose precise nature is difficult to define. The distinction between a "guild" and a "fraternity" is not always clear, and a man formally classified, say, as a fishmonger, might find that a large part of his livelihood was derived from wholesale transactions in goods other than fish. A blurring of lines also appears in the jurisdiction of the courts. Adultery, for example, might place the offender either before the archdeacon or the mayor. The same kind of overlapping appears in the royal government, where, to cite one instance, the Court of Chivalry heard cases involving debt and generally encroached on the jurisdiction of the Common Bench, in spite of protests against the practice in Parliament.

[122] *Cal. Wills*, II, 276. Cf. p. 300.

This vagueness concerning precise distinctions probably arose in part from the fact that medieval men tended to react to immediate situations, without reference to long-term policy. Generally, long-term considerations in organizational procedure seem to accompany the possibility of long-term financial involvements, which place wealth and, at times, sustenance itself in the future. It is true that a man might buy a "corrody" in a monastery or obtain income from royal or noble patronage. But the first is an investment of extremely modest potentiality, and the second is simply traditional feudal practice. The concept of usury still to a large extent prevented payment for the use of money in fourteenth-century England, and this in turn meant that investment in future income was for the most part investment in real property or in merchandise. Real property has no "responsibility" and may fluctuate in value or depreciate in a relatively short time, and the same is true of merchandise. In consequence, men operated, so to speak, "in the present." No steady inflation tempted them into the future very far, and neither financial nor social dynamism appealed to them as a desideratum.

These facts have widespread implications in every aspect of medieval English life. Men looked at the "future" as an extension of the "present," rather than as an opportunity for "progress." Meanwhile, the "past" was the model and guide for policy in the "present." When changes were desired, the desire was usually expressed in terms of the past rather than in terms of new developments possible in the future. Organizations were instruments of preservation, devices to maintain the traditions of the past in the light of present contingencies. They were, in consequence, extremely flexible. Time was not, as it is now, a salable commodity, and it was unnecessary to secure it by insisting on precise and self-perpetuating group structures.

It follows that medieval society was profoundly nonrevolutionary. The Peasants' Revolt, which seems at first to be an exception to this generalization, developed no long-term policies, and the short-term demands it generated were mere absurdities that had no practical significance. Aside from the extreme demands of the peasants and of some "Lollards," social criticism and social theory generally centered on moral rather than on organizational questions. If the morality of kings, princes, noblemen, clergy, merchants, laborers, and peasants could be preserved, then, it was felt, society would function smoothly and efficiently. The most popular treatise on government in late fourteenth-century England was the *De regimine principum* of Aegidius Romanus, which looks today like a rather tedious and irrelevant excursion into elementary morality. No one of any education felt seriously that if the interests of one group could be properly appreciated, then all the rest would automatically adjust themselves so as to create an earthly paradise.

Earthly paradises were, in fact, regarded as delusions of self-love. Chaucer gives us a fine example in the garden constructed by old January in the "Merchant's Tale," which is a figurative exemplar of what Dr. Johnson called a "Happy Valley" of self-satisfaction on earth. Christianity taught that life on earth is a trial or testing, a voyage or journey through a wilderness where true happiness may be found only by wisely avoiding the temptation to settle down and enjoy the amenities of lush islands or shady vales or the even more delusive temptation to create such amenities through wealth, power, or policy. This does not mean that Christian teaching frowned on national prosperity or peace within a realm. On the contrary, the clergy exerted themselves to achieve these goals by insisting on "common profit" rather than self-satisfaction as the only worthy motive for endeavor. But the goals were, by modern standards, modest. They could neither offer permanent satisfactions nor bring a halt to the "Wheel of Fortune." Chaucer states the attitude of enlightened fourteenth-century opinion well:

> Tempest thee noght al croked to redresse,
> In trust of hir that turneth as a bal.
> Gret reste stant in litel besinesse.
> And eek be war to sporne agayn an al.
> Stryve noght, as doth the crokke with the wal.
> Daunte thy self, that dauntest otheres dede,
> And trouthe thee shal delivere, it is no drede.

He who sets out to reform the world simply subjects himself to Fortune, and the only road to freedom is through self-control.

The essential dynamism of medieval Christian life was a dynamism of the spirit, rather than a social, economic, or political dynamism.

There were, in consequence, no medieval equivalents of modern "social criticism," in the sense that we find such criticism in Flaubert, or Zola, or Dickens, or their successors. Since medieval men were lacking in humanitarian piety, they had no concern for theories like socialism, Marxism, or fascism, which are, in essence, long-range efforts to create earthly paradises at the expense of large segments of the population. Neither politicians nor social theorists had sought to convince them that the world is not essentially a "wildernesse," as Chaucer called it in the poem quoted above, and they did not look forward to any glorious future on earth just around the corner. They lacked therefore much of our disillusionment, just as they lacked our hope. For the most part, they were content with their hierarchial structure, although they might argue about qualifications for the exercise of authority in the higher degrees or about the relative jurisdictions and powers of ecclesiastical and lay hierarchies. Typically, medieval "criticism of society" involves an analysis of the moral state of the various groups and degrees in the social structure. When, in the Prologue to *The Canterbury Tales*, Chaucer tells us that he will explain concerning his pilgrims

> . . . whiche they weren, and of what degree
> And eek in what array that they were inne,

he is suggesting that he will actually be portraying groups by means of which individuals are classed, the degree of the specific individual in the group, and the "array" of an individual of a given degree within the group with the question in mind as to whether the "array" is appropriate to the degree. The disparity between actual degree and "array," or outward pretense, both sartorial and social, is fundamental to the technique of his criticism, which is not directed at individuals, but at groups of individuals exemplified in the pilgrims and in the implications of their tales.

The tendency of individuals to form small, relatively independent groups, each with its own kind of community spirit, is quite evident in medieval London. Although the formal organization of a group might be vague, this does not mean that the members were not tightly bound within the group by personal relationships. Parish fraternities were originally communities of neighbors that might well contain members of various degrees. They afforded a stability that was not furnished by the parish itself, where frequent changes of rectors were common. Guilds were principally organizations of men engaged in a common industry, but some members might be very poor, while others, "more substantial," became aldermen or mayors. Nevertheless, the factor of mutual interest was strong in such organizations. In the prologue to the "Reeve's Tale," Chaucer tells us that the Reeve, who has just heard a story about a carpenter, was angry "By cause he was of carpenteris craft." Unfavorable reflections on any carpenter were felt to be detrimental to all carpenters, great or small. A fraternity or guild was, like society itself, a hierarchy, but a closely knit one, that usually provided its members with social and religious satisfactions, as well as material benefits.

The large number of churches and other ecclesiastical institutions in London is testimony to the fact that the religion of the time was an integral part of community life, and not simply a "thing in itself" to be supported by a reluctant population interested primarily in other matters. Religious ceremonies contributed to the social cohesion of parishes, fraternities, guilds, and the city as a larger community. At the same time, preachers furnished the moral and philosophical attitudes necessary to maintain the integrity of communities large and small. Morality as it was understood in the Middle Ages afforded practical guidelines for the efficient operation of individuals within a group. That is, the vices usually condemned by fourteenth-century priests gave rise to behavior that would be detrimental to the welfare of a closely knit community of any kind. Hence morality was a practical matter in the community, not something purely personal to be left to the discretion of the individual. It is true that the increasing importance of money in the economy tended to produce a conflict between ordinary economic behavior and moral belief, but this conflict became much more critical after our period.

Although many members of the feudal aristocracy resided in the city, they had no formal part in its government. Some indica-

tion of aristocratic polite manners may be found in the pages of
Chaucer, although he treats them in a satiric context so that what
he tells us must be used with some caution. When Pandarus ap-
proaches Criseyde in Book II of *Troilus,* he finds her with "two
other ladys" seated in a "paved parlour" listening to a recital of
"the sege of Thebes." We should probably imagine the parlor as
being near one end of the hall of Criseyde's Inn, and the ladies
seated on draped benches while a clerk standing before a lectern
near the window reads to them. Pandarus greets Criseyde:

> ". . . madame, God yow see,
> With al youre book, and al the compaignie."

Criseyde welcomes him and leads him graciously to a seat:

> And up she roos, and by the hond on hye
> She took hym faste, and seyde, "This nyght thrie,
> To goode mot it turne, of you I mette."
> And with that word she down on bench hym sette.

The polite and inconsequential remarks here and elsewhere in
their conversations and the gesture with the upraised hand convey an impression of studied elegance. Listening to a book being
read was probably a common diversion of well-to-do London
ladies. This kind of reading has social advantages. That is, the
ladies can at any time stop the clerk and discuss anything that
interests them especially, and even have him repeat passages. On
the other hand, they may simply gesture or make brief observations as he reads. The process was undoubtedly much slower than
modern silent reading, but it must have encouraged alertness and
the exchange of opinions. At the close of the "Miller's Tale" in
The Canterbury Tales Chaucer gives us a glimpse of such an
exchange:

> Whan folk hadde laughen at this nyce cas
> Of Absolon and hende Nicholas,
> Diverse folk diversely they seyde,
> But for the moore part they loghe and pleyde.

Chaucer's poetry was probably "read" in this way, but to a somewhat larger group than that in Criseyde's parlor.

A city garden, fifteenth century (copyright British Museum).

Troilus also furnished us a brief description of a well-kept garden of the kind that one might find in a large London inn. When Criseyde has been meditating in the evening about the possibility of loving Troilus, she descends from a solar in her house with her three nieces into the garden.

> The yerd was large, and rayled alle thaleyes,
> And shadwed wel with blosmy bowes grene,
> And benched newe, and sonded alle the weyes . . . .

We can imagine the garden divided into small square plots most of which contain fruit trees as well as herbs, flowers, and vegetables. The benches are probably of turf, and the many paths between the squares are covered with white sand. While the ladies are there, one of them sings a song. It is not unlikely that

125

on a summer evening one might hear ladies singing in the gardens of the London aristocracy, both noble and "city." As we learn
a little later in the poem, gardens also afforded places for private
conversation in a society where privacy of any kind was rare and
seldom cherished.

The manners of lesser folk in the city are probably reflected
with some accuracy in *The Canterbury Tales*. The Wife of Bath,
who is something of a scold and certainly a gadabout, likes to go

> To vigilies and to processiouns,
> To prechyng eek, and to thise pilgrimages,
> To pleyes of myracles, and to mariages,

although her motive for doing so—"for to se, and eek for to be
seye of lusty folk"—is dubious. London offered plenty of opportunity for activity of this kind. If there is one salient characteristic
of all the persons of lower degree in Chaucer's *Tales* it is the
heartiness of their expression. Whether they are simply saying,

> "Hayl, maister Nicholay!
> Good morwe,"

or using foul language—"Ye, Goddes armes!"—they create an
impression of vigorous life. It is quite likely that the lack of a
general long-term outlook with its attendant worries, a lack of
concern for "social" causes or "psychological" problems, and an
immersion in some kind of community activity on every possible
occasion gave actual Londoners of every degree an outward-
going freshness of manner that we, in a more advanced, prosperous, but gloomier age, if we were to confront it in the streets
rather than in the dreamworld of history, might condemn as
insensitive.

FOUR

A Brief Chronicle

On Monday, November 12, 1312, the mayor and aldermen of the City assembled at the Guildhall at Vespers, sang carols, and then proceeded through the city with torches, trumpets, and minstrels. On Tuesday the shops were closed, and everyone went in procession to St. Paul's to praise God. Afterward, they sang carols through the streets to the sound of trumpets. On the following Monday the mayor and aldermen went in procession richly dressed in colorful robes to make an offering. They returned to the Guildhall, dined, and "went in carols throughout the city all the rest of the day and great part of the night." The Conduit in Cheap ran with wine, and a tun of wine was set up near St. Michael le Quern. The city was celebrating the birth of the young prince who was to become Edward III.[1]

Fourteen years later, after Isabella and Mortimer had landed at Harwich and Edward II had fled to Wales, the Queen issued an order to the city to arrest Despenser. Their quarry had fled, but the Londoners broke out into the streets on October 15, beheaded John le Marshal, secretary to Despenser, and attacked the Bishop of Exeter as he sought sanctuary in St. Paul's. They hacked off his head with a butcher's knife in Cheap. There followed a period of uncontrolled rioting, looting, private vengeance, and gang murders, in which aliens especially were victims. On November 15, Prince Edward restored the franchise of the city, appointing Richard de Bethune and John de Gisors

---

[1] H. T. Riley, *Memorials of London and London Life in the XIII, XIV, and XV Centuries* (London, 1861), pp. 105–107.

Keepers of the Tower. Bethune became Mayor. The city made all who came within its walls swear allegiance to Prince Edward. When Parliament met in January, it was dominated by the London mob, demanding the deposition of the old King. Finally, Bethune gathered an assembly of lords spiritual and temporal at the Guildhall, including the Archbishop of Canterbury, and made them swear to agree to a deposition. On March 7, 1327, the new King, Edward III, issued to the city a new charter of liberties, which was read and explained in English to a meeting at the Guildhall on March 9. A new day had dawned for England's international chivalric prestige under Edward III and for the prosperity and independence of the city. The exposition of the city charter in English, meanwhile, was an event presaging the time when a great poet could address an aristocratic London audience in the English language.

Chaucer grew to maturity during a period of rising fortunes for the kingdom. On August 26, 1346, the English won a spectacular victory at Crécy, for which they were commended in a great ceremonial sermon by Bishop Thomas Bradwardine, who accused the French of moral weakness, especially in their pursuit of Cupid and Venus.[2] In 1347 the English took Calais, and Londoners were invited to take up residence there. Misfortune appeared in the following year in the form of the Black Death, which is said to have destroyed between thirty and forty percent of the population. But in 1355 King Edward was victorious in Scotland, and in the following year the Black Prince sent a letter to the city announcing the capture of King John of France. It was alleged that a third of the city of London was uninhabited because of the pestilence, but the Black Prince and his captive king were led across London Bridge and through the city to Westminster with great ceremony and pageantry, and royal jousts were held at Smithfield. In 1359 the Londoners were able to outfit eighty vessels and fourteen thousand men to pursue the Normans who had attacked Winchelsea.

The year was one of great hopes for the English. King Edward

[2] *Sermo Epinicius*, eds. H. A. Oberman and J. A. Weisheipl, *Archives d'historie doctrinale et littéraire du moyen âge*, XXXIII (1958), esp. pp. 323–324.

set out on a campaign in France, expecting to be crowned at Reims. Among the prisoners he ransomed in this campaign was young Geoffrey Chaucer, who was probably in the company led by Lionel of Ulster.[3] Edward's venture failed, and the result, in 1360, was the Treaty of Bretigny, not so favorable as had been hoped, but still a valuable achievement. In 1362 John of Gaunt was made Duke of Lancaster, receiving the sword and cap of his investiture from the King in Parliament in November. As the inheritor through his wife, Blanche, of Duke Henry's estates, he became the most wealthy and powerful subject in the realm. The Black Prince had gone in that year to Gascony as Prince of Aquitaine. Meanwhile, in London, the misteries began a period of organization and development. In 1364, Pierre de Lusignan, who had recently visited England, in a campaign that fired the imagination of poets, captured Alexandria. Chaucer included the idealized knight of *The Canterbury Tales* among his followers:

At Alisaundre he was whan it was wonne.

The English knights who were there brought back cloth of gold, gems, clothing, and other luxuries with which to adorn themselves and their ladies, stimulating a taste that London merchants could find profitable. In 1366 Chaucer, now a squire, probably undertook a visit to Spain, and later in the year married Philippa, a lady of the Queen's chamber. One more great victory, that of the Black Prince at Nájera, heartened the English in 1367, but when the Prince returned to England in 1371, he was a sick man, and the fortunes of his kingdom had passed a turning point.

After about 1362 King Edward began to lose his grip on the affairs of the realm, gradually devoting more of his time to hunting and relaxation on his country manors. The great offices of the realm passed under the control of a group of clerical ministers led by William of Wykeham, who became Bishop of Winchester in 1367 and enjoyed enormous influence until 1371. The decisive year, both for the King and for the realm was 1369. In that year

[3] Martin M. Crow and Clair C. Olson, *Chaucer Life-Records* (Oxford, 1966), pp. 23–28.

the war with France resumed. The Queen died of the plague on August 15. Chaucer and his wife Philippa were granted liveries for mourning as members of the royal household.[4] On September 12, Blanche, Duchess of Lancaster died of the plague also, and Chaucer soon set about the composition of his first great poem, *The Book of the Duchess*. Meanwhile, the French became more successful in frustrating English efforts in the field. Charles V was a much more astute and less scrupulous leader than his predecessor King John, and France began to regain its position as the leading nation of Europe. After the death of the Queen, King Edward's distractions began to include Dame Alice Perrers, "Lady of the Sun," who, in 1374, "rode from the Tower of London, through Cheape, accompanied by many Lords and Ladies, every Lady leading a Lord by his horse bridle, till they came into West Smithfield," where there was "a great Iust, which endured seven days after."[5] Whatever her character may have been, her presence at the court in a position of prominence was hardly conducive to high morale. John of Gaunt, either ambitious to become ruler of Spain or anxious to secure the southern flank of England's Continental holdings, married Constance of Castile in Gascony.[6] London welcomed the newly wedded pair in 1372, leading the Duke and the new Duchess, whose beauty made a great impression on the spectators, through Cheap to the Savoy. However, the Duke was soon openly maintaining Katherine Swynford, the sister of Chaucer's wife Philippa, as his mistress. Two years later, in 1374, Chaucer, having returned from a mission to Italy, took up residence at Aldgate, where he remained, except for some trips abroad, until 1386. The history of the rest of the century is characterized by a steady deterioration in the realm as a whole, by financial crises, the spread of heresy, and revolt.

The great problem of the period was taxation made necessary by the expenses of war. Even the clergy suffered. Their property yielded an income more than three times that of the King, but most of them were poor. The rest, "possessioners," as they were called, were extremely wealthy. On the whole, they were reluc-

[4] *Ibid.*, pp. 85, 98–100.
[5] J. Stow, *A Survey of London*, ed. C. L. Kingsford (London, 1908), II, 29 ff. In a procession of 1386 the lords, more properly, led the ladies.
[6] *Anonimalle Chronicle*, ed. V. H. Galbraith (Manchester, 1927), p. 69.

tant to subject themselves to royal subsidies, a fact that produced a great deal of animus against Wykeham and his clerical ministers, who were removed in 1371. Wykeham was an able administrator, but, like a number of other men, a victim of circumstances. Lords and Commons alike began desperately to seek scapegoats to blame for the financial condition of the kingdom. Since there was no real long-term financial "policy," and since individual men tended to think in terms of personal relationships and personal responsibility, the last years of the century were marked by the condemnation of a number of individuals who were actually not very much at fault, the greatest of whom was King Richard himself.

The symptoms of this kind of reaction became unmistakable in the Good Parliament of 1376, over which John of Gaunt presided. The Commons introduced a long series of petitions and declared themselves too poor to endure further taxation. Peter de la Mare, who was elected their spokesman, asked that twelve peers be appointed to assist in the reform of the realm. After consultation with these peers, and probably at their instigation, with special impetus from William of Wykeham, who was among them, the Commons announced that the realm suffered chiefly because a number of councillors and royal servants were becoming wealthy at the expense of the King. In circumstances where no annual budget was kept and there was little understanding of planned expenditures, this was a natural if somewhat shortsighted reaction. The chief victims named were Lord Latimer, the Chamberlain, who had won distinction at Crécy, and a London merchant, Richard Lyons. Two other Londoners, John Pecche and Adam de Bury (Mayor, 1373–1374), were also condemned for corrupt practice. Alice Perrers was accused of being responsible for royal expenditures of two or three thousand pounds a year. King Edward was a generous man and probably did not regard two or three thousand pounds as an extravagance for a royal mistress.

It used to be fashionable for historians to take the charges brought forward in the Good Parliament quite seriously, and Latimer and Lyons have had an enduring evil reputation.[7] Recent

[7] For example, see T. F. Tout, *Chapters in Administrative History* (Manchester, 1923–1935), III, 288 ff.

scholars have become more skeptical.[8] It is unlikely that the charges were literally true, except for the fact that Alice Perrers was undoubtedly expensive. Even if there was some truth in the allegations, punishing a few men would do nothing to solve the basic financial difficulty. However, the public charges were detrimental to the reputation of London, and Chaucer's friend Ralph Strode, the Common Pleader of the City, complained that the mayor and aldermen had made grants to individuals without consulting the commonality. At his instigation, John Warde, Grocer, who was Mayor, with the advice of John of Northampton, John More, Nicholas Twyford, and others, called a great assembly at the Guildhall. Lyons, Pecche, and Bury were ousted as aldermen and deprived of citizenship. Pecche was accused of having cornered the market in sweet wines and taken 40d on every butt sold, although he had a royal license to do these things and had hardly been secretive about it. It was agreed that the mayor and aldermen could do nothing without the consent of the twelve principal misteries at least. Furthermore, to implement this policy, it was decided that the Common Council was to be elected by the misteries, as follows:

6 each: Grocers, Mercers, Drapers, Fishmongers, Goldsmiths, Vintners, Tailors, Skinners

4 each: Saddlers, Weavers, Tapicers, Fullers, Brewers, Girdlers, Dyers, Ironmongers, Cordwainers

3 each: Salters, Butchers

2 each: Leathersellers, Founders, Joiners, Tallowchandlers, Curriers, Fletchers, Bakers, Broiders, Haberdashers, Brasiers, Cappers, Pewterers, Bowyers, Hatters, Lorimers, Horners, Armorers, Cutlers, Spurriers, Plumbers, Waxchandlers, Shearmen, Painters, Tanners, Pouchmakers, Woolmongers, Pinners

1 each: Farriers, Bladers, Blacksmiths, Heumers.[9]

---

[8] For example, see May McKisack, *The Fourteenth Century* (Oxford, 1959), p. 391.

[9] R. R. Sharpe, *Calendar of Letter-Books Preserved among the Archives of the City of London* (London, 1899 *et seq.*), *Letter-Book H*, pp. 38 ff. For discussion, see Ruth Bird, *The Turbulent London of Richard II* (London, 1949), pp. 17–24. The return to elections by wards is discussed above, Chapter III.

The hierarchy thus established was still based largely on wealth and prestige, but did tend to spread the responsibility for municipal action. The treatment of Lyons, Pecche, and Bury was probably in part due to a desire to clear the city's reputation, and in part a concession to the jealousy of the members of the lesser crafts.

Aside from this reaction in London, the efforts of the Good Parliament were soon dissipated. During its session the Black Prince died of the malady he had contracted in Spain. He had enjoyed a large following that included both prominent noblemen and distinguished clerks, and his death was a severe blow to the morale of the kingdom. At a council called by John of Gaunt in October, the acts of the Good Parliament were annulled. Wykeham was condemned for his actions before 1371, and Peter de la Mare was imprisoned. At Gaunt's inspiration, Wyclif moved throughout London churches preaching against "Caesarian clergy," possesioners in high office whose multiple benefices were a drain on the finances of the Church.[10] Londoners, who enjoyed Wykeham's new buildings at St. Martin le Grand and who took pride in their youthful and aristocratic Bishop, Wiliam Courtenay, were not likely to be much impressed. The Duke's motives in sponsoring Wyclif had nothing whatsoever to do with the reformer's more radical doctrines, for John of Gaunt was an extremely conservative man. He was not basically anticlerical, but he probably thought of the large number of clerics in high office as a dangerous innovation, a threat to the power of the baronage, and an indication of ecclesiastical corruption. However, Wyclif was the Duke's "man," and until his rather curious views became unmistakable, the Duke would protect him. Meanwhile, there were among the Duke's followers a number of conservative individuals whose firm conviction that the traditional moral values of the past ought to be revered should not be mistaken as evidence for the influence of Wyclif. As the century wore on, anyone who took a firm stand on moral questions might loosely be called a "Loller" by the vulgar or uninformed, but the majority of such persons would have been deeply shocked by the more radical ideas of the Oxford philosopher.

[10] See K. B. McFarlane, *John Wycliffe* (London, 1952), pp. 69 ff.

The reasons behind the summoning of Wyclif to St. Paul's to be tried before Bishop Courtenay early in 1377 are not altogether clear. Courtenay had been among the peers who condemned Latimer at the Good Parliament, and it is likely that he was motivated in part by an effort to discomfort John of Gaunt for restoring Latimer to his post and refusing to forgive Wykeham. He must have found Wyclif's activities extremely irritating, and he was himself a young man, somewhat headstrong and not so judicious as his episcopal office might indicate. The Duke seems to have regarded the impending trial of his preacher as a personal affront and to have been generally impatient with the government of London, whose reaction to the Good Parliament may have irritated him and offended his aristocratic sensibilities. He went so far as to suggest in Parliament that the mayor be replaced by an appointed captain and that the Marshal of England, Henry Percy, have power to make arrests in the city. Quite naturally, the Londoners were in turn alarmed and deeply offended. The prospect of losing their traditional self-government and being subject to the whims of the Court of Chivalry, which had no interest in their welfare, must have seemed disastrous.

When Wyclif was brought before Courtenay at St. Paul's on February 19, he had become a mere pawn in a controversy whose real issues had very little to do with him. He was accompanied by John of Gaunt, by four friars, one each from the mendicant orders who offered to defend him, and by Henry Percy, the Marshal. Courtenay was hardly a theologian, so that actually there was little point in his carrying out a trial in the face of this array of clerical and secular power. However, he was supported by a great crowd of Londoners, who thronged into the church to maintain their rights and to defend their bishop. Percy, who was not noted for calm restraint, began to order them about. He was reprimanded by the Bishop, who was, in turn, reprimanded by the Duke. Gaunt probably regarded Courtenay as an upstart member of the minor aristocracy whose qualifications for the episcopate were tenuous. An argument concerning whether Wyclif should be seated or forced to remain standing terminated with the Duke's saying to Courtenay, with complete disregard for his office, "You trust in your parents, who will not be able to assist you, for they will have enough to do defending themselves."

When the altercation became even more heated, the Londoners rioted. The meeting broke up, and Wyclif went for the moment free of examination.[11] The likelihood that an examination would have resulted in any action was small, for Wyclif was clever, shifty, and no more candid than he had to be when confronted by his superiors. Moreover, he was in this instance powerfully supported by the fraternal orders.

On the following day, the Londoners met in a great assembly, worried by the possibility that they might lose their liberties and probably further excited by the malicious and unfounded rumor that John of Gaunt intended to seize the kingdom on the death of Edward III. During the meeting they were informed that one of their fellows, John Prentig, had been arrested by Percy in his capacity as Marshal for slandering the Duke and that he was being held prisoner in Percy's Inn near Aldersgate. This infringement of their prerogative infuriated them, and a mob departed from the meeting, broke into Percy's Inn, and released the prisoner. Gaunt and Percy, who were dining in the Vintry at the house of Gaunt's steward, John Ipris, heard that the mob was after them and fled by water to the residence of Princess Joan in Kensington. The mob headed for the Savoy, beating and critically wounding a priest they met who called Peter de la Mare a traitor. But Courtenay arrived before the mob and turned them away with soft words. The destruction of the Savoy by a London mob would certainly have endangered the liberties of the city, and would have made Courtenay's position untenable. On the way home, the mob reversed the Lancastrian arms wherever they found them. Reversed arms were recognized as a sign of treason and disgrace throughout Christendom.[12] The Duke, who was proud of his chivalry and sensitive about his loyalty, did not regard this action lightly.

A delegation of Londoners appealed to the Princess Joan in behalf of Wykeham and Peter de la Mare. But they were told that they had best approach the King and offer apologies for their conduct. In the royal presence the Londoners explained that they

[11] Cf. *ibid.*, pp. 69 ff., and Joseph Dahmus, *William Courtenay* (University Park and London, 1966), Ch. III.
[12] See M. H. Keen, *The Laws of War in the Late Middle Ages* (London and Toronto, 1965), pp. 54–55, 57, 173.

were fearful for their liberties and that the mob that attacked Percy's Inn and marched on the Savoy was not made up of citizens, but of the lesser sort of unenfranchised residents. The old King assured them that he had no intention of removing their liberties. Some leading citizens then persuaded the Bishop of Bangor, who held a large inn in Farringdon below that of the Bishop of Ely, to excommunicate all persons who had defamed the Duke. At a further meeting between a group of citizens and a royal representative, it was suggested that the Londoners obtain a wax taper bearing the Duke's arms and carry it to the shrine of the Virgin in St. Paul's to demonstrate their contrition. The mayor and aldermen performed this ceremony with great solemnity, but not much to the satisfaction of the Duke, to whom it seemed somewhat funereal. Finally, the mayor and aldermen resigned, and a new mayor, Nicholas Brembre, was elected. Meanwhile, Wykeham, about whom the Londoners had been concerned, approached Alice Perrers, who persuaded the King to restore his temporalities. What John of Gaunt thought of this we do not know, but at least the situation had its amusing aspects.

On June 21, 1377, King Edward, long a promoter of London's interests, died. He had been a great warrior in his youth, and his son the Black Prince had been one of the finest exemplars of European chivalry. Even in his decay, Edward was a genial and generous man, who, in spite of his weakness, lent a certain dignity to the court. Now England had only a boy to take his place. As if in respect for his memory and in recognition of the difficult responsibilities that lay ahead, everyone seemed anxious to settle differences and begin afresh. A deputation from the city led by John Philpot sought a reconciliation with John of Gaunt before the young King Richard. Lancaster graciously asked pardon for the citizens, as he had pardoned them, he said, himself, and publicly made peace with Wykeham. King Richard released Peter de la Mare from prison, and the new reign began with an atmosphere of goodwill. Richard took up residence in the Tower, and on the day of his Coronation, July 16, rode through the City in procession to Westminster, followed by the Duke of Lancaster, Henry Percy, the mayor, sheriffs, aldermen, and the men of the misteries in their liveries. In the midst of Cheap the citizens had erected a great decorated castle with four towers. Young virgins dressed as queens cast golden leaves and flowers on the King, and a golden Angel descended from the top and presented him with a crown. Wine flowed in the Conduit, as it had on the occasion of King Edward's birth many years before, and the citizens proclaimed not only their new King, but the Duke of Lancaster as well. At the Coronation itself, whose ceremonies had been carefully arranged by John of Gaunt, Richard, attended by his mother and by Sir Simon Burley, made Thomas of Woodstock Earl of Buckingham, Thomas Mowbray Earl of Nottingham, Henry Percy Earl of Northumberland, and Sir Guichard d'Angle, his military tutor, Earl of Huntingdon. Next day the King proceeded on a ceremonial visit to St. Paul's, where he and the assembled Londoners heard a sermon by Thomas Brinton, Bishop of Rochester, urging the people to reconcile themselves to their lords. Chaucer had been away in France since February 17, assisting in negotiations for a marriage between Richard and a French princess, but he was back in London in time to witness the splendor and pageantry of the Coronation.

Meanwhile, the war with France continued. The French took the Isle of Wight, captured Rye, and would have taken Winchelsea if they had not been repulsed by the Abbot of Battle. The gates of London were fortified with portcullises and barbicans, the aldermen made their wards ready, and the wharves were guarded.[13] The Scots attacked along the border. Percy resigned as Marshal and set out for the north. Four Londoners, including William Walworth and John Philpot, collected £10,000 to lend the King, and the city added £5,000 more. In October Parliament met to organize the new government. Archbishop Simon Sudbury, who had been Bishop of London (1362–1375), opened the proceedings with an address on the theme *Rex tuus uenit tibi* (Zach. 9. 9), which he divided into three parts "as if it were a sermon." His thesis was that the new King had come "as our good and entire friend," and as a natural liege lord, "not by election nor by any other collateral means, but by right succession of heritage." Thus the people were bound to him by natural love, and in the

---

[13] For details, see *Letter-Book H*, pp. 64–68.

present evil times, with enemies attacking the kingdom, they should offer him aid and counsel and help him with the expenses necessary for defense.[14]

Next day Parliament reassembled in the White Chamber to hear an address by Richard Scrope on the dangers to the realm and the need for money. The Duke of Lancaster, who had been appointed a receiver of petitions for England, France, and Wales, arose to present a moving defense of his own integrity. After kneeling before the King, he called attention to the fact that the Commons had accused him of acts that amounted to treason and stated that he wished to do nothing further before the truth could be made known. He said that none of his ancestors on either side had been traitors and that it would be a marvelous thing if he were a traitor, simply in accordance with nature, if for no other reason. However, he pointed out that he had more to lose by treasonable activity than any other man in England. Finally, he said that if anyone accused him of disloyalty, or of any other act prejudicial to the realm, he was ready to defend himself either by his body or in any other way before the lords and the King, like the poorest bachelor of the realm. The lords lay and spiritual hastened to reassure him, and to assert that accusations against him or any other words that would move debate among the lords should be considered treasonable and punished accordingly. There can be no doubt of Gaunt's sincerity. As he grew older, he became the most important stabilizing influence in the kingdom.

Near the opening of his address for the Commons, Peter de la Mare, who was once more Speaker, complained bitterly of the condition of English chivalry. It was once, he said, "most energetic, ardently desirous of great enterprises, each man eager to perform great deeds of arms, one above the other." But, he lamented, chivalry is now "together with all other virtues placed behind, and vice is praised, advanced, honored, and not at all punished or chastised."[15] To men of the fourteenth century chivalry did not mean a set of dead ideals out of the past, or the

[14] *Rot. Parl.*, III, 3–4.
[15] *Ibid.*, III, 5.

assiduous and frivolous cultivation of the ladies. It was instead the only available instrument of defense and just conquest, a source of national prosperity and international prestige. Without "virtuous" chivalry, England might be harassed continuously by its enemies, its trade would suffer, and its people would become impoverished. Peter de la Mare was not employing empty rhetoric. The enemy was quite obviously at the gates. Geoffrey Chaucer, meditating at Aldgate on the lessons of *The Consolation of Philosophy*, was preparing the groundwork for his great poem of warning to the chivalry of England, *Troilus and Criseyde*, and probably completing *The House of Fame*, a contrast between the fickleness of earthly fame and true fame of a kind pleasing to God.[16] Parliament appointed nine councillors for the King, demanded a trial for Alice Perrers, granted subsidies, and gave London a new charter and a confirmation of its liberties.

In May 1377 the Pope, perhaps warned by Bishop Brinton, issued a series of bulls to Archbishop Sudbury and Bishop Courtenay complaining of the heresies of Wyclif and demanding action. Bulls were also addressed to the King, the Chancellor, and the University of Oxford. Most of the propositions attributed to the reformer had to do with legal matters—"binding and unbinding" by persons not conforming to the Law of Christ, the power of temporal lords to deprive ecclesiastical lords of their temporalities, and so on. A group of Oxford scholars commented that although the propositions as stated were ill-sounding, they were nevertheless orthodox. No one felt that a curse by an irate archdeacon who simply wanted money or an absolution by a priest or friar who wanted a fee without reference to the contrition of the penitent was necessarily efficacious. Theologians had long insisted that confession was not valid without contrition of heart. Nevertheless, it was dangerous to allow laymen to think that they could avoid ecclesiastical correction because they felt it to be unjust, and in the early months of 1378 Wyclif was called to Lambeth to answer to the charges. At the trial itself, Wyclif interpreted his own views in such a way as to make them seem quite ordinary. Moreover, the proceedings were interrupted by

---

[16] See B. G. Koonce, *Chaucer and the Tradition of Fame* (Princeton, 1966).

Chaucer's friend Sir Lewis Clifford, who brought a message from Princess Joan demanding Wyclif's release.[17] Insofar as Wyclif's ideas represented an effort to correct abuses in the ecclesiastical hierarchy, especially where the neglect of spiritual considerations for money was concerned, they probably generated a great deal of sympathy in intellectual circles. Chaucer's ironic remark,

> For curs wol sle, right as assoilyng savith,

in a discussion of archdeacons who act as though a man's soul were in his purse, probably struck a sympathetic chord in many members of his audience. It is not necessary to regard the appearance of Clifford at Lambeth as an underhand "political" move inspired by the Duke of Lancaster. The royal desperation for money in the second half of the fourteenth century was symptomatic of a malady that was corrupting all ranks of society, but it was especially distasteful as it appeared among spiritual leaders. Wyclif was, however, creating a scandal, and some months later the government ordered him to desist from discussing his controversial theses, much in the same way that it had silenced Fitzralph some years earlier when he was violently attacking the friars in London.

The year 1378 was a memorable one for Londoners, for it was in this year that John Philpot equipped a fleet and captured the son of the Scots pirate, Mercer, who had been harassing English shipping. At some time during his office as Mayor, Nicholas Brembre asked that the charters of the misteries be submitted at the Guildhall, an act that has caused historians to attribute unworthy motives to him. But he may have been merely seeking useful administrative information. The mayor and aldermen were required to pass judgment on matters of standards, apprenticeship, and so on. Their task was made somewhat more complex because of the increasing number of chartered misteries. The war continued to go badly. John of Gaunt was not very successful on the Continent, and, to make matters worse, Castilian galleys

---

[17] Among Joan's executors were Chaucer's friends Sir John Clanvowe and Sir Richard Stury, in addition to Sir Lewis Clifford. It is quite probable that the Princess was devoutly interested in ecclesiastical reform.

attacked Cornwall. A local outrage, meanwhile, unsettled the community as a whole. In 1367 Robert Haulay and John Shakyl had captured a Spanish nobleman, the Count of Denia, at Nájera and were holding his son as a hostage for ransom. Ten years later the King's Council decided that the Spaniard should be released in an exchange of prisoners, but Haulay and Shakyl refused to give him up. They were imprisoned in the Tower, but their prisoner could not be found. Nine months later they escaped, fled to Westminster, and took sanctuary in the Abbey. Sir Alan Buxhill, Keeper of the Tower, pursued them with a troop of soldiers. Shakyl was captured, but Haulay, who was hearing Mass, attempted to evade his pursuers by running around the choir. He was intercepted by two soldiers, one of whom cleft his skull while the other ran him through. Meanwhile, a sacristan, who sought to keep order in the church, was also killed, and Haulay's body was dragged out into the street.

Archbishop Sudbury excommunicated those guilty of the murder, and in London Bishop Courtenay published a condemnation at St. Paul's, repeating it thrice weekly. In it he specifically exempted the King, Princess Joan, and the Duke of Lancaster from guilt, probably hoping by this means to suggest that they might all be involved. The King, who was a boy without much voice in decisions of this kind, was obviously not involved, and Princess Joan was too widely admired, both as a great beauty and a great lady, to suffer from the Bishop's efforts; but Londoners were always ready to suspect John of Gaunt of almost anything, in spite of the fact that he was on the Continent at the time Haulay was killed. He had in the past taken some interest in the prisoner. The result of the Bishop's action was a great deal of whispering in the City to the effect that the real villain in the affair was the Duke. The government finally ordered Courtenay to be silent about the matter.

Parliament was convened at Gloucester in October, a location that may have been selected to avoid the London mob, of which John of Gaunt had just reason to be suspicious. On the advice of certain clerks, including Wyclif, who here acted for the government for the last time, it was decided that "in case of debt, or of an accounting, rather than for a deed of trespass, wherein a man would not be in danger of life and limb, no one ought to have immunity in Holy Church."[18] There is nothing new or startling about this decision, duly defended by the rather pedestrian Wyclif in a treatise, but it avoids the issue, which was not actually the question of sanctuary, but bloodshed in the choir of a church during Mass. It was, however, about as much as the government could expect. The Gloucester Parliament produced a statute allowing alien fishmongers to sell as they pleased in London and elsewhere. Finally, it was at this Parliament that the English government formally proclaimed its allegiance to Pope Urban VI, who had been elected on April 9. The cardinals declared the election void on August 9, thus beginning the Great Schism. Sir Edward Berkeley and Chaucer were in Milan at the time of this announcement, where they had been on a mission to Barnabo Visconti and Sir John Hawkwood. They had left England on May 28, after Urban's election, and returned on September 19. It is quite likely that they brought news of the Schism with them, and it is possible that they may also have heard some of John of Legnano's arguments in favor of Urban. We do know that Chaucer's Clerk, a reliable spokesman, said that Legnano "enlumyned al Ytaille . . . of philosophie."[19] Relationships between London and the nobility, which were sufficiently strained to move Parliament to Gloucester, were further weakened during the year when Thomas of Woodstock accused Brembre of attacking his inn. Brembre vigorously denied the charge, but the Londoners were forced to raise a bribe to keep the noblemen and their considerable trade in the city.

Events of 1379 demonstrated still further decay in the morale of the kingdom. A Genoese merchant who had promised the King to make Southampton the most prosperous port in Europe, and who held royal letters of safe-conduct, was murdered by a London merchant. Sir John Arundel, the brother of the Bishop of Ely, had succeeded Henry Percy as Marshal and had been placed in charge of the defense of the south coast. A petition in Parliament complained that men-at-arms stationed there awaiting departure for the war had been ravaging the countryside, not sparing

[18] *Rot. Parl.*, III, 37.
[19] See John P. McCall, "Chaucer and John of Legnano," *Speculum*, XI (1965), 484–489.

the church in their depredations.[20] Walsingham alleges that when Sir John and his men finally set sail, they took with them women, some of them nuns taken by force. A great storm arose, and the women were cast into the sea to lighten ship.[21] Walsingham had an old maid's delight in scandal, but whether there were any women involved or not, the storm was real, Sir John was shipwrecked and drowned, and the expedition was a failure. The proceeds of a graduated poll tax granted earlier in the year were dissipated. In 1380 a new poll tax was granted, and this one precipitated the greatest disaster of the century, the Peasants' Revolt.

After the ravages of the Black Death and the efforts to fix wages and prices, there had been considerable unrest among the peasants generally. A petition before Parliament in 1377 pointed out that villeins and tenants of both ecclesiastical and lay lords had "with the counsel, procurement, and aid of certain persons" purchased in the royal court "exemplifications" of Domesday Book, misinterpreted them, and, on the basis of these misinterpretations, forcibly refused the customs and services due their overlords, threatening them with death. They were said also to have collected sums of money to aid the rebellion.[22] It seems reasonable to conclude that the basis for their action was the theory that the land they worked had at one time been royal demesne and that they owed only the services of tenure on such demesne. The petition reveals in any event that men in villein tenure were beginning in a significant way to be dissatisfied with their lot, the advantages of which were not so apparent as they had been during the preceding century. Other sources indicate that some of them were especially incensed by *merchetum*, a traditional fee for the marriage of a daughter, and *heriot*, a customary reversion of a part of a peasant's goods to his overload at death. The decay of the manorial courts and the intrusion of royal courts where the traditions of Roman law, as distinct from feudal custom, were strong, may have contributed to the uneasiness of the tenants; and they were undoubtedly envious of men working freely on leased lands. The latter were also enjoying a new sense of the power of money and were anxious for more. The further

[20] *Rot. Parl.*, III, 81.
[21] *Historia Anglicana*, ed. H. T. Riley (London, 1863–1864), II, 420–422.
[22] *Rot. Parl.*, III, 21–22.

fact that literate persons, probably friars, were assisting the discontented peasants and helping to collect money for them indicates a certain amount of organization. Both villeins and free peasants had, in any case, rising economic expectations and were especially sensitive to taxation. In the long view, the growth of a monetary economy in a society organized along feudal lines was bound to produce dislocations. These dislocations were not finally settled until the eighteenth century. However, modern writers should not look upon medieval peasants as their own revolutionary forebears. We are today the cultural descendants of the rootless proletariat of the late eighteenth and nineteenth centuries, not of medieval peasants.

The immediate cause of the outbreak on a large scale was the imposition of the new poll tax and the high-handed behavior of the commissioners sent out to collect it. Shakespeare, although he is describing other events at another time, expresses what must have been the feeling of a great many people in the fourteenth century rather well:

> The subject's grief
> Comes through commissions, which compel from each
> The sixth part of his substance, to be levied
> Without delay; and the pretense for this
> Is named your wars in France. This makes bold mouths:
> Tongues spit their duties out, and cold hearts freeze
> Allegiance in them. Their curses now
> Live where their prayers did, and it's come to pass
> That tractable obedience is a slave
> To each incensed will.

If the King had been a mature warrior successful in battle and forceful in his domestic administration, it is possible that the tax might have been endured; but the King was a boy, and the most powerful man at court, the Duke of Lancaster, was decidedly unpopular.

Large-scale revolt began in Essex among fairly well-to-do peasants. They were encouraged by two butchers of London, Adam atte Welle and Roger Harry, who in the days after May 30 rode through Essex urging the rebels to attack London.[23] Adam

---

[23] See Charles Petit-Dutaillis in André Réville, *Le soulevèment des Traivailleurs d'Angleterre en 1381* (Paris, 1898), LXXII.

was a regular supplier to the Savoy who probably had a personal grudge against John of Gaunt. The men of Kent under Wat Tyler, who was not a peasant, sacked Canterbury on June 7, opened the prison at Maidstone on June 11, and proceeded toward London, attacking royal and ecclesiastical officials and collecting followers along the way. When they reached Southwark on June 12, they attacked the residence of Richard Imworth, the Marshal, released the prisoners in the Marshalsea, and attacked the Flemish women of the Stews because they were foreigners. Then they proceeded to Lambeth, where they destroyed some chancery records and the records of Archbishop Sudbury. That night they assembled on Blackheath on the south side of the river below the Tower.

Next day, June 13, the rebels from Kent proceeded to London Bridge, perhaps under the inspiration of John Horn, Fishmonger, who was an alderman. There Walter Sybyll, Stockfishmonger, was guarding the gate. It was later alleged that Walter refused help from Thomas Cornwallis, who had been sent by the mayor with a force to assist in keeping the portal closed, and that he conspired with John Horn to open the gate.[24] The rebels managed to get in somehow in any event. Aldgate was opened by William Tonge, Vintner, although his motives are not altogether clear. The rebels entered and, under the leadership of Adam atte Welle, Roger Harry, Thomas Farndon, a member of a well-to-do London family, and other local residents, attacked the Temple, where they destroyed legal records and burned the Savoy, Fleet Prison, and the Hospital of St. John. Farndon bore a grudge against the Master of the Hospital who, as Royal Treasurer, had, he thought, unjustly deprived him of his inheritance. Those who burned the Savoy refrained from looting, seeking instead to destroy everything, but personal malice did not long restrain the mob in this respect elsewhere. The rebels released the prisoners in Newgate. A number of London tradesmen, chiefly fishmongers, butchers, and brewers, evidently assisted these operations, taking the opportunity to settle private grievances at the same time. John Horn took upon himself the office of a judge and went about the city holding court for the benefit of his friends.

[24] *Ibid.*, pp. 190–191.

Meanwhile King Richard and his Council were meeting in the Tower. They could see the smoke and flames rising from the city in the long summer afternoon and hear the cries of the mob and the screams of their victims. On the following day, Richard is said to have mounted a turret toward St. Katherine's to address a mob outside the walls, promising them pardon if they would go home and submit a schedule of written grievances. This offer, however, was rejected, and the young King, accompanied by some members of his Council, Sir Robert Knolles, Mayor William Walworth, some citizens, and squires, set out for Mile End to meet the rebels who had assembled there. According to some accounts, Princess Joan accompanied him in a chariot. On Tower Hill Thomas Farndon seized the King's bridle and demanded vengeance on the Prior of St. John's. Richard, who was fourteen, sagaciously replied, "You shall have what is just." As the party was riding through Aldgate a brewer, William Trewman, attacked Nicholas Brembre, who was among the citizens in the party, and accused him of offenses during his term as Mayor. Later in the day, he made an "affray" at Brembre's house in La Reole, making him give up five marks.

At Mile End, where Richard was virtually a prisoner, the rebels demanded justice for traitors against the king and the law. Richard replied that the people could have their will with "all who were traitors and could be proved traitors by the law."[25] The mob petitioned further that no man should be servile by birth, nor do homage for service to any lord, but be able to buy land for 4d an acre and to serve only by a contract with a definite term. There was, of course, no way to implement this demand in the fourteenth century. Richard, however, replied that they should be free generally and that he would execute proven traitors brought to him safely as the law demanded. There was little else he could say. Many of the men of Essex seemed satisfied by his assertions and returned home, some with royal charters prepared by clerks.

But while these negotiations were proceeding, Thomas Farndon, still seeking vengeance on Robert of Hales, Prior of St. John's, led a mob to the Tower. They broke in, seized Archbishop

25 *Anonimalle Chonicle*, p. 144.

Sudbury, Robert Hales, Fr. William de Appleton, physician to the Duke of Lancaster, and John Legge, Sergeant at Arms, led them to Tower Hill, and summarily beheaded them. This was a procedure not altogether synonymous with "proving them traitors by the law." The heads of these men were paraded through the city to Westminster and back to London Bridge, where they were mounted on stakes with several others on the tower. The head of the Archbishop was placed a little higher than the rest and decorated with a red hood. Meanwhile, the mob raged through the streets. They beheaded Richard Lyons formally in Cheap, slaughtered thirty-five Flemings who had sought sanctuary in St. Martin le Grand, killed a number of other Flemings in the Vintry, and massacred all the Lombards they could find. The city record observes that "hardly was there a street in the city in which there were not bodies lying of those who had been slain. Some of the houses also in the said city were pulled down, and others in the suburbs destroyed, and some too, burnt."[26] A London brewer, one Walter atte Keye, went searching for a standard book of city customs called *Jubilee*, proposing to burn it, and generally the lower elements in the population gave reign to their impulses.

That evening King Richard and his mother took refuge in the Great Wardrobe. In the morning, he went to Westminster Abbey to hear Divine Service. While he was there, some rebels broke into the Abbey, seized Richard Imworth the Marshal, who was clinging to a pillar of the shrine of St. Edward, and dragged him off to Cheap to be beheaded. When Richard arrived at Smithfield, according to the account in the *Anonimalle Chronicle*, he stationed himself to the east near St. Bartholomew's and ordered the rebels to array themselves on the west. The King commanded Walworth to bring the rebel leader before him, and Wat Tyler rode out on a small horse with banners flying. He approached the King, dismounted, seized him by the hand, and shook it vigorously, saying, "Brother, be of good comfort and joyful, for you shall have within fifteen days forty thousand soldiers of the commons more than you have had before, and we shall be good

[26] Riley, *Memorials*, p. 450.

companions." He then demanded a charter granting six points, the first of which is obscure and may result merely from a misunderstanding on his part:

1. That there should be no law except the Law of Winchester.
2. That there should be no outlawry.
3. That there should be no seignory except that of the King.
4. That the goods of the Church should be divided among the parishioners.
5. That there should be only one bishop in England, and that possessioners should be deprived of everything except their sustenance.
6. That there should be no serf in England.

Richard replied that Tyler could have what he could well grant, saving the regality of his crown. Needless to say, it would have been impossible to regard these demands seriously, and Richard's reply was hardly a "promise" to fulfil them. The statement is sometimes made that it is doubtful that the King had much sympathy for the rebels. It is quite evident, and only reasonable, that he had no sympathy for them at all.

It was a hot day. Tyler rinsed out his mouth with water before the King, spat on the ground, and mounted his horse. A valet in the royal retinue, recognizing Tyler, observed that he was "the greatest thief and robber in Kent." When Tyler offered violence before the King, Mayor Walworth arrested him. At this, Tyler drew a dagger and attacked Walworth, but the latter was armed and suffered no injury. He drew his baselard and wounded Tyler on the neck and head. A valet of the King ran him through with his sword, mortally wounding him so that he fell from his horse. The King rode forth and told the rebels to follow him to Clerkenwell. Walworth rode hastily to London, where he summoned Sir Robert Knolles, the ward captains, and their men. They were said to have been impeded somewhat by Walter Sybyll, who is pictured riding about crying "All is lost!" and closing Aldersgate. But Walworth and his men soon returned to Smithfield, where they found Tyler dying at St. Bartholomew's. They beheaded him and carried the head to Clerkenwell, where the men of the wards surrounded the rebels. The latter, finding themselves surrounded and without a leader, asked mercy, which the King granted. When the affray was over, the King knighted William Walworth,

Death of Wat Tyler, fifteenth century (copyright British Museum).

John Philpot, and Nicholas Brembre. Charters of pardon were granted to those rebels who lingered suspiciously in London. All that remained was the punishment of the guilty, a procedure that was characterized in London by great moderation, so that only Jack Straw and a few others were executed.

Chaucer, who probably witnessed many of the events just described, has very little to say about the revolt in his poetry. The only direct reference is a jocular one in the description of the chase after the fox in the "Nun's Priest's Tale":

> Certes, he Jakke Straw and his meynee
> Ne made nevere shoutes half so shrille
> Whan that they wolden any Flemyng kille,
> As thilke day was maad upon the fox.

The poet had no patience with hierarchical disruptions and would probably have agreed with the "sadde folk" in the "Clerk's Tale":

O stormy peple! unsad and evere untrewe!
Ay undiscreet and chaungynge as a fane!
Delitynge ever in rumbul that is newe,
For lyk the moone ay wexe ye and wane!
Ay ful of clappyng, deere ynogh a jane!
Youre doom is fals, youre constance yvele preveth;
A ful gret fol is he that on yow leveth!

Chaucer's friend and fellow poet John Gower, addressing himself to Thomas Arundel, devoted the first book of his *Vox clamantis* to an account of the revolt, wherein he described the rebels as mad beasts entering New Troy and committing the most despicable crimes. Historically speaking, the revolt accomplished nothing beyond much senseless bloodshed and destruction. The peasants were not, on the whole, hopelessly oppressed; on the contrary, Froissart's observation that they were too fat and prosperous probably has a certain amount of justification. In spite of their theoretical attacks on the hierarchy of the kingdom, what they wanted actually was the same thing the government wanted: more money. Most of their leaders in London seem to have been interested primarily in private vengeance, and many members of the mob devoted their attention to looting. The revolt did succeed in convincing many Englishmen for years to come that there is nothing so dangerous as a mob.

In October 1381 Walworth was succeeded as mayor by John of Northampton, a friend of the Duke of Lancaster, who set about instituting reforms, among them the regulations concerning prostitutes and bawds discussed earlier. These proved relatively innocent, but Northampton attacked the fishmongers, who were suspected of maintaining unnecessarily high prices. The decision of the Gloucester Parliament to allow alien fishmongers to sell as they pleased was probably a first step in preventing local merchants from purchasing fish from strangers and reselling them at higher prices. Northampton issed a series of more specific regulations. Local fishmongers were to desist from harboring or associating with alien (nonresident) fishmongers bringing fish for sale. Strangers bringing salt fish or other nonperishable victuals, like garlic, onions, or salted eels, were to sell them directly to royal purchasers and others, and local fishmongers were not to buy them until after three days. Alien fishmongers were to sell their fish at their vessels or in Cornhill and West Cheap. Fish-mongers purchasing fish from aliens after the three-day period were to sell them only between 11 A.M. and 1 P.M., or, if they made their purchases after 11 A.M., they could not sell them until after 1 P.M. Freshwater fish were to be sold only by those who caught them.[27] The effect of these regulations was to limit severely the activity of local fishmongers as distributors or mid-dlemen. The fishmongers were asked to bring their charter to the Guildhall, were carefully watched for the use of false measures, and the price of herring was fixed.[28] The regulations concerning nonperishable foodstuffs may have affected grocers as well as fishmongers. In any event, Northampton's actions aroused the hostility of a great many London merchants, who, under the leadership of Nicholas Brembre, referred to contemptuously by Gower as "Bramble," began a quarrel with Northampton and his followers that lasted many years and at times erupted into violence.

In 1382 Northampton and his aldermen and council offered a petition in Parliament complaining that London fishmongers seized the fish of aliens, sold them at high prices, and paid the aliens at their pleasure. They had oppressed strangers with threats of violence and claimed jurisdiction in their own courts. Although Nicholas Exton and Walter Sybyll objected, alleging prejudice, John More, speaking for Northampton's party, accused the fishmongers generally and Sybyll in particular of having assisted the rebels in the revolt.[29] There may have been some truth in this charge, for many fishmongers were probably angry because of the action of the Gloucester Parliament, but it was essentially irrelevant. In any event, the Parliamentary response forbade fishmongers to have judicial power, and a statute made it illegal for fishmongers to buy any fish for resale except fresh eels, luces, and pike. But this statute was repealed in the follow-ing year.[30]

The Peasants' Revolt inspired new interest in Wyclif. Before 1382, however, the reformer's ideas had been confined largely to

27 *Letter-Book H*, pp. 190–191.
28 *Ibid.*, pp. 193, 194, 196.
29 *Rot. Parl.*, III, 141 ff.
30 *Statutes of the Realm*, II, 29, 34.

Oxford and Leicester, although Wat Tyler's demands and John Ball's teaching suggest attitudes reminiscent of the reformer. Ball confessed to having been influenced by Wyclif, but the idea may have been suggested to him by one of Gaunt's enemies. It is difficult, in any event, to imagine Wyclif approving of Ball's ambition to be Primate of England. Walsingham thought that Wyclif on the one hand and the friars on the other had been influential in bringing about the revolt, but he also blamed the bishops generally for laxness. In 1382 Courtenay, elevated as Archbishop of Canterbury after the murder of Sudbury, called a Council at Blackfriars in London to discuss a series of propositions, most of which were undoubtedly derived from the writings of Wyclif. Many distinguished theologians were present, including Henry Crump, a Cistercian, who was Regent in Sacred Theology at Oxford. Crump had recently created a furor by calling Wyclif's followers at Oxford "Lollards."[31] This was a term of opprobrium, suggesting that the person so designated was an idle babbler about doctrinal subjects, or, in the Pope's words, a "dry tare." It was by no means a synonym for "Wyclifite." Thus Sir John Clanvowe, contrasting worldly wisdom and true wisdom, says that those who live wisely and "would fain live meekly in this world, and be out of . . . riot, noise, and strife, and live simply, and customarily eat and drink in measure, and clothe themselves meekly, and suffer wrongs patiently . . . the world [namely the worldly-wise as a group] scorns and calls 'lolleris.' "[32] The word *lolleris* does not here designate a sect, but is a term of contempt, and its misuse by the worldly-wise does not mean that it had no just application. That is, there were undoubtedly idle and loquacious persons who deserved it. Clanvowe does not designate himself here as a "loller." He simply shows a traditional orthodox sympathy for those who seek what Bishop Brinton called "clerical wisdom." The Council of 1382 set out to examine erroneous doctrines. It did not mention Wyclif or attack "Lollards" specifically, but it was clear at the outset that many of those present shared Crump's contempt for Wyclif.

[31] Dahmus, *Courtenay*, p. 99.
[32] *The Two Ways*, ed. V. J. Scattergood, *English Philological Studies*, X (1967), 48.

The Council convened on May 17, but the deliberations were interrupted by an earthquake that toppled pinnacles and chimneypots in the city and frightened the inhabitants. It also disturbed the members of the Council. However, Courtenay assured them that just as the earth required an earthquake to purge it, so also the Church required great upheavals to purge it of heresy. Thus reassured, the members condemned ten of the propositions before it.[33] Four of them concerned the Eucharist, having to do with the confusion that arose from the introduction of Aristotelian categories into discussions of this subject and with the problem of whether or not Christ ordained the Mass in the Gospels. One concerned the ability of a priest in mortal sin to administer the sacraments; one questioned the need for confession when the penitent was contrite; two attacked Papal power; one denied the clergy the right to temporal possessions; and one stated that "God must obey the Devil." The fourteen remaining propositions were said to be erroneous. These attacked the friars, the religious orders, and the administrative privileges of the Church. On May 26 Parliament enacted a statute authorizing sheriffs and other officials to arrest anyone preaching heretical doctrines, and Courtenay issued a decree a few days later placing all persons who accepted, preached, or listened to any of the condemned propositions under excommunication. Courtenay then moved to Oxford, where the followers of Wyclif still expected protection from the Duke of Lancaster. But when the Duke learned, through two of Wyclif's followers, what they were actually saying about the Eucharist, he was outraged and gave them a long lecture on the orthodox interpretation of the subject.

Meanwhile, in January 1382, King Richard married Anne of Bohemia and shortly thereafter began his practice of granting lands escheated to the Crown for one reason or another to his household followers. This was not in itself a strange thing for a feudal king to do, but the royal treasury was in no condition to give up any of its potential assets. The lack of a budget made the basic situation difficult to understand, but the steady pressure of indebtedness was unmistakable, and Richard began to acquire a

[33] For the circumstances and the propositions themselves, see Dahmus, *Courtenay*, pp. 78–83.

reputation for extravagance. Parliament had turned down funds for a campaign in France, and in 1382 the alternatives of an attack on Spain under Gaunt and a Crusade against Clementist heretics in Flanders under Bishop Despenser of Norwich were considered. The bishop had acted firmly in the Peasants' Revolt, attacking and routing the rebels in his area with force of arms. Attacks on peasants were contrary to the laws of chivalric warfare, so that his victory in that respect lacked a certain luster. However, the Duke of Burgundy had taken Bruges, and Calais was threatened. Moreover, the wool trade with Ghent was cut off. It was decided, therefore, in 1383, to allow the Bishop to have his Crusade. His army was made up mostly of undisciplined apprentices and runaway clerics interested in loot, his strategy was indecisive, in spite of the efforts of Sir Hugh Calverley to alter it, and the "Crusade," in which the Bishop attacked perfectly good Urbanists at Ypres, was a dismal and disgraceful failure. Many pious ladies and gentlemen who had generously donated gifts to the multitude of friars who moved about England preaching the Holy War were woefully disappointed, and it was necessary to send John of Gaunt abroad to arrange a truce. The new Chancellor, Michael de la Pole, condemned the Bishop in Parliament, forcing him to give up his temporalities for a time. Some of his captains, found to have taken bribes from the French, were imprisoned. English chivalry had indeed reached a low ebb in 1383. Chaucer, wishing to show the contrast between the chivalry of his youth and that of the eighties, depicted his dandified young squire, an obvious "soldier of Venus," as having distinguished himself with Despenser

> . . . in chyvachie
> In Flaundres, in Artois, and Pycardie.[34]

A Parliament at Salisbury in April 1384 marked the decisive beginning of strained relations between King Richard and his elders. When the Earl of Arundel denounced the government, and predicted the downfall of the realm, Richard flew into a rage, telling

---

[34] See Alan Gaylord, "Chaucer's Squire and the Glorious Campaign," *Papers of the Michigan Academy of Science, Arts, and Letters,* XLV (1960), 341–361.

him to go to the devil. In Richard's behalf it might be said that he was not the master of his kingdom and that many of the mistakes that had led to the decay of the realm were no fault of his; but his burst of temper was a sign of weakness. The Duke of Lancaster, who had just returned from an excursion into Scotland, arose and smoothed things over. While Parliament was still in session, an Irish friar who had just celebrated Mass before the King and the Earl of Oxford, denounced Gaunt as a traitor, alleging that he was plotting to kill the King. Gaunt defended himself convincingly, and the friar was sent to prison. However, many were curious to know who had inspired the friar. He was intercepted on the way to his imprisonment by Sir John Holland, Sir Peter Courtenay, and two other knights, who tortured him unmercifully to discover the instigator of the plot. They were unsuccessful, and the friar died. Thomas of Woodstock, Earl of Buckingham, who shared the King's weakness for rash action, became so enraged at the incident that he burst into the royal chamber, drew his sword, and threatened to kill anyone who accused his brother the Duke of Lancaster of treason. Altogether, the whole series of events must have been considerably unsettling for Richard. The atmosphere of amnesty and goodwill with which his reign had opened would never return.

In London John of Northampton was reelected Mayor in 1382 at the suggestion of the King.[35] At the end of his second term of office, however, Nicholas Brembre was elected, perhaps by "stronge honde" or intimidation.[36] In any event, Northampton had many followers, especially among those who benefited from his efforts to keep the price of victuals low or who maintained resentment for one reason or another against fishmongers. Neither Northampton nor his followers were willing to give up their agitation in the city. On January 22 he was forced to find sureties for £5,000 to keep the peace, and on February 9 a writ for his arrest on the ground that he was planning insurrection in the city was issued. In a disturbance on February 11, one of Northampton's adherents, John Constantyn, Cordwainer, was arrested for alleging that Brembre planned to murder Northampton's followers.

[35] *Letter-Book H*, p. 200.
[36] *Ibid.*, p. 220 and note.

Letters patent were issued by the King permitting Constantyn's execution. In September Northampton and two of his closest associates—Richard Norbury, Mercer, and John More, Mercer—were brought to trial at the Tower before the royal justices. It was alleged that they "did feloniously and traitorously . . . rise in rebellion against Nicholas Brembre, the Mayor, the Aldermen, and other governors of the said City, and did cause many conventicles, assemblies, and covines to be made . . . whereby many doors and windows of houses and shops in Westchepe, Bugerow [Budge Row], Fletestrete, and elsewhere in the City and suburbs that were open early in the morning were afterwards closed, as a sign of insurrection, and locked, and as much as in them lay they assembled the populace, feloniously and traitorously aiming at the death of the said Nicholas, the Mayor, and certain Aldermen, and other good and wise men of the City."[37]

According to the record, Northampton and his friends pleaded guilty at the Tower and were condemned to be taken through the city to Tyburn to be hanged. But Michael de la Pole, the Chancellor, is said to have appeared with writs ordering them to be imprisoned instead. They were sentenced to confinement for ten years and were forbidden to come within a hundred miles of London.[38] One chronicler relates that Thomas Usk, who was Northampton's secretary, had revealed "multa enormia et sinistra" concerning his master at a council on August 18. Northampton is said to have denied the charges and offered wager of battle. He is also said to have angered the King by objecting to a judicial decision at a time when the Duke of Lancaster was not in the kingdom. Exactly what his relation with the Duke may have been is not clear. However, on May 7, 1386, Gaunt wrote to Brembre, who was enjoying his third consecutive term as Mayor, concerning Northampton "against whom the mayor's wishes and purposes were outrageous." The King, he said, had promised to pardon Northampton, More, and Northbury, provided that they did not come within forty miles of the city. But because of Brembre's intervention, the Duke complained, the King had not done so. On May 12, Gaunt wrote again, saying that Northampton planned

37 *Ibid.*, pp. 264–265.
38 Monk of Westminster in Higden's *Polichronicon,* ed. J. R. Lumby, IX (London, 1886), pp. 30–31.

to go with him to Spain and asking that Northampton's wife and children be allowed their inheritance.[39] The Mayor and Aldermen replied that they agreed to allow Northampton to approach no farther than eighty miles from the city, characterizing him and his followers as "rioters, brawlers, disturbers of the peace, initiators and maintainers of common quarrels in the city."[40] The quarrel was still active in 1387, when Nicholas Exton, who succeeded Brembre as mayor, confirmed the cancellation of Northampton's London citizenship.[41] At a meeting on April 17, it was revealed that Lord la Zouche had been pleading with the King to restore Northampton's citizenship. The Mayor and Aldermen expressed surprise.[42] At a conference with the King they obtained assurances that he would be cautious in showing favor to the still imprisoned Northampton, Northbury, and More. They also sought to persuade the Minister of the Friars Minor to cease pleading for Northampton. On June 3, 1387, the King finally announced that he had pardoned Northampton and his companions at the behest of the Duke of Lancaster, although they were not to come within eighty miles of London.[43]

The quarrel between Northampton and Brembre probably involved commercial interest at the outset, but the personal involvement of the King and the Duke of Lancaster undoubtedly complicated matters. The Duke needed "a friend in London." It is possible that Michael de la Pole, who was brother-in-law to Sir Richard Scrope and had been attached to the retinues of the Black Prince and John of Gaunt successively, may have helped to persuade the King not to allow Northampton to be executed in the first place, although one story has it that the Queen prayed that he be spared. Richard probably came to favor Brembre because of his behavior during the revolt of 1381 and, having knighted him, took it upon himself to protect his interests. And Brembre, for his part, probably allowed his relationship with the Crown to overcome his discretion in the pursuit of personal ag-

[39] A. H. Thomas, *Calendar of Select Pleas and Memoranda of the City of London* (Cambridge, 1932), pp. 109–110.
[40] *Ibid.*, pp. 111–112.
[41] *Letter-Book H*, p. 304.
[42] *Ibid.*, p. 305.
[43] *Ibid.*, p. 307.

grandizement. In the long run, Brembre got the worst of it, for he was a victim of the Merciless Parliament. Northampton eventually returned to London. However, Richard had meanwhile confiscated much of his property and distributed it among his immediate followers. This action, which became somewhat characteristic, was not entirely judicious. The whole affair must have been irksome to Chaucer, who knew Brembre at the Custom House, but had, at the same time, close connections with the Duke of Lancaster. Whatever the complications of the conflict in London may have been, the issues remained alive for some time, and an air of uneasiness in the city accompanied the uneasy air at court.

The year 1385 was marked by omens of disaster: a conjunction of Jupiter and Saturn was noted by Walsingham, and there was an earthquake as well. Richard set out on a campaign against the Scots, who were being aided by the French as a part of their plan for a large-scale invasion of England. In London preparations were made to defend the city. A proclamation was issued urging all those who could go to the coast to defend the city and the realm to report to the Guildhall for pay—12d a day for men-at-arms and 6d for archers. The expedition was to be led by Sir Robert Knolles. A defense tax was imposed on victuals and other merchandise.[44] The French invasion of the south did not, however, take place. Richard's campaign in the north, his first personal military venture, was not crowned with much success and was marred by a brawl at York as a result of which Sir John Holland murdered the young heir of Stafford and fled into Lancashire. Richard swore that he would treat Holland, who was his half brother, like any other murderer, but he failed to carry out this threat. Princess Joan, saddened by the incident, fell ill and died. Once over the border of Scotland, Richard made his younger uncles Duke of York and Duke of Gloucester, and made Michael de la Pole Earl of Suffolk. After burning some abbeys and taking Edinburgh, Richard returned home without encountering the main military power of the Scots. Robert de Vere, Earl of Oxford, whom the King stubbornly and foolishly trusted,

[44] *Ibid.*, pp. 269–271.

had been largely responsible for the inconsequential nature of the expedition. He took every occasion to prejudice the King against Lancaster and to see to it that the Duke's advice was received with suspicion. Richard was thus alienated from his most powerful and most loyal uncle, a fact that was to have disastrous consequences.

In the following year John of Gaunt set out for Spain. The English had been heartened by the news of a great Portuguese victory at Aljubarotta, and Gaunt was eager to exploit the potentialities of his Spanish marriage. The war was declared a Crusade, opened officially with a sermon at St. Paul's on February 18 and preached throughout the country by Lancaster's friends the Carmelites. Even King Richard seems to have shared in the general enthusiasm for the venture. Gaunt took with him Sir Thomas Percy and Sir John Holland, who, by virtue of an impetuous wooing and an ensuing pregnancy had married Elizabeth of Lancaster, formerly betrothed to the Earl of Pembroke. He also took Constance of Castile and their two unwed daughters Philippa and Katherine, doubtless with a view to finding profitable marriage partners for the latter. "King John," as he was called, and his Queen accepted golden crowns from Richard and departed for Plymouth on March 16. After the usual delays, the expedition set forth on July 7. The army paused to relieve Brest, besieged by the Duke of Brittany, sailed thence to Coruña, and then moved, with a certain crusading appropriateness, to Santiago de Compostella. John of Gaunt was to be away from England for almost three years, leaving Richard to contend with a dissatisfied Commons, a rebellious baronage, and his own quick passions and foolish prejudices.

On October 1 the Wonderful Parliament met amid renewed threats of invasion from abroad and the nuisance of armed bands of returned soldiers and outlaws roaming the country. Chaucer attended as a representative from Kent, although, in the fourteenth century, this was not an especially noteworthy honor. Richard was interested only in obtaining revenue for an offensive against the French and retired to Eltham to await a decision concerning the large subsidy he had requested through Michael de la Pole, the Chancellor. The Commons, probably at the instigation of Thomas of Woodstock, Duke of Gloucester, and other lords, who were irritated because Richard had made his friend Robert de Vere Duke of Ireland, demanded the replacement of Michael de la Pole as Chancellor and of John Fordham, Bishop of Durham, as Treasurer. These men were not especially culpable, but, as usual in the fourteenth century, individuals were made to accept the blame for economic situations beyond their control. Richard was quite naturally irritated and replied brashly to a request that his officials be removed. The Commons then demanded that Richard return to Parliament. When this failed to move him beyond an acknowledgement that he would be happy to receive a petition from the Commons, Gloucester and Bishop Thomas Arundel approached the King, reminded him that the Commons could leave Parliament after forty days if the King were not there, and deplored the decay of English chivalry, heavy taxation, and the evil counsellors of the King; finally, they suggested that Richard might, like Edward II, be deposed if he did not act favorably. Needless to say, things would not have gone so far if the Duke of Lancaster had been in England.

The young King had little choice but to return to Parliament, although he must have regarded Gloucester with a certain impatience. He dismissed Michael de la Pole and Fordham from office. Gloucester and Arundel inspired an attack on Michael de la Pole somewhat like that staged against Wykeham earlier. The charges had little substance, but the former Chancellor was deprived of his irregular grants, made to pay a fine (later remitted), and imprisoned "at the King's pleasure." Bishop Arundel was made Chancellor and the Bishop of Hereford, John Gilbert, was made Treasurer. A commission was formed to save the King from his favorites, to reform the government, and to plan countermeasures against France. Any hope that these or any similar measures could effectively assist the financial condition of the kingdom was, of course, futile.

Meanwhile, certain of the London guilds entered a series of petitions against Nicholas Brembre. They undoubtedly represented Northampton's faction, but, at the same time, they were probably encouraged to present their complaints at this time by those wishing to discomfort the King. The mercers complained that Brembre "wyth his upberers, proposed hym the yere next after John Northampton Mair of the same Citee, with stronge honde, as is ful knowen, and thourgh debate and strenger partye ayeins the pees bifore purveyde was chosen Mair, in destruccion of many ryght." Furthermore, Brembre made "dyverse enarmynges bi day and eke by nyght, and destruyd the Kynges trewe lyges, som with open slaughtre, some bi false emprisonement, and some fledde the Citee for feere, as it is openlich knowen." At the next election, the only persons summoned were "of his ordynance and after hys avys." Moreover, Brembre had, it was alleged, run his office "as it were of Conquest," imprisoning or impeaching his enemies, whom he called traitors to the King. During the time of Brembre's successor, Nicholas Exton, the ancient customs of the City, in the book called *Jubilee*, were burned, and Exton, it was alleged, continued to imprison those opposing him. Similar complaints were registered by the cordwainers, saddlers, painters, armorers, pinners, broiders, spurriers, and bladesmiths.[45] The tailors complained further that Brembre had seized their charter.[46] Generally, these misteries desired a reinstatement of the statute forbidding members of the victualing trades to hold judicial office. Although it is probable that these petitions were exaggerated, it is also probable that Brembre had been high-handed. It is difficult to discover any real clue to the nature of the London quarrel from these petitions. The mercers and tailors were relatively wealthy, while the pinners and spurriers were relatively poor. It is clear that the general animus was directed against the victualing trades.

Altogether, the Wonderful Parliament hardly marked a step toward "constitutional government," and the temporary muzzling of the King, who had not yet been declared of age in any event, was nothing of which anyone could be proud. The new Commission, probably inspired by Gloucester, whose share of the London customs was in arrears, deprived Chaucer of his position at the Custom House. The collectors with whom he worked were Brembre and Exton. It may well be, as has been suggested, that the unfavorable account of the Trojan Parliament in *Troilus*, wherein the chivalry of Hector is overruled by "noyse of peple,"

---

[45] *Rot. Parl.*, III, 325–327.
[46] I. S. Leadam and J. F. Baldwin, *Select Cases Before the King's Council* (Cambridge, Mass., 1918), pp. 74–76.

reflects the poet's experience at the Parliament of 1386.[47] As *The Parliament of Fowls* reveals, Chaucer was not especially enthusiastic about parliaments of any kind, and this one, with its rash accusations and ineffective measures, probably deepened his conviction that disorder in the political hierarchy could be the only result of allowing clamorous commoners to have too much voice in national affairs. The year was marked by only one piece of good news. The Earls of Arundel and Nottingham were victorious over a large French and Spanish fleet. They destroyed the fortifications of Brest and returned home with large quantities of wine, which sold at low prices in England.

Matters were to grow worse. In February 1387, Richard set out on a tour of the midlands and the north, which kept him away from the new Commissioners for ten months. He continued to cultivate Robert de Vere and probably helped him to put aside his wife, Philippa de Coucy, in favor of a Bohemian woman, Agnes Lancecrona, an act that was not of a kind to win much respect either for himself or for the Earl of Oxford. The absence of the Duke of Lancaster and his forces and Gloucester's threat to depose him probably suggested to the King the need for military support. Although he had no means to acquire a large force, he did succeed in assembling some Cheshire archers and Welsh pikemen. In August he called together his chief judicial authorities: Tresilian, Chief Justice of the King's Bench, Belknap, Chief Justice of the Common Bench, and others. At two meetings, he put certain questions to them concerning his royal estate. Was the statute of the last Parliament derogatory to the regalia and prerogative of the King? The justices said that insofar as it was contrary to the royal will, it was derogatory. What punishment did this offense imply? The answer was death, unless there were a royal pardon. The same punishment was said to be appropriate for those who consented. Those who forced the King or impeded royal rights were said to be traitors. It was agreed that the King could determine what should be taken up in Parliament and that he could dissolve Parliament at will. Anyone who opposed these rights or who tried to use the precedent of the deposition of Ed-

[47] See J. P. McCall and George Rudisill, "The Parliament of 1386 and Chaucer's Trojan Parliament," *Journal of English and Germanic Philology*, LVIII (1959), 276–288.

ward II was said to be a traitor. These judgments are not revolutionary, since Parliament did not customarily reach decisions contrary to royal consent. They were witnessed by the Archbishop of York, who probably found nothing new or startling in them. There can be no real question of Richard's rights; the only problem was whether he had sufficient power to maintain them. It is quite probable that Gloucester desired either to rule the kingdom from his own position or to usurp Richard's power altogether if that failed. In his behalf it may be said that he was acutely conscious of the loss of national power and prestige during Richard's reign and that Richard himself had shown more concern at times for his immediate satisfactions than for the welfare of the realm as a whole. But the idea that Richard was personally responsible for what had happened to the realm was mistaken, although it was consistent with the medieval tendency to seek full responsibility for the condition of any human hierarchy at its apex and could thus win wide popular acceptance.

On November 10 Richard entered London, where he received an enthusiastic formal welcome from the city. He was escorted in procession through Cheap to St. Paul's and thence to Westminster amid loud acclamations from the populace. On the next day, he summoned Gloucester and the Earl of Arundel to appear before him. But Gloucester, who had learned of the decisions of the justices, refused to appear. Richard responded by demanding that Londoners refuse to sell anything to Arundel, relying too heavily on the enthusiasm exhibited at his homecoming. Gloucester and Arundel gathered a large military force north of the city, where they were joined by Thomas Beauchamp, Earl of Warwick. Their combined force took up a position at Waltham Cross, from which point they began to circulate propaganda against the royal favorites in the city and managed in this fashion to recruit large numbers of Londoners to their cause. It is probable that they also thoroughly intimidated the city government. A delegation sent to them from the King, including Archbishop Courtenay, Bishop Wykeham of Winchester, and Thomas Arundel of Ely, sought a compromise. They were obliged to listen to a series of "appeals," or formal charges of felonious conduct, against Michael de la Pole, Robert de Vere, Tresilian, Nicholas Brembre, and Alexander Neville, Archbishop of York.

The "appeal" was the customary feudal action against a felon, largely replaced during the later fourteenth century by the indictment. If a man were stabbed and robbed, for example, he could recite in detail before the proper justice the time and place of the event, the size and nature of the wound received, his efforts to raise a hue and cry, and his complaints to neighboring authorities. The appeal was carefully checked as it was being made against a written version in the hands of the authorities. Any discrepancies would invalidate the appeal. Recitals of this kind sometimes filled a whole day. If the appeal seemed accurate, and was in proper form, the accused had the alternatives of submitting his case to a jury of persons assembled from near the scene of the crime or offering trial by battle. Since persons from the neighborhood were likely to be friends of the appellant, and the battle was frequently long and inconclusive, appealed felons usually demanded battle. For these reasons "appeals" were discouraged in the later Middle Ages. They were still used, however, in the Court of Chivalry, where battles were carried out more efficiently and appeals were not necessarily so circumstantial. Gloucester was expert in the procedures of this court, and probably regarded the appeal as a means of getting rid of his enemies in the present instance without the embarrassment of allowing them any opportunity for public defense. Moreover, the appeals would effectively prevent the King from doing whatever he might have been contemplating as a result of the decisions of his justices. They had the further advantage of suggesting that the use of force, which the King was in no position to counter, might be imminent.

The appellants, having stated their case, came before the King in Westminster Hall, where Sir Richard Scrope, acting as their spokesman, but actually not very sympathetic with their cause, asked for a trial in Parliament under common law, if any means could be found for holding it. The request for "common law" effectively removed the case from the Court of Chivalry. Richard agreed to hold Parliament on February 3, 1388. Although the appellants had no legal basis for any action, they did have obvious military power. Archbishop Neville fled to his diocese in disguise, Robert de Vere disappeared in the direction of North Wales, Suffolk managed to get out of the country, and Tresilian went into hiding in Westminster. Brembre, who probably thought the charges brought against him too fantastic to be taken seriously, rashly remained in London. An effort by Robert de Vere to bring a military force southward in the King's support failed when he and his men were trapped by Gloucester and Gaunt's son, the Earl of Derby, at Radcot Bridge. De Vere escaped, however, and fled the country. Richard took up residence in the Tower for safety, but was unable to get any support from the Londoners who had greeted him with such enthusiasm a short time before. They now refused to billet his men in the city. The country was, in effect, in a state of insurrection.

In December 1387 the appellants settled their forces at Clerkenwell. Among their activities was an effort, at the Guildhall, to persuade the Mayor, Nicholas Exton, the aldermen, and the men of the misteries to settle their differences and join the anti-Ricardian faction. During the last days of December, the appellants, who now included the Earl of Derby and Thomas Mowbray, Earl of Nottingham, entered the Tower with some five hundred retainers and confronted Richard. Exactly what happened there is obscure, although it is clear that Derby and Nottingham acted as moderating influences on Gloucester. Threats of some sort were brought against the King, which may have included withdrawal of homage and some form of deposition. The legal heir apparent was Roger Mortimer, Earl of March, but Gloucester seems to have entertained the idea of seizing the throne for himself. Any such move could hardly have appealed to Derby, and there was, moreover, the added deterrent that the Duke of Lancaster might return to England in the near future. The result of the conference was that the list of "traitors" drawn up by the appellants was extended to include Sir Simon Burley, Sir John Beauchamp, and the justices who had advised Richard concerning his Parliamentary rights. A number of clerks and lesser ladies and gentlemen were dismissed from the court.

Parliament met on February 3 in Westminster Hall. The appellants, dressed in surcoats of gold, were said to have come before the King, who occupied his throne in the center, to have their charges read by a clerk, Geoffrey Martin. The specific items in the appeal are in part simply a record of events clothed in derogatory language. For example, the judgment of Tresilian and the other justices concerning the King's rights is called "false" and is said to have been inspired by Bishop Neville, Robert de Vere, and Michael de la Pole. Other charges consist merely of derogatory language. For example, those mentioned above "with the assent of Brembre" are said to have "accroached" royal power, with the result that taxes and subsidies were necessary. The taxes and subsidies were real enough, but they would have been necessary whether the persons mentioned had "accroached" anything or not. Brembre was accused specifically of having executed some felons and accused felons taken from Newgate and of having caused it to be proclaimed in London that no one should speak evil of the "traitors." Altogether, the appeal hardly justified the use of the word *treason,* but what was worse, it had no legal basis at all. A body of legal experts consulted by the King and the lords affirmed that it was invalid, under either civil law or common law. At this, Gloucester and his friends declared that in matters of the kind the lords in Parliament should be judges, with the king's assent. It is obvious that he was simply seeking to achieve his personal ends by appealing to the vanity of the lords and by intimidating the King. In other words, he was seeking to turn Parliament into an instrument of lynch law.[48]

On February 14, the "absent traitors"—Suffolk, Robert de Vere, Tresilian, and Alexander Neville—were judged guilty of treason by the lords alone and sentenced accordingly. Neville's punishment was left to the Pope. Three days later Brembre, showing remarkable courage, appeared to defend himself. He requested counsel, but this was denied him. He asked to see a copy of the accusations in order to prepare a defense. This was also denied. The charges were read to him one by one, and he declared himself not guilty on each count. Since he was facing an appeal, he quite rightly demanded trial by battle. Next day Richard spoke movingly in his defense, but was answered by the appellants and many of the lords, who summarily cast their gloves at his feet. The young King retired in confusion, but the enormous insult those gloves implied was unlikely to be soon forgotten. Much of Richard's curious behavior in his last years

[48] On the "constitutional principles" of this parliament, see Anthony Steel, *Richard II* (Cambridge, 1962), pp. 152–153.

was triggered by threats of a recurrence of this kind of treatment, and the responsibility for his "tyranny" should be placed
where it belongs, on the shoulders of the rash and impetuous
men who surrounded him. Brembre was denied trial by battle,
but a committee of lords was appointed to investigate the charges
against him. It could find no grounds for judging Brembre guilty
of treason.

Meanwhile, Gloucester found Tresilian disguised in the house
of a tenant of the Sacrist of Westminster and dragged him from
sanctuary. Since he had already been sentenced, he was drawn
on a hurdle to Tyburn and executed. Returning to Brembre, the
lords consulted representatives of the guilds to determine whether
Brembre had planned to make himself "Duke of Petty Troy" and
execute a great number of persons opposing him. No conclusive
answer was forthcoming. When the Mayor and aldermen were
interviewed, they replied that Brembre was more likely than not
to know about the charges brought against him and that he was
deserving of execution if he was guilty. Undeterred by lack of
evidence, the lords condemned Brembre, who was drawn on a
hurdle to Tyburn and executed. It is said that at the last moment
he acknowledged that he had been malicious toward John of
Northampton, and asked pardon of Northampton's son, who was
standing nearby. Whatever we may think of Brembre in other
respects, he was a courageous and forthright man, worthy of
considerable admiration. The lords then turned for the moment
to lesser victims. They impeached Nicholas Blake and John of
Northampton's old secretary, later Sheriff of Middlesex, Thomas
Usk. The execution of Usk was slow and awkward. He is said
to have denied giving false testimony against John of Northampton. A book, *The Testament of Love*, a somewhat unsophisticated
but very pious imitation of *The Consolation of Philosophy* of
Boethius, survives him.[49] In it he pays high tribute to the poetry
of Geoffrey Chaucer.

The appellants had other victims to consider: Burley, Beauchamp, Berners, and Salisbury. The first three were accused of

---

[49] The work contains allegorical elements that are fully explained in the
text. The notion sometimes entertained by literary historians that it reveals
elements of "courtly love" is absurd.

corrupting the King in his youth, and Salisbury of conniving with the French. The specific charges against Burley, a distinguished companion of the Black Prince and the King's tutor in his youth, were either patently fictitious or clearly not treasonable. For example, it was said that he had conspired to kill the members of the recent Commission, an obvious fiction. Or, it was said that he had helped keep Michael de la Pole in office. He may or may not have done so, but if he did, his action was hardly treasonable. The "color of words" that Gloucester and his friends used in this instance to excuse their intended murder was very transparent indeed. Richard did everything he could to save Burley. It is said that Queen Anne knelt before Gloucester to pray for him, but was told that she had better pray for herself and the King. Derby and Nottingham attempted to prevent the sentence of execution, but the lords had tasted blood and were anxious for more. In March, Burley, Beauchamp, and Berners were taken to the block, and Salisbury was hanged and drawn. The appellants concluded their business by awarding themselves £20,000 for their trouble and by bribing Sir John Holland, who had returned from Spain, with the Earldom of Huntingdon and 2,000 marks a year not to interfere with them. These measures were not exactly designed to improve the condition of the treasury, about which they pretended to be concerned. A committee was left to clear up the unfinished business of Parliament.

Among the lesser accomplishments of the Merciless Parliament was a statute that all merchants anywhere in England could buy or sell freely, a measure designed especially to inconvenience the followers of Brembre among the victualers of London.[50] At a Parliament held in Cambridge in September the earlier statute against victualers holding judicial office was renewed, as was the Statute of Laborers. An effort was made to impose sanitary regulations, referred to earlier, and an ordinance was passed to the effect that guilds and fraternities could be abolished and their wealth used for purposes of war at the discretion of the lords. The last regulation was, fortunately, not implemented in the fourteenth century. In October, Nicholas Exton was succeeded as Mayor by Nicholas Twyford, Goldsmith. Meanwhile, in Au-

[50] Monk of Westminster, p. 179; *Rot. Parl.*, III, 247.

gust, Douglas defeated the English at Chevy Chase, taking young Henry Percy prisoner. The war was by no means ended, but the appellants, in spite of Gloucester's military ambitions, did very little about it except to arrange a truce at Calais.

On May 3, 1389, at a meeting of the Council King Richard announced that he was of age and intended to rule as a monarch should. There was nothing the Commissioners could do about this decision, and no one, including the King, engaged in any drastic action. In considering Richard's relations with Gloucester, we should remember that the latter was his uncle and that family squabbles may be very bitter on the surface without disturbing a certain substratum of affection. William of Wykeham replaced Thomas Arundel as Chancellor, and Bishop Brantigham of Exeter, a seasoned administrator, was made Treasurer .A distinguished scholar, Edmund de Stafford, was made Keeper of the Privy Seal. He was to become Chancellor in 1396 and to serve again in the same capacity under Henry IV. In the new administration Geoffrey Chaucer was made Clerk of the King's Works, the most important post of his career.

Looking back over the twenty years since Chaucer's "goode faire White" died in 1369, we can see that events in England must have been a continuing series of disappointments to the poet. The decline of English prestige during the last years of King Edward, the upheavals of the Peasants' Revolt, the wild charges and countercharges among the various court and city factions, the apparently continuous decay of the clergy, and the irresponsible actions of the Merciless Parliament must have impressed him deeply. During his residence at Aldgate, he apparently found some satisfaction in *The Consolation of Philosophy*, a book that urges its readers to set their hearts on the realm of the intangible rather than on the frustrating satisfactions of the material world. *Troilus and Criseyde* is permeated with the spirit of Boethius. In it a young Prince of Troy, who is an exemplar of the weaknesses of English chivalry, abandons the interests of Old Troy for the sake of a shallow and selfish woman whose falseness is suggestive of the flitting delights that brought Old Troy to destruction by fire and might well destroy New Troy as well. The actions of English parliaments may well have helped to inspire the bitter words of the balade "Lak of Stedfastnesse," addressed to King Richard:

Somtyme the world was so stedfast and stable
That mannes word was obligacioun;
And now it is so false and deceivable
That word and deed, as in conclusioun,
Ben nothing lyk, for turned up-so-doun
Is al the world for mede and wilfulnesse,
That al is lost for lak of stedfastnesse.

. . . .

Trouth is put doun, resoun is holden fable;
Vertu hath now no dominacioun;
Pitee exiled, no man is merciable.
Thurgh coveitise is blent discrecioun.
The world hath mad a permutacioun
Fro right to wrong, fro truth to fikilnesse,
That al is lost for lak of stedfastnesse.

When he began work on *The Canterbury Tales*, he was able to choose as his chief weapon, not the plodding seriousness and strong language of Gower, but humor. Much of the sting has gone out of this humor today, for it has been smothered in sentimentality, "psychology," and aesthetic seriousness, but in its own time it must have been singularly biting. To appreciate it, we should try to envisage as much as we are able the actual problems with which Chaucer and his contemporaries lived and worked. Poetry was not then a separate entity, an "art" divorced from everyday reality. The realm of "aesthetics" had not been invented. It was an integral part of the life of the times.

The seven years after Richard's assumption of full powers were relatively uneventful, and there is no reason to suppose that Richard spent them mulling over ways to avenge the transgressions of the appellants. The Duke of Lancaster returned to England at Plymouth on November 19, 1389. He was no longer "King of Spain," but his daughter Philippa had married the heir of the Spanish throne, and his daughter Katherine was Queen of Portugal. He had himself received £100,000 and an annuity of £6,000. Westminster and London welcomed him with enthusiasm, and there were special ceremonies at the Abbey and at St. Paul's. His son, the Earl of Derby, distinguished himself at the great jousts at St. Ingelvert, proclaimed by the Lancaster Herald, wherein Sir Regnault de Roye and Marshal Boucicault challenged the chivalry of Europe. He later undertook a pilgrimage to Jerusalem. The return jousts for those at St. Ingelvert were held with great pomp at Smithfield. Chaucer, as Clerk of the Works, supervised the erection of the lists and probably helped design some of the formal pageantry. The quarrels at court subsided. Lancaster was made Duke of Aquitaine for life, and the Palatinate of Lancaster was granted to him and to his heirs male in tail. William Venour, Grocer and Mayor of London, and his aldermen swore before the King that John of Northampton had been unjustly accused, and a petition in Parliament asked that all judgments against him be repealed. The petition was granted, and in 1391 it was decreed that his property be restored, and that similar treatment be accorded Richard Norbury and John More. A few years later Northampton was restored to the freedom of the city.[51] London's foreign trade prospered, and in spite of a dearth of grain in 1390 and six weeks of overcast weather in 1391, both noted by Walsingham, the general outlook was better than it had been in many years. Lancaster pursued a policy of peace with the French and used a firm hand against unrest at home.

The peaceable atmosphere of the new regime was marred temporarily by occasional minor conflicts. In 1392 the King asked that citizens of London with the necessary income take up knighthood. The same request had been made in the past at various times, and the citizens replied, as usual, that their incomes were not sufficiently secure to warrant their compliance. Richard then asked for a loan, but the merchants of London refused, alleging that because of their recent loss of liberties in such a way that strangers enjoyed as much liberty as they did, they were too poor to afford a loan. This was a reference to the decree of the Merciless Parliament allowing strangers to buy and sell freely. The loan, however, was supplied by a Lombard. When the King inquired as to its source, he was angered to find that the Lombard had borrowed the money from the very merchants who had refused it to him in the first place.[52] The King's reaction was, unfortunately, extreme. He moved the Exchequer, the Common Bench,

[51] Rot. Parl., III, 282–283, 291–293; Letter-Book H, pp. 359, 370–371, 419–420, 428–429.
[52] Monk of Westminster, p. 270; Letter-Book H, pp. 379–382.

and the Chancery to York, an action that involved long trains of
packhorses bearing records and great convoys of clerks riding
northward along the muddy roads of the country. Farringdon
became very quiet. The King also removed the Mayor and
sheriffs from office and set up a commission of inquiry. The Londoners, whom Richard had some reason to distrust, finally made
him a free grant of £10,000 and reconciled themselves to him in
a magnificent formal ceremony involving an elaborate procession across London Bridge and through Cheap. It is described
for us in detail in a Latin poem by Richard of Maidstone.[53] In
the following year a rising in Cheshire was tactfully put down
by the Duke of Lancaster, but his action resulted in a quarrel
with Earl Richard of Arundel, who berated the Duke in Parliament. The Earl was forced to apologize, however, and to find
sureties for good behavior on pain of forfeiting £40,000. He
caused trouble again in 1394. Queen Anne died on June 7. Arundel arrived late at her funeral and then asked permission to
leave before the ceremonies at Westminster were concluded.
Richard struck him down in anger and disgust. Arundel had be-
haved boorishly and certainly deserved a reprimand, but Richard's hot action demonstrated a disquieting lack of self-control.

The King departed for Ireland in 1394, accompanied by
Gloucester, Sir John Holland, and other notables, with a large
army. Although he was not especially successful with the "rebel
English," he did draw up a plan for the pacification of the country and succeeded in making knights of four native chiefs. Others
promised good behavior, but, as Richard was to learn, the Irish
are a mercurial people. In any event, the King enjoyed his visit
to Ireland immensely. He seemed to be making real headway
with a knotty problem, and he returned home reluctantly in May
1395, perhaps somewhat alarmed by evidence of spreading Lollardy. During a session of Parliament some Lollard manifestos
were affixed to the doors of Westminster and St. Paul's. Walsingham's gossip has it that these were the work of Sir Lewis Clifford,
Sir Richard Stury, Sir John Latimer, and Sir John Montagu. It is
very unlikely that Stury or Clifford entertained Lollard ideas,

---

[53] The pageant is described and some parts of the poem are translated in
G. Wickham, *Early English Stages* (London, 1959), I, 64 ff.

and improbable that any of the men mentioned had anything to do with the manifestos. Meanwhile, the Irish venture had enabled Richard to obtain household troops. Yeomen and archers were enlisted, especially from Cheshire, and granted the privilege of wearing the badge of the White Hart. In this year Jean Froissart, who had been secretary to Queen Philippa before her death and whom Chaucer had succeeded as the most prominent poet of the English court, returned to England for the first time in many years. He visited the shrine of St. Thomas at Canterbury and saw the tomb of the Black Prince in the cathedral. Sir Thomas Percy offered to take him to see the King, to whom he wished to present a book of his poems "touching morality and love" that he had written during the past thirty-four years. During his visit, he met his old friend Sir Richard Stury, who told him of the King's plan to ask Lancaster to return from Aquitaine, of the opposition of Gloucester, and of the impending marriage between Richard and the little daughter of the King of France. When Froissart saw King Richard, he noticed that he spoke French very well. Richard received another communication from an aging poet, this one a long epistle from Philippe de Mézières, who had once been Chancellor to Pierre de Lusignan, urging him to marry Isabella, make peace with France, and join in a new crusade. Late in the following year, John of Gaunt was recalled from Aquitaine, where he had spent ten months.

Early in January 1396 the Duke of Lancaster, who was fifty-six, married his mistress, Katherine Swynford, who had given him four children, the Beauforts. The marriage was sanctioned by the Pope in September, and the Beauforts were granted letters patent of legitimacy by the King in the following year. In October Gaunt and his new Duchess went to France to arrange the formalities of a meeting between Richard and Charles VI. Late in the month the two rulers met amidst much pomp and ceremony. They agreed to build a chapel to Our Lady of Peace, and Richard received Isabella, who was not quite eight years old, from her father. They were married by the Archbishop of Canterbury at Calais on November 4 and shortly thereafter were welcomed in London amid much pageantry. For the moment all seemed well. But the Duke of Gloucester had not given up his warlike ambitions or his enmity to the King, and Richard himself was soon to be distracted by ambitions to become Emperor of the Romans.

Events of the last years of the century are confused. England was full of inspired propaganda, rumors, slanderous accusations, and idle gossip, much of which is reflected in the chronicles. The "verdict of history" concerning King Richard rests on very shaky foundations. Since London was involved only occasionally and indirectly, we may treat these years very briefly. It seems evident, however, that Gloucester had been systematically making friends among influential Londoners and was successfully influential on London opinion. Gower, who probably had ties of some sort with the Arundel family, treats him with great sympathy. Chaucer is, as usual, silent about particular persons and events. According to one account, sympathetic to Richard and not necessarily reliable, Gloucester was responsible for precipitating a new quarrel between Richard and the former appellants of the Merciless Parliament. At a banquet in June 1397 Gloucester, irritated over the quite legitimate return of the fortress of Brest to the Duke of Brittany and angered by the presence of returned knights from Brest at the banquet, remarked that these knights were badly paid and had no further employment. Richard replied to the effect that he had provided for them. At this, Gloucester said, "Sire, you ought first to hazard your life in capturing a city from your enemies before you think of giving up any city that your ancestors have conquered." Angered, Richard asked Gloucester whether he thought him a merchant or a traitor. Gloucester is said to have retired. But he arranged a meeting of his friends at St. Alban's, which resulted in an assembly of the old appellants at Arundel Castle, where they swore to stand together against the King and the Duke of Lancaster. The conspirators were betrayed, however, by Nottingham, who brought news of their action to Richard while he was dining at Cold Harbor in London. Richard ordered the arrest of Arundel and Warwick, who were imprisoned in the Tower. He rode out himself to Pleshy with some retainers and sympathetic Londoners to arrest Gloucester. The Duke was ill, but was sent to Calais under Nottingham's care, and there died.

In an ironic repetition of the pattern of events in 1388, Richard arranged for eight new appellants to "appeal" Gloucester, Arundel, and Warwick. Parliament met at Westminster on September

17, 1397. Since Westminster Hall was being reroofed and was un-
available, the meeting was held in a large open structure erected
temporarily for the occasion. It was surrounded by Richard's
archers. No one would now throw down his glove before the
King. The new appellants were the Earls of Nottingham, Rutland,
Kent, Huntingdon, Somerset, and Salisbury. They were allowed
to attend armed, as were the Dukes of Lancaster and York and
Henry of Derby.

Sir John Bushy, with the assistance of Bagot and Green, represented the Commons, who began by revoking the general pardon
granted to the Commissioners of 1386 and the special pardon
granted to Arundel in 1394. The Lords Spiritual, in view of an
impending judgment of blood, appointed Thomas Percy as their
proxy and retired. Richard announced that the other members of
the Commission of 1386 still had valid pardons, to the special
delight of Wykeham. Archbishop Arundel was impeached and
exiled. The new appellants, dressed in red silken robes trimmed
with white bands and embroidered with gold lettering, first appealed the Earl of Arundel. He demanded trial by battle, which
was refused. Richard accused him, with some justice, of the murder of Simon Burley; and Gaunt, acting as Seneschal, condemned
him to death with forfeiture of his properties. Arundel was executed on Tower Hill. The death of Gloucester was announced,
and a confession written by him in English was read before Parliament. In it he acknowledged various offenses—taking upon
himself royal power, coming armed before the King, opening
messages, slandering the King, denying him homage, and threatening to depose the King. He denied, however, engaging in any
recent conspiracies, whether truthfully or in an effort to protect
his friends we do not know.[54] Warwick confessed openly, and his
death sentence was commuted to perpetual exile on the Isle of
Man. Richard's answer to the Merciless Parliament was neither
so outrageous nor so merciless as the Merciless Parliament itself.

Richard proceeded to create five new dukes. Henry of Derby
was made Duke of Hereford, Thomas Mowbray Duke of Norfolk,
John Holland Duke of Exeter, Thomas Holland Duke of Surrey,
and Edward of Rutland Duke of Aumale. Various other persons,

[54] *Rot. Parl.*, III, 379.

including Thomas Percy, received new titles. After four months, Parliament was convened again at Shrewsbury. Mowbray was absent. Henry, the new Duke of Hereford, appeared before Parliament and, on the advice of his father, alleged that Mowbray had told him in confidence that Richard was planning to dispose of both of them in the same way that he had disposed of the other appellants. This was, as it turned out, an injudicious action. A commission was set up to investigate the matter, and another to consider petitions remaining after the close of Parliament Since the commission to examine Hereford's petition could reach no conclusion, a judicial duel was arranged to take place between the two lords on September 16 at Coventry. The lists were set up and the combatants made ready with great pageantry and display. But at the last moment Richard ordered them to lay down their arms. He banished Norfolk for life and Hereford for ten years, later commuted to six. This decision met with general approval at the time. Norfolk made a pilgrimage to Jerusalem in penance for his transgressions and died in Venice a year after he left England.

On February 3, 1399, John of Gaunt died. With him went the strongest moderating influence at the English court and its most distinguished and respected representative abroad. His absence in 1388 permitted the extremes of the Merciless Parliament, and his absence now permitted the extremes of Richard's impulsiveness during the last months of his reign. He had already begun to charge fees for pardons issued to all those who had been in any way involved with the original appellants. Now he levied fines ranging from 1,000 marks to £1,000 on the seventeen counties that supported them, and demanded "blank charters," or, in effect, blank checks, from the wealthier men of the realm. He needed money desperately, not only for the pomp and circumstance he cherished, but also for a new expedition to Ireland, in spite of the fact that the Shrewsbury Parliament had granted him the subsidies and customs on wool and leather for life. On March 18, with the cooperation of his Council and much legal advice, he annulled the grant of the Palatinate of Lancaster to John of Gaunt and to his heirs forever, thus depriving the new Duke of Lancaster of his inheritance. At the same time, he changed Henry's sentence of banishment to perpetual exile. The announcement of these acts did not take place until May, when the King was on his way to Ireland. They must have seemed outrageous and frightening to a people who felt themselves overburdened by taxation and miscellaneous fines. Neither accumulated wealth nor inherited property seemed safe from a monarch whose acquisitiveness was apparently unbounded.

In Ireland Richard pursued the rebel MacMurrough through forests and bogs, only to have his men face starvation and slow attrition in the face of the guerrilla tactics of the enemy. In Dublin the army found fresh supplies and, finally, the news that Henry, together with the former Archbishop and some knights and retainers had landed in England. The propaganda efforts of the new Lancastrian faction were enormously successful, and they were themselves quick to use trickery, false oaths, and lynch law to achieve their ends. The Londoners under Drew Barentyn flocked to the rebel cause. Richard landed at Milford Haven on July 25. By September 2 he was being paraded through London on a small horse to be imprisoned in the Tower. He had faced the mobs of Kent and Essex, overcome the ambitions of Gloucester and the intransigence of Arundel, but in the end he failed to win the loyalty of his greater magnates. By February 15, 1400, King Richard was dead at Pontefract Castle. His body was taken slowly to London, with the face exposed to public view. In this state, he made one more progress through Cheap to St. Paul's, where, it is said, he was seen by some twenty thousand people in two days.

John of Gaunt's great speech on the state of the realm delivered at the Bishop of Ely's Inn in Shakespeare's play contains a magnificent tribute to the traditional glory of England:

> This royal throne of kings, this scept'red isle,
> This earth of majesty . . . .

But it closes on a note of extreme pessimism:

> That England that was wont to conquer others
> Hath made a shameful conquest of itself.

A pessimism akin to this must have occupied the mind of Chaucer as, in his last days, he addressed Gaunt's son, the new King

Henry, from his residence at Westminster. In need of a renewal of his pension, he composed a jocular poem to his empty purse, the Envoy of which stated Henry's claim to the throne:

> O conquerour of Brutes Albion,
> Which that by lyne and fre eleccion
> Been verray king . . . .

The traditions of "Brutes Albion" with its ancient city of "New Troy" were soon to fade into the mists of historical mythology.

FIVE

London as an Intellectual Center

Ordinarily we think of Oxford and Cambridge as the important intellectual and cultural centers of late medieval England, and of London as a largely commercial city in which intellectual and cultural activities were of only minor importance. In a way, this is obviously a fair estimate, but we must not turn an obvious truth into an exaggeration. Insofar as the visual arts are concerned, London was, of course, of primary importance. The activities of more prominent masons, painters, goldsmiths, and other craftsmen involved in the production of what we should call "works of art" centered in the court, and in the later fourteenth century the "court" implied the London area. As the center of England's luxury trade, London was also, almost automatically, a center of the minor arts. To a certain extent, the same consideration applies to literature. Chaucer, the acknowledged master of late medieval English craftsmen in words, was a royal servant first, and a poet only by virtue of court patronage. Insofar as intellectual activity, as distinct from artistic activity, is concerned, it is also true that a great many men of learning and intellectual distinction formed, at one time or another, a part of the floating population of the city. Sermons, often a vehicle for the dissemination of current ideas, were nowhere so efficaciously delivered as at Paul's Cross, which was the central pulpit of the kingdom. Again, as we have seen, many prominent lords lay and spiritual had London residences, and these residences implied the presence of learned clerical advisers as well as administrators. Finally, London's larger ecclesiastical institutions were never without men of some intellectual distinction.

St. Paul's tended to favor men of administrative ability among its canons and officials, but many of them were university men, and a few were thinkers of real distinction. Between 1337 and 1348 the Chancellor, who had charge of the school, was Thomas Bradwardine, whose *De causa Dei contra Pelagianos* was one of the most important theological works of the century in England.[1] It attacks the problem of reconciling free will (or free choice) on the one hand and the doctrine that real virtue is impossible without grace on the other, emerging with a "Boethian" position on free choice and an anti-Pelagian view of grace. The book is not a dry scholastic treatise confined to the pedestrian rhetoric of the syllogism, but a wide-ranging discussion containing incidental material on such topics as dreams or the philosophy of Ovid, so that it is of interest to literary and cultural historians as well as to historians of philosophy. The prominent place of *The Consolation of Philosophy* in Bradwardine's discussion of free choice should help us to understand the timeliness of Chaucer's translation of that work and its significance in relation to the philosophical problems of the day. Bradwardine's presence must have made a lasting impression on St. Paul's and on the traditions of its school. Chaucer refers to him when his Nun's Priest brings up the problem of foreknowledge and necessity:

> Witnesse on hym that any parfit clerk is
> That in scole is greet altercacioun
> In this mateere, and greet disputisoun,
> And hath been of an hundred thousand men.
> But I ne kan nat bulte it to the bren
> As kan the hooly doctour Augustyn,
> Or Boece, or the Bisshop Bradwardyn,
> Wheither that Goddes worthy forwityng
> Streyneth me nedely for to doon a thyng—
> "Nedely" clepe I "symple necessitee."

[1] Gordon Leff's study, *Bradwardine and the Pelagians* (Cambridge, 1957), probably exaggerates the revolutionary and "deterministic" aspects of Bradwardine's conclusions. Bradwardine quotes Boethius at length and with obvious approval.

Or elles, if free choys be graunted me
To do that same thyng, or do it noght,
Though God forwoot it er that (it) was wroght,
Or if his wityng streyneth never a deel
But by "necessitee condicioneel."

The distinction between "simple" and "conditional" necessity is, for purposes of this discussion, Boethian, and the obvious answer to the problem from the point of view of Chaucer and his audience was that so long as man is reasonable he is free to choose. The "conditional necessity" concomitant with "foreknowledge" does not influence his choice. It is also very probable that Chaucer felt that this conclusion could be found in any of the three authorities mentioned. This view is not without some justification. In any event, the mention of Bradwardine's name in the same breath with Augustine and Boethius is a very high compliment.

Bradwardine was one among an influential group of scholars at Merton College, and he became a member of the circle of distinguished thinkers who surrounded Richard de Bury.[2] Richard had been a canon of St. Paul's between 1331 and 1333, although it would be wrong to assume that he spent a great deal of time there. Richard is best remembered today for his *Philobiblon*, a treatise on the love of books. It contains a spirited defense of poetry based on a concept of the art very similar to that held by Petrarch and Boccaccio in Italy.[3] He is addressing himself to such lovers of the Naked Truth as Plato or St. Bernard:

All the various missiles by means of which those who love only the naked Truth attack the poets are to be warded off with a double shield, either by pointing out that in their obscene material a pleasing style of speech may be learned, or that where the material is feigned but a virtuous doctrine is implied, a natural or historical truth is enclosed beneath the figurative eloquence of fiction.

[2] For a brief account of the Mertonians and of the circle of Richard de Bury, see W. A. Pantin, *The English Church in the Fourteenth Century* (Cambridge, 1955), pp. 136–140.
[3] Boccaccio's views, which elaborate those of Petrarch, are conveniently available in C. G. Osgood, *Boccaccio on Poetry* (New York, 1956). A collection of Petrarch's writings on poetry in translation is being prepared by Peter Marinelli for the University of Nebraska Press.

Although most men by nature desire to know, not all of them are equally delighted by the process of learning. Indeed, when the labor of study is tasted, and the fatigue of the senses is perceived, many throw away the nut unadvisedly before the shell is removed and the kernel extracted. For a double love is inborn in man, that is, a love of liberty is his own guidance, and a certain pleasure in work. For this reason no one willingly subjects himself to the rule of others, or unwillingly pursues a labor that involves any effort. For pleasure perfects work, just as beauty perfects youth, as Aristotle most truly asserts in the tenth book of the *Ethics*. Concerning this matter the prudence of the Ancients devised a remedy by means of which the wanton will of man might be captured as if by a certain pious fraud, when they hid away Minerva [i.e., wisdom] in secret beneath the lascivious mask of pleasure. We are accustomed to lure children with rewards so that they will wish to learn those things to which we force them, though unwillingly, to apply themselves. For corrupted nature [i.e., the nature of man after the Fall] does not migrate toward virtues with the same impetus with which it supinely thrusts itself toward vices. Horace tells us about this in a little verse, when he is speaking of the art of poetry, saying,

> Poets wish either to teach or to delight.

He implies the same thing in another verse of the same book more openly, writing,

> He hits the mark who mingles the useful and the sweet.[4]

The mask of pleasure that hides wisdom is exactly the same thing that Petrarch described as "the poetic veil." The figurative or fictional surface of poetry was thought to conceal wisdom. If a man does not spontaneously admire Naked Truth, she may be clothed in attractive garments. When the labor of removing these, revealing the lady's charms one by one, is presented to the reader, he can be led to embrace her with more avidity. The attractive exterior may be very cleverly contrived, but the real purpose of studying poetry is to remove it. Now, this attitude, which is very different from modern attitudes that attribute to

---

[4] *Philobiblon,* XIII. The best edition is that of A. Altamura (Naples, 1954). English translations usually miss the frequent allusions in the text, which are an essential part of its meaning.

figures and symbols a "truth" of their own, undoubtedly characterized the analysis of classical poetry as it was taught at St.
Paul's School. It was certainly the attitude of Geoffrey Chaucer
in clothing his *sentence* with attractive tales, traditional figurative devices, and the rhetoric of poetic expression. Efforts to an-
alyze his work on the basis of more modern attitudes suited to a
different stylistic language must inevitably be misleading.

The Archdeacon of London at St. Paul's between 1350 and
1354, and Dean of the Cathedral from 1354 to 1362, was another
member of the circle of Richard de Bury, Richard Kilvington. He
had been Richard's chaplain in 1342 and 1344. In 1350 he became
a Doctor of Theology. Kilvington was the author of two treatises
on Aristotle, one of which was on the *Ethics*, a commentary on
the *Sentences* of Peter Lombard, and other works, including, it is
said, treatises against the mendicant orders. He is remembered
for having sponsored a series of sermons delivered in London in
1356 and 1357 by another member of the circle of Richard de
Bury, Richard Fitzralph. The evidence thus indicates that the
"humanistic" tradition manifested in the *Philobiblon* was fairly
strong at St. Paul's from the time of Chaucer's birth (probably
between 1340 and 1345) until he was a young man. If, as has
been suggested, he attended St. Paul's School, he could hardly
have escaped being exposed to it. The *Philobiblon* is thus an excellent introduction to some of the fundamental attitudes that
shaped the mind of the poet, who, like Richard de Bury himself,
was a lover of "bokes" and of the wisdom they contained:

> For out of olde feldes, as men seyth,
> Cometh al this newe corn from yer to yere,
> And out of olde bokes, in good feyth,
> Cometh al this newe science that men lere.[5]

[5] Certain scholars have recently treated the accomplishments of Richard
and his circle with extreme condescension. However, few English Latin
books of the later Middle Ages equal the *Philobiblon* in the compact allusive-
ness of its style. Medieval and modern contentions that Holcot either wrote
the book or rendered Richard considerable assistance in its composition
cannot be supported by reference to Holcot's other writings, which display
neither the intellectual discipline nor the felicity of phrasing of Richard's
book. I do not here refer to his use of the *cursus*. Holcot, like Berchorius, is
usually diffuse and extremely fond of highly miscellaneous "examples" of a
kind not much in evidence in the *Philobiblon*.

Since the London sermons of Fitzralph were attacks on the fraternal orders, it is appropriate here to digress on the subject of the controversy that arose in the thirteenth century between the friars on the one hand and the "secular" clergy, sometimes assisted by monastic regulars and occasionally by a few members of the fraternal orders themselves, on the other.[6] This controversy stirred thoughtful men and engaged the attention of poets throughout Europe, and, in fact, still echoes in the writings of Erasmus, St. Thomas More, and Rabelais. Briefly, it was begun at Paris by William of St. Amour, who attacked the friars vigorously in Scriptural language, much of which became more or less standard weaponry for fraternal opponents during the following centuries. That is, there is a whole realm of antifraternal "iconography." The conflict appeared on various levels. First of all, in their activities as preachers, confessors, and administrators of the sacraments generally, as funerary supervisors, and beggars, the friars entered into an administrative and economic rivalry with the parish clergy. Their very existence as "regulars" on the one hand and as "prelates," wandering at large out of the cloister, on the other seemed to give them an anomalous position in the traditional ecclesiastical hierarchy. Furthermore, they tended to develop their own theological and exegetical traditions, partly intended to support their position. The controversy touched on a wide range of subjects: spiritual perfection, and legitimacy of begging, the essential innocence of the Blessed Virgin, voluntarism, Aristotelianism, and so on. It thus became one of the most fruitful sources of miscellaneous intellectual activity during the later Middle Ages. Since it had many ramifications, it is difficult to generalize about it, but we can touch upon the high points of its effect in London.

In 1309 the rectors and curates of the city lodged a series of formal complaints at a council held at London and Lambeth.[7]

---

[6] For a brief account of the early development of the controversy with a fraternal bias, see D. L. Douie, *The Conflict Between the Seculars and the Mendicants of the University of Paris in the Thirteenth Century* (London, 1954). Most scholarly treatments of the subject favor the friars.

[7] W. Page, *The Victoria History of London*, I, 200–201; F. M. Powicke and C. R. Cheney, *Councils and Synods with Other Documents Relating to the English Church*, II, Part II (Oxford, 1964), pp. 1255–1264.

The friars, they said, were actually possessioners, although they pretended to possess nothing. They built large buildings, were personally ambitious, and were, in spite of their pretense of poverty, wealthy. By preaching, hearing confessions, and burying the dead they deprived the ordinary parish priests of their incomes. They engaged in litigation of all kinds, defamed the parish priests, and claimed special powers as confessors. They sought out the wealthy rather than the poor; moreover, they stationed themselves like *quaestores*, or pardoners, about the city, taking alms that should have gone to the churches. These complaints are fairly typical of the usual pastoral objections to the mendicant orders, although the case was often stated more vigorously and in more abusive language. There can be no doubt that there was considerable truth in the charges.

The friars also alienated a great many persons by engaging in political activity. Chaucer's Summoner charges that

> . . . a flye and eek a frere
> Wol falle in every dyssh and eek mateere,

a saying in which there seems to have been an element of truth. For example, many friars became partisans of Edward II, who felt obliged to issue the following writ to the Mayor and sheriffs of London in 1314 to defend the Dominicans:

We do commend you, strongly enjoining, that on our behalf you will cause in the city aforesaid strict prohibition to be made that any person shall, on pain of heavy forfeiture to us, write any such manner of writings containing defamation of the said order (of Preachers), or publish the same, or give aid to those writing or publishing the same, either secretly or openly.[8]

The French Chronicle of London records that in 1327 "the Friars Preachers took to flight, because they feared that they should be maltreated and annihilated; seeing that the community entertained great enmity against them by reason of their haughty carriage, they not behaving themselves as friars ought to behave."[9]

[8] H. T. Riley, *Memorials of London and London Life in the XIII, XIV, and XV Centuries* (London, 1861), p. 112.
[9] Translated by Riley (London, 1863), p. 264.

Friars receiving their privileges from the Pope (copyright British Museum).

An awareness of William of St. Amour's specific arguments in London is attested by the appearance of some of them in an encyclopedia compiled in the area by one Jacobus, a Cistercian, around mid-century.[10] This work also contains a sermon by Fitzralph.

When Fitzralph took up the quarrel in London, therefore, he was elaborating a familiar theme. He may have been encouraged to develop it earlier by Richard de Bury, who, in the *Philobiblon*, acknowledges that the libraries of the friars contain many books, but accuses the friars nevertheless of neglecting them:

Not only these Preachers [i.e., Dominicans], but others who follow their example, have been withdrawn from the paternal care and study of books by a superfluous triple solicitude: that is, for the belly, for clothing, and for houses. Having neglected the Providence of the Savior, whom the Psalmist promises to be solicitous for the needy and the poor [Ps. 39: 18 Vulg.], they are occupied with the needs of the failing body in order that their feasts may be splendid [cf. Ecclus. 28: 28] and their vestments rich in a manner contrary to the rule of their order, not to mention the fabric of their houses erected like

[10] *Omne Bonum*, BM Royal MS 6E6 and MS 6E7. The discussion of the friars appears in MS 6E7, esp. fol. 161 verso. Brother Jacobus, MS 6E6, fols. 249ff., was also deeply concerned about nonresident clerics.

fortified castles to a height hardly suited to the poverty they profess. On account of these things, we books, who have always sought their advancement and have conceded them such seats of honor among the powerful and noble [cf. Matt. 23: 6], are now estranged from the affections of their hearts and rated as superfluous, except that they hold fast to certain quartos of little value from which they bring forth their Iberian laments and apocryphal ravings [e.g., the work of Gerard de Borgo San Donino], not as food for the refreshment of souls, but rather for the itching ears of the listeners [cf. 2 Tim. 4: 2–4]. Holy Scripture is not expounded, but altogether set aside, as though it were commonplace and already made known to all. Yet hardly any have touched its hem [cf. Matt. 14: 36]; for such is the profundity of its words that it cannot be comprehended by the human understanding, even if it devotes its greatest effort and most profound study to it, as St. Augustine asserts [Epist. to Volusianus]. He who gives himself to it assiduously, if only He who created the spirit of piety will open the door [Col. 4: 3], may extract from its nucleus a thousand lessons of moral discipline, which will not only be powerful in most recent newness [cf. Rom. 7: 6], but will also refresh the understanding of the auditor with a most savory sweetness.[11]

In the last part of this passage, Richard is accusing the friars of neglecting the "spirit" of the Scriptures; a close adherence to the "letter" was regarded as a "carnal" trait, consistent with a concern for the belly, clothing, and houses. The idea is elaborated further on, where Richard says that distrust in Providence has caused the friars to rely on their own understandings, and this in turn has brought about a reliance on material things, which has resulted in a neglect of books. Finally, he accuses the mendicants of fostering unlearned and incompetent preachers.

It is not at all difficult to find reflections of some of these ideas in Chaucer. Solicitude for the belly is ludicrously apparent in the friar of the "Summoner's Tale," even while he is denying its existence:

> "Now dame," quod he, "now je vous dy sans doute,
> Have I nat of a capon but the lyvere,
> And of youre softe breed nat but a shyvere,
> And after that a rosted pigges heed—
> But that I nolde no beest for me were deed—

> Thanne had I with yow hoomly suffisaunce.
> I am a man of litel sustenaunce:
> My spirit hath his fostrying in the Bible."

He goes on to explain at length the wonderfully virtuous absti-
nence of the friars. He also shows some interest in "houses":

> "Thomas, noght of youre tresor I desire
> As for myself, but that al oure covent
> To preye for yow is ay so diligent,
> And for to buylden Cristes owene chirche."

Not only his house, but the books it contains as well are objects
of solicitude:

> "Yif me thanne of thy gold, to make oure cloystre,"
> Quod he, "for many a muscle and many an oystre,
> Whan other men han ben ful wel at eyse,
> Hath been oure foode, our cloystre for to reyse.
> And yet, God woot, unnethe the fundement
> Parfourned is, ne of our pavement
> Nys nat a tyle yet withinne oure wones.
> By God! we owen forty pound for stones.
> Now help, Thomas, for Him that harwed helle!
> For elles, moste we oure bookes selle."

But the books may be sacrificed for stones. Finally, the friar is
not above "glosing" without textual support:

> "But herkne, now, Thomas, what I shal seyn.
> I ne have no text of it, as I suppose,
> But I shal fynde it in a maner glose,
> That specially oure sweete Lord Jhesus
> Spak this by freres, whan he seyde thus:
> *Blessed be they that povere in spirit been.*"

This friar, like those about whom the London rectors complained,
claims that his ministrations are more efficacious than those of
ordinary curates:

> "Thise curatz been ful necligent and slowe
>   To grope tendrely a conscience."

Whatever the earlier influence of Richard de Bury may have been, Fitzralph was encouraged by Kilvington and by Thomas de la Mare, the great Abbot of St. Alban's.[12] He preached at Paul's Cross on December 18, 1356, on "dominion" and on the validity of mendicant poverty. Roughly, his contention was that since the friars had departed so scandalously from their stated ideals and engaged themselves heavily in worldly concerns, they had no right to preach, or to hear confessions, or to have any dominion of any kind. Since the privileges of the friars were relatively new, and had been subject to controversy in the past, this was not a strange position to take. But when Wyclif in 1376 used a similar argument to attack the secular clergy, whose participation in the Apostolic succession at ordination was traditionally accepted, he succeeded in pleasing some friars, but he also raised questions that were to shake English society to its foundations in years to come. The question whether outward status had any true validity without inward virtue, or, to put it bluntly, whether dominion was justified in those not in a state of grace, began to disturb men in all walks of life. As a curious side effect, an awareness of the problem also produced ancestors of "Holy Willie," for no one in authority liked to admit to not being in a state of grace. It also gave rise eventually to the kind of introspective concern evident in Bunyan's *Grace Abounding*. The poem *Piers Plowman* even goes so far as to suggest that no representatives of the true priesthood of God, exemplified in the person of Piers, could be readily found in the Church Militant. But it lays the blame squarely on the friars, who are accused of such malpractice in the administration of Penance that true contrition is rare, so that the New Law, in effect, is left inoperative:

> The frere with his physik   this folk hath enchaunted,
> And plastred hem so esyly   thei drede no synne.

In a sermon on January 22 Fitzralph again attacked the theory and practice of mendicant poverty and on February 26 severely condemned London merchants who went to the friars for absolu-

---

[12] See David Knowles, *The Religious Orders in England* (Cambridge, 1955), II, 43.

tion and did not pay their tithes. On March 12, again at St. Paul's, he attacked the wealth and pride of the friars. Aubrey Gwynn, whose studies have done much to increase our knowledge of Fitz-ralph, quotes him on this subject:

They have churches finer than our cathedrals, their cellars are full of good wine, they have ornaments more splendid than those of any prel-ate in the world, save our Lord Pope. They have more books, and finer books, than any prelate or doctor; their belfries are more costly; they have double cloisters in which armed knights could do battle with lances erect; they wear finer raiment than any prelates in the world.[13]

Greyfriars, with its marble floor and great marble columns, stood just across Cheap as Fitzralph spoke; and it is not unlikely that friars dressed in richly embroidered copes and semicopes were in evidence in the streets of the city. After a sermon preached by Fitzralph on March 25 at St. Mary Woolchurch, the royal gov-ernment asked him to give up his attacks on the friars in London, probably to keep the peace.

There is some evidence that the friars themselves engaged in attempts at reform. In 1376 the Master General of the Domini-cans, Elias of Toulouse, visited England, where he found many abuses. The English friars succeeded in resisting his demands, but at the expense of strained relations with the Master General for a number of years.[14] One of the most striking charges brought against the friars by William of St. Amour was that, contrary to the injunctions of Matt. 23:8 and 23:10, they liked to be called "masters." The other characteristics of the Scribes and the Phar-isees—their tendency to say one thing and do another, their pride, ostentation, and, above all, their hypocrisy—were often attributed to the friars. But all could be summed up in the epi-thet "Master." Rather amusingly, the mendicants expressed a complaint in Parliament in 1397 alleging that members of their orders had been purchasing degrees of Master of Theology abroad, so that many illiterate friars claimed it. They asked that

[13] *The English Austin Friars* (London, 1940), p. 87.
[14] Beryl E. Formoy, *The Dominican Order in England before the Refor-mation* (London, 1925), p. 23.

no mendicant claim such a degree without the approval of his Provincial Chapter.[15]

Fitzralph's silence in London after 1357 by no means brought an end to attacks on the friars. In 1382 Bishop Brinton, who enjoyed preaching in London, complained that the friars claimed to be more competent in converting the people than the parish priests, so that parishioners throughout the world were abandoning their curates for strange and unknown confessors, a practice that resulted in widespread contempt on the part of parishioners for their churches and for their priests.[16] The friars were usually accused, as they are in *Piers Plowman*, of luring parishioners away by administering easy penances and of not paying sufficient attention to whether or not persons confessing to them were contrite. Since, in accordance with the New Law, mercy was available only to the penitent, this was a serious spiritual matter. But it was also a serious social matter. We should understand in the first place that contrition is not synonymous with a modern sense of guilt. A man is "contrite" because he has offended against God's love, which is something outside of himself. He may feel "guilty," on the other hand, because he has a sympathetic feeling for any suffering he may have caused someone else. That is, "guilt" is an inward-looking feeling depending on subjective considerations for its solution. It is difficult to resolve and may lead to aberrant behavior. Contrition results in a renewed impulse not to offend against God's love, which should lead to virtuous, or, in a medieval context, harmonious social behavior. An Old Law attitude, demanding an eye for an eye and a tooth for a tooth, regardless of the attitude of the transgressor, would easily lead to tyranny in any social hierarchy, and at a time when social hierarchies might be very small and intimate, this was a matter of everyday concern. At the same time, a leader of a small group might find it difficult to manage if persons in it refused to be contrite. Under these circumstances, an Old Law attitude was an attitude associated with selfishness and a ruthless concern for personal satisfaction at the expense of the com-

[15] *Rot. Parl.*, III, 341–342.
[16] *Sermons*, ed. Sister Mary Aquinas Devlin, O. P. (London, 1954), No. 99, p. 455.

munity. Hence the emphasis on the subject of penance in the literature of the period. It finds an important place in *Pearl, Sir Gawain, Piers Plowman,* and *The Canterbury Tales,* which ends with a sermon on the subject. It was, in the fourteenth century, by no means a "theoretical" or "purely theological" concern. If the friars were actually arranging matters so that no one feared sin, they were rendering the community as a whole a singular disservice that had very practical ramifications in the life of every man.

A number of incidents marred the reputation of the friars during the later years of the century, and, at the same time, a popular reaction to fraternal abuses became evident. In 1385 Bishop Braybrook found it necessary to forbid the citizens to confess to a certain Dominican, who, posing as a bishop, had obtained large sums of money from the citizens.[17] In 1387 an Augustinian friar, Peter Pattishall, purchased a Papal chaplaincy from an itinerant vendor. Outraged by the fact that such purchases were possible, he abandoned his order and preached a violent sermon against it at St. Christopher's by the Stocks. His facts were challenged by the London Augustinians, some citizens rioted, and Pattishall succeeded in nailing his charges to the door of St. Paul's.[18] Bale attributes to him a work in defense of Kilvington and Fitzralph, and other attacks on the friars, including a song. Popular sympathy for antifraternal propaganda is often revealed in songs. In his employment of the Scriptures to attack the friars William of St. Amour had made good use of the beginning of II Tim. 3, where "lovers of themselves" who are "lovers of pleasures more than of God" are said to "creep into houses, and lead captive silly women that are laden with sins." This charge, frequently interpreted spiritually to mean that the friars were seducers of sinful souls rather than of warm female bodies, might appear in a stanza such as this one:

> Thai dele with purses, pynnes, and knyves,
> With gyrdles, gloves, for wenches and wyves;
> Bot ever bacward the husband thryves
>   Ther thai are haunted tille.

[17] *Victoria History of London,* I, 216.
[18] K. B. McFarlane, *John Wycliffe* (London, 1952), pp. 138–139.

> For when the gode man is fro hame,
> And the frere comes to oure dame,
> He spares naither for synne ne shame
> That he ne dos his wille.[19]

We may remember the words of Pees in *Piers Plowman:*

> And at the last this limitour   tho my lorde was out
> He salved so oure wommen   til somme were with childe!

Toward the end of his career, Wyclif, who had at first won some sympathy among the friars, began to attack them, so that the old language of William of St. Amour began to echo among Lollards as well as among learned men of conservative inclination.

All this does not mean that there were no good friars, or that most friars, or friars "typically," were hypocrites, or loved pleasure more than God, or seduced women under a cloak of piety, or administered easy penances to those who wished to avoid the embarrassment of confession to their own parish priests. Robert Pynk, an Oxford Doctor of Theology, who was Lector at Blackfriars between 1348 and 1361, was especially commended by the Mayor of the City, who wrote to Pope Urban V in 1365, saying that Pynk had "for twenty years and more preached the Word of God in the . . . city in the presence of the King, the Queen, the Prince, dukes, earls, and other nobles of the kingdom, as well as before archbishops, bishops and other prelates of the Church, as also the common people in nearly every part of England."[20] The city did not wish to lose him. The good work of the friars in the city is also attested to by the frequent bequests made to them in wills. Attacks made in highly conventionalized language against the new and relatively successful mendicant orders were not "realistic" appraisals of "things as they are." The friars suffered from the same weakness that plagued the rest of the fourteenth-century community, a desire for money. They did maintain their own theological traditions, they did concentrate in densely populated areas, and they did become favorite confessors to the wealthy and

[19] T. Wright, *Political Poems and Songs* (London, 1859), p. 264.
[20] R. R. Sharpe, *Calendar of Letters from the Mayor, Aldermen, and Commonality of the City of London* (London, 1885), p. 111.

the noble. They were, moreover, very numerous, perhaps not "as thikke as motes in the sonne-beem," but sufficiently numerous to be much in evidence, and it was inevitable that many of them should be of small intellectual and moral stature. Their defenses of their own position often sounded hypocritical, and hypocrisy was the chief characteristic anticipated in the followers of Antichrist, with whom the friars were sometimes associated. We should not dismiss the controversy between the friars and the remainder of the ecclesiastical hierarchy as a mere "jurisdictional" affair; nor should we, on the other hand, take all the accusations against the mendicants as literal truth, and add "hypocritical and vicious friars" as a generalization to the "lustful nobility" and "Caesarian clergy" already conjured up by our more pious historians to characterize "the waning Middle Ages."

Chaucer quite obviously made use of antimendicant propaganda. One of his favorite poems, the *Roman de la rose*, defends William of St. Amour at some length, discusses his views of mendicancy, and makes its chief exemplar of hypocrisy most typically a friar. Oton de Grandson, whom Chaucer admired as a knight and as a poet, speaks well of William. The language and attitude of William's attacks reappear in Boccaccio's *Decameron*,[21] and in the *Genealogy of the Gods* Boccaccio describes the friars as being among the chief enemies of poetry.[22] In Italy the Dominicans especially adopted an attitude toward poetry very much like that taken by the Puritans in England many years later, and there may well have been friars of similar persuasion in England. In any event, the Friar of the "General Prologue" to *The Canterbury Tales* reflects the familiar charges. He

> . . . hadde maad ful many a mariage
> Of yonge wommen at his owene cost,

being, as it were, in a very vulgar sense, a "noble post" in his order. This is an indirect reflection of the charge that the friars

---

[21] There is a great deal of anticlericalism of one kind or another in *The Decameron*, and there are, in addition, some salacious stories. But the author was nevertheless a very pious man. Modern readers, trained in the traditions of the Reformation, often find it hard to understand this fact.

[22] See Osgood, *Boccaccio on Poetry*, pp. 32–36 and xxxii–xxxiii.

"lead captive silly women." Moreover, as the rectors and curates of London had suggested many years before, this mendicant

> hadde power of confessioun
> As seyde hymself, moore than a curat.

He was, furthermore,

> an esy man to yeve penaunce
> Ther as he wiste to have a good pitaunce.

He carried "knyves and pynnes" for "faire wyves," frequented the wealthy, engaged in litigation, and dressed "lyk a maister or a pope." Harry Baily calls him "my leeve maister deere," or "myn owene maister deere." That Chaucer was not innocent of the implications of this epithet is revealed in the "Summoner's Tale," when the friar there, who has not objected to being called "maister" by Thomas and his wife, confronts a lord:

> "Now, maister," quod this lord, "I yow biseke—"
> "No maister, sire," quod he, "but servitour,
> Thogh I have had in scole that honour.
> God liketh nat that 'Raby' men us calle,
> Neither in market ne in youre large halle."

The "Summoner's Tale" itself, the story of an amusingly unsuccessful effort on the part of "Sir *Penetrans-domos*," as he is called elsewhere, which leaves him in a very bad odor indeed, is a compendium of antifraternal allegations, involving many rather subtle reflections of the traditional language of the controversy. But we should be careful to distinguish the words of the irate Summoner, a corrupt minister of God's wrath wrathfully telling a tale that shows the dangers of wrath, and Geoffrey Chaucer. The well-dressed Friar of loose morals and easy penances in the Prologue, who does not object to being called "maister" by the Host is not to be taken as a "typical" or "realistic" friar. He is rather a vivid exemplar of mendicant weaknesses described in Chaucer's imaginative variation on a series of conventional themes. Historians, literary and otherwise, who regard Chaucer's figures as "personalities" or as "realistic" reflections of the times only deceive themselves. However, the fictional Friar does demonstrate that Chaucer took a position very similar to that of Richard de Bury, Kilvington, and Fitzralph in one of the major controversies that was stirring the intellectual world of his time.

To return to St. Paul's, it is not always easy to determine at this distance what kind of intellectual interests the officials of the cathedral pursued. Among the bishops, Ralph de Baldock left the cathedral a large library, including works by St. Augustine, Cassiodorus on the Psalms, St. Gregory on Ezechiel, various other glossed Scriptural books, the *De sacramentis* of Hugh of St. Victor, the Epistles of Peter of Blois, and William of Conches on Plato's *Timaeus.*[23] The dominant position held by St. Augustine in fourteenth-century libraries is a mark of intellectual activity, not of mere authoritarianism. As F. M. Powicke observed in connection with the library at Merton College, "The influence of St. Augustine can be traced in every revival of ordered or mystical piety, every stage of ecclesiastical reform, every fresh tendency in thought. . . . That the fellows of Merton read St. Augustine and possessed so much of his work is in no way surprising."[24] In the later part of the century, Bishop Michael of Northburgh (1355-1361) seems to have been interested chiefly in law, and was the author of a *Concordancia legum et canonum.* Sudbury, who succeeded him, was educated at Paris. Courtenay had been Chancellor at Oxford, but was clearly not a profound theologian, although he was extremely active in opposing heresy. Braybrook, like Courtenay, was educated at Oxford. Among the Chancellors after Kilvington, Nicholas Hereford, who held the office for a brief time in 1395 and 1396, had been a leading Wyclifite, but after a very sincere conversion, engaged actively in attacking heresy. The Treasurer of St. Paul's between 1373 and 1387 was John Maundour, a Mertonian and a Doctor of Theology.

A number of university men may be found among the canons of the cathedral, but it is impossible to maintain that the canons necessarily spent a great deal of time in London. John Lecche, who had been Chancellor at Oxford in 1338 and 1339, became a

---

[23] A. B. Emden, *A Biographical Register of the University of Oxford to A. D. 1500* (Oxford, 1957–1959), III, 2147–2148.
[24] *The Medieval Books of Merton College* (Oxford, 1938), p. 23.

canon in 1345 and held a prebend between 1351 and 1361. His intellectual interests are attested by the fact that he left Llanthony Priory fifty-seven volumes, including law books, a copy of Aegidius Romanus, *De regimine principum,* which was one of the more popular books in England during the later fourteenth century, a copy of the Pauline Epistles glossed, St. Jerome on the Psalms, Lombard's *Sentences,* Bartholomew's *De proprietatibus rerum,* the *Rationale* of Durandus of Mende, the works of Albertanus of Brescia, which include the source of Chaucer's *Melibeus,* and other books. John de Wylyot, a Doctor of Theology, became a canon in 1371. He is remembered for having left Merton College lands to support poor scholars.

The Archdeacons of London between 1384 and 1400, Thomas de Baketon and Thomas Stowe, were both university men. The latter became Dean in 1400. It is quite likely that Robert Hallum, who was in the service of Archbishop Courtenay between 1389 and 1394, spent a great deal of time in London. His friend Nicholas Bubwith, a chancery clerk as early as 1380, became Bishop of London in 1406. Hallum and Bubwith were together at the Council of Constance, where they succeeded in persuading Giovanni Bertoldi de Serravale to make a Latin translation of Dante's *Commedia.* This work contains the Italian text with a running translation and commentary in Latin.[25] Altogether, there is every reason to suspect that most persons associated in one way or another with St. Paul's were actively interested in the intellectual issues of the day and that many of them had literary interests as well.

Among the friaries in the London area, it is possible that Whitefriars was most active in intellectual affairs. The Carmelites maintained a flourishing school of theology there, which produced a substantial number of exegetical works at a time when exegetical activity in England was comparatively rare. In this connection, exegesis was, in effect, the fruit of theological study and the basis for teaching and instruction. The most influential theological work of the Middle Ages, the *Sentences* of Peter Lombard, was regarded as an introduction to the study of the Scriptures. Today we are likely to think of medieval exegesis as dull

25 BM Egerton MS 2629.

and uninteresting, but it often reflects the intellectual interests of the time and their practical ramifications in everyday affairs much more clearly and vividly than the more refined works of theological controversy that have largely occupied students of the history of thought. Many theoretical works, especially those of a controversial nature, were exciting only to persons in academic circles and had little relevance elsewhere. Unfortunately, the exegetical writings of the London Carmelites do not survive, or have not been "discovered," but the fact that they existed is nevertheless of some importance to our understanding of the intellectual life of the city.

For example, Thomas Brome, who died in 1380 in London, is said to have been the author of a commentary on Romans. John de Elm, who was Prior for a time, wrote a gloss on the Apocalypse. Robert Ivory, who became Lector in Theology at Whitefriars in 1372, studied philosophy and theology for twenty-two years at Oxford and Cambridge. He is reported to have donated many books to the Convent library and to have done much to increase its holdings. Among the works attributed to him is a commentary on Ecclesiasticus. John of Gaunt's confessor, John Kynyngham, was Provincial Prior between 1393 and his death in 1399. He was an active opponent of Wyclif and preached the closing sermon for the Blackfriars Council of 1382, probably at Paul's Cross. Various works are attributed to him, including commentaries on the Lamentations of Jeremias and on Ezechiel. He was succeeded as Provincial Prior in 1399 by Stephen Patrington, noted for his London preaching. He is said to have addressed a defense of the mendicant orders to John of Gaunt, who was an active patron of the London Carmelites. Richard Lavenham, who became Prior of the London Convent in 1399, was confessor to Richard II, and the author of some commentaries on Aristotle and on the Scriptures, a translation of four books of the Revelations of St. Brigit, and a compilation of excerpts from Cicero's *De natura deorum,* as well as a short treatise on the sins in English. Altogether, the work of the London Carmelites, which may have been much more extensive than our account indicates, suggests a great deal of learning and considerable scholarly industry, as well as a substantial library at Whitefriars.

By far the most famous scholar at Blackfriars during the fourteenth century was Nicholas Trivet, who was Lector there for some years after 1324.[26] He was a prolific writer, who composed commentaries on Genesis, Exodus, Leviticus, and the Psalms, treatises on the Mass, chronicles, and commentaries on the classics. His classical studies include Livy, the elder Seneca, the younger Seneca, Juvenal, Cicero, Virgil, and Boethius. He also commented on *The City of God* and on Walter Map's *Epistle of Valerius,* a favorite text during the later Middle Ages. The commentary on *The Consolation of Philosophy* replaced the earlier standard commentary by William of Conches and was probably used by Chaucer. In spite of its curious "allegorizing" of specific passages, it probably demonstrates a better understanding of the general import of the *Consolation* than that usually found in modern discussions of the work, which are vitiated by extreme literalism, prejudices derived from post-Kantian philosophy, and pedestrian "philological" methods. The "allegorizing" itself sheds considerable light on literary attitudes of the time. Although Trivet complained about the availability of books, his presence at Blackfriars probably indicates that the library there was respectable from a medieval point of view. Dominicans and Franciscans in the later fourteenth century are chiefly noted for their attacks on Fitzralph and Wyclif. We have little information about the Augustinians, although they became noted on the Continent for their scholarship, especially for their interest in the classics.

One Augustinian who may have visited London occasionally was Giovanni Becchetti, Lector at the Oxford Convent between 1385 and 1390, when he returned to Italy. He claimed to be a member of the "Italian branch" of the family of St. Thomas Becket. He wrote a treatise on the harmony between Plato and the Sacred Scriptures, a commentary on the Gospels, and other works, although these were probably not composed in England. It may be possible to obtain some idea of the content of the library of the Austin Friars in London by consulting the surviving records of their library at York. M. R. James suggested that the libraries at London, Bristol, Hereford, Oxford, Cambridge, Norwich, and Ipswich were "at least equal in extent to that of the

[26] Trivet's life and works are being carefully studied by R. J. Dean. For an account of his work on the classics, see Beryl Smalley, *English Friars and Antiquity* (New York, 1960), pp. 58 ff.

York friars."[27] The library contained, as might be expected, texts of the Bible and accompanying reference works, such as glosses, running commentaries, concordances, and dictionaries. Among Patristic authors, St. Augustine was especially well represented, although the library contained works by Chrysostomos, Basil, Ambrose, Jerome, Gregory, Bede, Isidore of Seville, St. Bernard, and Hugh of St. Victor. The *Consolation* of Boethius and that author's theological treatises were there. The York friars also had a copy of the works of William of St. Amour. Among classical authors we find Cicero, Sallust, Vegetius, Seneca, Plato, Aristotle, Macrobius, Claudian, Horace, Persius, Virgil, and Ovid, the last with commentaries, including that of Petrus Berchorius. To assist in reading such authors, the friars had a copy of "the Third Vatican Mythographer," a more or less standard introduction to the allegorical significances of the pagan deities and their activities. Among medieval works and authors the library included the Epistles of Peter of Blois, the treatises of Albertanus of Brescia, Giraldus Cambrensis, the *Policraticus* of John of Salisbury, Neckam's encyclopedia, the *Moralium dogma philosophorum*, Martianus, Prudentius, the *De planctu Naturae* of Alanus, Bernard Silvestris, Walter Map's *Epistle of Valerius*, the *De regimine principum* of Aegidius Romanus, and some works of Holcot. There were also numerous works of scholastic philosophy, a very full collection on astrology and astronomy, some books on law and medicine, and some collections of sermons. Both Richard de Bury and Fitzralph commented on the extensive libraries of the friars, and it is quite likely that the London convents, which were of special importance, contained very full collections.

As we noticed in Chapter II, university men appear occasionally among rectors of London churches. London attracted clerics of all kinds, some of them well-educated and respectable. Thomas Worminghall was residing in London in 1366, when he was made Master of Peterhouse. And Thomas Wymbledon, who may have been a Fellow of Merton, gained fame in London as a preacher. On the other hand, some of the straying clerics of the period were university men. In 1366 William le Pyle, an Oxford Master of

---

[27] "The Catalogue of the Library of the Augustinian Friars at York," *Fasciculus Ioanni Willis Clark dicatus* (Cambridge, 1909), p. 17.

Arts and a canon of Exeter, was reported to be spending a great deal of time in London; and the Dean of Exeter himself between 1362 and 1378, one Robert Sumpter, was reprimanded by his bishop for spending too much time in the city.

One of London's most distinguished citizens was its Common Pleader after 1373, Ralph, or as Chaucer calls him, "philosophical" Strode. Strode was a Mertonian who was much admired for his work on logic both in England and in Italy. He was the author of five logical texts and of a poem, now lost, called the *Fantasma*. The city was fortunate in some of its officers. The Common Clerk or "secretary," as he called himself, after 1417 was John Carpenter, who directed the compilation of the *Liber Albus*, left the city some land to be used for educational purposes, and left a collection of books that included, among other works, a copy of the *Anticlaudianus* of Alanus de Insulis, two copies of the same author's *De planctu Naturae*, Innocent's *De miseria humanae conditionis*, Petrarch's *De remediis utriusque Fortunae*, and the *Philobiblon* of Richard de Bury.

The wills of other London citizens also mention books from time to time. Thus Thomas Giles of Fleetstreet, a clerk, left to his son Thomas in 1349 "all his books, bound and unbound, on the canon and civil law, grammar, dialectic, theology, as well as geometry and astronomy."[28] Works of "grammar" might well have included classical texts. Another will of the same year mentions the *Pars oculi sacerdotis*, that is, the first part of the *Oculus sacerdotis* of William de Pagula, a confessional manual. The same work appears in a will of 1393.[29] A fishmonger in 1350 left his son some unidentified "Books of Romance."[30] Various portions of the Bible either in Latin or in translation were evidently to be found among the citizens. Thus a wealthy vintner in 1350 left a book called "le Byble" and a Psalter written in Latin and English;[31] and a grocer in 1351 left a copy of the *Parabola Salomonis* (the Book of Proverbs) to his son.[32] The Bible occurs again in

[28] R. R. Sharpe, *Calendar of Wills Proved and Enrolled in the Court of Husting, London* (London, 1889), I, 557.
[29] *Ibid.*, I, 606–607; II, 297. Cf. Pantin, *The English Church,* pp. 197–198.
[30] *Cal. Wills,* I, 627.
[31] *Ibid.*, I, 636.
[32] *Ibid.*, I, 649–651.

wills of 1368, 1389, 1394, and 1397.[33] The *Catholicon*, here probably the Catholic Epistles rather than the encyclopedia, appears
in 1375 and 1393.[34] The *Legenda Aurea* is mentioned in several
testaments. Somewhat more varied fare occurs in the will of Sir
William de Thorp, Knight, registered in 1397. Sir William left, in
addition to a Bible, a Breviary, a Psalter, and a book by Richard
Rolle, a copy of Higden's *Polichronicon* and another of Aegidius
Romanus, *De regimine principum*.[35] In general, the wills surviving have little value as statistical evidence, since they sometimes omit important bequests to elder sons made privately as
well as other private bequests and do not, in any event, constitute a complete record. They do show, however, that fishmongers
and their fellows owned books and sometimes valued them highly
and that their tastes were seldom frivolous. Sometimes books
appear in records of litigation. Thus in 1382 William Walworth
seized some property of John Salmon, Burgess of Bruges, because of the latter's failure to pay a debt. The property included
a book of "The Romance of King Alexander" described as "curiously illuminated" and said to be worth £10. There was also a
dorser of Arras nine yards long and three yards wide showing the
Coronation of King Arthur and worth £6.[36] These were luxury
items to be offered for sale to the nobility. A few wills contain bequests for educational purposes. Thus Henry de Yerdlee, Skinner,
left a residuary bequest "to be devoted to the education of poor
children, and to the marriage of poor girls."[37]

The library at Westminster Abbey should probably be included
among facilities available to London readers. In 1376 Simon
Langham left a large collection to the Abbey,[38] which included,
in addition to the Bible, a number of glossed texts of individual
books, and the moralization of the whole Bible by Nicholas de
Lyra, a good collection of the works of St. Augustine, St. Gregory

[33] *Ibid.*, II, 115, 272–273, 312, 326.
[34] *Ibid.*, II, 169, 297.
[35] *Ibid.*, II, 326.
[36] A. H. Thomas, *Calendar of Select Pleas and Memoranda of the City of London 1381–1432* (Cambridge, 1932), pp. 10–11.
[37] *Cal. Wills*, II, 132. Cf. p. 161.
[38] J. A. Robinson and M. R. James, *The Manuscripts of Westminster Abbey* (Cambridge, 1909), pp. 4–7.

on Ezechiel, his *Cura pastoralis* and *Dialogi,* the *Hexaemeron* of St. Ambrose, some works of Bede, Chrysostomos on Matthew, the *Consolation* of Boethius, the *Speculum historiale* of Vincent of Beauvais, the encyclopedia of Bartholomew, a "Dictionarius" in three volumes, and Aegidius, *De regimine principum.* It becomes fairly obvious from any account of medieval libraries that students of medieval literature who wish to know something of the intellectual background of the authors they study should acquire some knowledge of the Bible, its glosses and commentaries, and the Fathers. In this connection, St. Augustine is clearly of primary importance, and St. Gregory is not to be neglected. The *Consolation* of Boethius is obviously a very important work. No one who wishes to approach the poetry of Chaucer, who translated it, can afford to neglect reading it carefully and sympathetically. Medieval readers apparently had no nineteenth-century or modern doubts about the Christianity of its author.

We have some information about books in London schools. In 1328 William de Tolleshunt, the master of the almonry school at St. Paul's, left his books to the library there. They included the *Derivationes* of Hugo of Pisa, a large encyclopedia containing a great deal of "iconographic" material, and the *Etymologiae* of Isidore of Seville, a standard source book of miscellaneous information throughout the Middle Ages. There were also books on grammar, dialectic, natural history, and medicine.[39] A larger collection was left to the school by William Ravenstone. It contained some classical texts including the *Ars poetica* and *Sermones* of Horace, the *Metamorphoses* of Ovid, the *De raptu Proserpinae* of Claudian, the *Thebaid* and *Achilleid* of Statius, the *Georgics* of Virgil, and works by Lucan, Juvenal, and Persius.[40] In considering these and similar lists, we should remember that young boys were, in earlier centuries, introduced to what we should consider to be very difficult tasks. In the early fifteenth century, John Seward maintained a school in Cornhill. Two manuscripts of Seward's works survive, one of which, at Merton College, contains the commentary on the *Metamorphoses* of Petrus Berchorius. Seward himself wrote a moralization of the account

[39] See Edith Rickert, *Chaucer's World* (New York and London, 1948), pp. 121–122 and the references there.
[40] *Ibid.,* pp. 122–126.

of the Harpies in the third book of the *Aeneid,* a series of fictional addresses by the Harpies, a treatise on the properties of the antelope together with their application to Henry V, a debate on the proper scansion of *O stelliferi conditor maris,* the first line of Meter 5 in the first book of *The Consolation of Philosophy,* and some epigrams.[41] It is quite likely that Chaucer as a boy read a great deal of Ovid, Virgil, and Statius with some care, together with medieval commentaries on the texts. The "moralizing" character of these commentaries is partly a classical inheritance and partly a medieval effort to make classical texts immediately relevant to the practical affairs of life. The commentaries are often faulty where factual information is concerned, but they are no more "outrageous" historically than the "aesthetic" or "psychological" commentaries being produced today, which are simply "moralizations" of a different kind, produced for a society in which traditional morality has little meaning.

Among educational institutions, we should not neglect the legal training centers in Farringdon. It has been suggested that Chaucer may have studied for a time at the Inner Temple. If he did, he probably devoted a great deal of attention to history and the Scriptures, as well as to the law. In any event, his Sergeant of the Law in the "General Prologue" to *The Canterbury Tales* should not be taken as a typical lawyer. He is, rather, an exemplification of the grasping qualities and worldly wisdom of lawyers that had been subjects of complaint for a great many years at the time Chaucer wrote. The traditional attitude of moralists toward these weaknesses was made somewhat more urgent in the fourteenth century by the widespread lust for money that was characteristic of the age. Richard de Bury had written of "the lucrative knowledge of positive law accommodated to dealing with earthly affairs" with some contempt. "The more useful it is," he said, "to the children of this world, the less it assists the children of light [cf. Luke 16:8] to comprehend the mysteries of the Holy Scriptures and the hidden sacraments of the faith, since it is especially conducive to friendship with this world, through which, as James testifies [Jac. 4:41], man becomes the enemy

---

[41] V. H. Galbraith, "John Seward and his Circle," *Mediaeval and Renaissance Studies,* I (1943), 85–104.

of God."[42] Chaucer's Sergeant, who "often hadde been at the Parvys" in St. Paul's, seemed to be a man of great reverence, for "his wordes weren so wise." This wisdom, however, enabled him to collect many fees and robes, so that he held a great deal of land in fee simple. To hear him talk, one would think that he knew all the cases and judgments since King William's time. This worldly wisdom, wealth, and pretentiousness place our representative of legal learning among those who

> Plededen for penyes   and poundes the lawe,
> And nought for loue of owre lord   vnlese here lippes onis.

But neither Chaucer's Pilgrim nor the description in *Piers Plowman* means that such lawyers were "typical." Both poets are, rather, emphasizing common weaknesses of the legal profession. These might appear to a greater or lesser extent, or perhaps not at all, in specific individuals. Most of Chaucer's criticisms of social groups have, like that of the friars, a long tradition behind them. Chaucer vivifies these traditions with local touches, like the mention of the "Parvys," and by arranging them so as to form portraits with a certain verisimilitude. In other words, he brings them to life for his audience.

In the fourteenth century physicians, as distinct from surgeons, who learned their trade as apprentices, were increasingly men of some university training. London had its share of distinguished medical men, the most famous of whom was John of Gaddesden (ca. 1280–1361). He became a canon of St. Paul's in the early thirties and probably spent a great deal of time in London. Today he is remembered for his book called *Rosa medicinae*. In the Preface he asserts that "nothing has been set down here but what has been proved by personal experience, either of myself or others." From a modern point of view, his empiricism leaves much to be desired, and few of his proposed cures sound attractive or promising. However, he does give some sound advice occasionally. For a "sweet savor," for example, he recom-

---

[42] *Philobiblon*, XI. For the applicability of similar attitudes to Chaucer's Man of Law, see Chauncey Wood, "Chaucer's Man of Law as Interpreter," *Traditio*, XXIII (1967), 149–190.

A visit by a physician, fifteenth century (copyright British Museum).

mends frequent baths and changes of underwear.[43] His attitude toward women, whom he classes as "venemous animals," was a trifle cynical, and he enjoyed occasional touches of humor, quoting, for example, the proverb

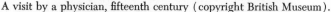

Pisces et uxores in cauda sunt meliores.[44]

John of Arderne, who recommends that a physician know proverbial expressions to cheer his patients, was a distinguished surgeon who may have spent some time in London. He was also the author of a number of treatises. Another medical author was John Mirfeld of St. Bartholomew's Hospital. His *Breviarium Bar-*

[43] See H. P. Cholmeley, *John of Gaddesden and the Rosa Medicinae* (Oxford, 1912), p. 60.
[44] *Ibid.*, pp. 61, 67.

tholomei is a treatise reflecting some knowledge of the prominent medical authorities of the time, including Bernard of Gordon
and John of Gaddesden. Mirfeld was also the author of a theological treatise, the *Floriarium Bartholomei*, which indicates some
knowledge of St. Augustine, St. Jerome, Isidore of Seville, St. An-
selm, St. Bernard, and St. Thomas Aquinas, as well as of Horace,
Virgil, Ovid, and Boethius.[45]

Some fourteenth-century physicians and surgeons in the London area are known only because their names appear among
sworn surgeons of the city or in legal records. As we have seen,
however, an educated physician like William Tanterville might
serve as rector of a London church. Thus the Rector of St. Mary
le Strand between 1375 and 1377 was one of the royal physicians,
William de Wymondham, an Oxford M. A.[46] A royal surgeon to
Edward III, Adam Rous was a London resident who was called
a "sworn surgeon to the City of London" in 1361.[47] John Bray
served as a physician in the households of Edward III and John
of Gaunt and was retained by Richard II. Like Fr. William de
Appleton, he was probably killed by the mob in 1381.[48] Occasional names of foreign physicians in London survive in the
records. Pascal de Bononia, who was a canon at St. Paul's, was
probably educated in Italy, as was Adam de Romanis, a native
of Naples. It is likely that better medical treatment, for what it
was worth, was available in London than in any other city of
the kingdom, and quite possible that the more educated medical
men exchanged ideas and methods of treatment.

Chaucer's Physician, like his Friar or Sergeant of the Law,
betrays typical weaknesses of his profession. He is, in the first
place, "grounded in astronomye" and uses "ymages." According
to Holcot, who considered this subject in his commentary on the
Book of Wisdom, these "images" have no more value than the
material from which they are made. Although John of Arderne

[45] Norman Moore, *A History of St. Bartholomew's Hospital* (London, 1918),
I, 608 ff.
[46] Emden, *Biographical Register of Oxford*, III, 2122; C. H. Talbot and E.
A. Hammond, *The Medical Practitioners of Medieval England* (London,
1965), p. 420.
[47] Talbot and Hammond, *Medical Practitioners*, pp. 7–8.
[48] *Ibid.*, p. 125.

seems to have had some regard for astrological considerations, Holcot probably represents enlightened opinion, and Chaucer's implication is thus that his Doctor was something of a quack. Moreover, the Physician connives with apothecaries for mutual profit, a practice long condemned in medieval attacks on medical abuses. The list of "authorities" known to the Doctor is probably intended to indicate pretentiousness rather than learning, and the remark that his diet was moderate followed by "His studie was but litle on the Bible" suggests strongly that he cared only for the nourishment of the flesh and nothing for that of the spirit. The final thrust, "he loved gold in special," is once more an attack on the great weakness of the age.

Some of the noblemen of the city showed considerable interest in the intellectual issues of the day, and a few had specifically literary inclinations. Queen Philippa maintained a poet, Jean Froissart, as her secretary, and, as we have seen, Froissart presented King Richard with a copy of his poetry. Unfortunately, we have little information about Richard's library, although we do know that in 1379 a copy of the *Roman de la rose* was purchased for him.[49] Among the effects of Sir Simon Burley, who had been Richard's tutor, were found a number of books, including nine romances in French and one in English. Sir Simon also had a French version of the *Historia scholastica* of Petrus Comestor, and a French translation of Aegidius Romanus, *De regimine principum*.[50] It is unfortunate indeed that we have no record of books at the Savoy. The presence of King John of France there suggests that books were obtained for him or by him, and the Duke of Lancaster himself was a man of considerable alertness. His patronage of Chaucer is a testimonial to his good taste. It is likely that Chaucer obtained his extensive knowledge of French poetry in the households of noblemen, and the Savoy represents by far the best possibility in this respect. Edward III gave King John an

[49] M. V. Clarke, *Fourteenth Century Studies* (Oxford, 1937), p. 122.
[50] *Ibid.*, pp. 120–121. The *De regimine principum* also appears in the library of the Duchess of Gloucester, who had, in addition, a French Bible, a Book of Decretals in French, a Book of Histories, *Vitas Patrum*, St. Gregory's *Cura pastoralis*, two glossed Psalters, a Book of Devotions, a Book of Vices and Virtues, a Chronicle of France, and the History of the Knight of the Swan. See J. Nichols, *Collection of Wills* (London, 1780), pp. 181, 183.

exchiquier, an early keyboard instrument. It would be interesting to know what kind of songs it was used to accompany.

Sir John Montague, third Earl of Salisbury, was a poet in his own right, although he may have composed in French. He was sufficiently familiar with the cultural traditions of France to be selected as tutor for the son of Christine de Pisan, a lady of rather meticulous tastes. A group of Salisbury's friends who had been associated with John of Gaunt or the Black Prince and later with Princess Joan were much disturbed by weaknesses in church and state and were interested in reform. They include Sir William Beauchamp, Sir Lewis Clifford, Sir Richard Stury, and Sir John Clanvowe, all of whom were friends of Chaucer's. Reform movements might be very diverse in the fourteenth century, including chivalric orders like the Order of the Passion of Our Lord established by Philippe de Mézières, which sought the unification of Europe in a new crusade, and various forms of what is loosely called "Lollardy." Wyclif's doctrines specifically had little appeal among the nobility.[51] Clifford once brought Chaucer a copy of a poem written in his honor by Eustache Deschamps, praising him for his wisdom and for his ability as a translator of the *Roman de la rose*. Deschamps was, as his poems testify, a considerable social critic in his own right. Stury owned a copy of the *Roman de la rose*, a poem that has been grossly misrepresented by literary historians. It has nothing to do with what they are pleased to call "courtly love," but is a satirical critique of false love and corrupt *mores*, much admired by Philippe de Mézières. Stury belonged to Philippe's Order, whose "Apostle" in England was the knight and poet Oton de Grandson. Clanvowe was the author of a moral treatise and the probable author of a poem, "The Cuckoo and the Nightingale." The character of Chaucer's courtly associates, his translations of Boethius and at least part of the *Roman de la rose*, and his obvious admiration for Deschamps hardly suggest that he could have been the carefree celebrator of "earthiness" critics have sometimes sought to make him. Neither he nor his courtly associates may be justly accused of what has been called "high frivolity."

[51] For biographical information concerning these man and the question of their "Lollardy," see W. T. Waugh, "The Lollard Knights," *Scottish Historical Review*, XI (1914), 55–92.

"The Cuckoo and the Nightingale" begins with an echo of Theseus' humorous comments on the foolishness of lovers generally and of Palamon and Arcite specifically in the "Knight's Tale":

> The god of love, a! *benedicite!*
> How mighty and how greet a lord is he!

After elaborating this theme, the poet comments, again humorously, on his own lovesickness in May, in spite of his advanced age. Recalling the doctrine of lovers that it is better to hear the Nightingale than the Cuckoo, he sets out to discover the truth of the matter for himself. He finds a bank covered with daisies, where the birds sing in pairs, maintaining their Valentine's Day choices. As Chaucer indicates at the beginning of "The Complaint of Mars" and in "The Parliament of Fowls," Valentine's Day, which was a standard festival in all ecclesiastical calendars, was associated with choosing mates, that is, wives and husbands, not with the choice of sweethearts or mistresses. There the poet falls asleep. In his dream, a Nightingale and a Cuckoo engage in a debate, in which the latter accuses the former of fostering wilful love that is unreasonable. The Nightingale denies the charge, weeping. Feeling sympathy for the Nightingale, the poet chases the Cuckoo away. He is then advised by the Nightingale to relieve the uneasiness of love in May by going out before dinner to contemplate "the fresshe deyeseye." At the close, the Nightingale complains to the other birds, who decide to hold a Parliament to consider her case on the next Valentine's Day at Woodstock before the chamber window of the Queen. All this is managed with considerable grace and fluency and is probably intended as a light and humorous but nevertheless telling tribute to married love, an emotion conventionally associated with Valentine's Day and the daisy.[52] We should probably think of the

---

[52] For St. Valentine's Day and the daisy, see D. W. Robertson, Jr., *A Preface to Chaucer* (Princeton, 1962), p. 225, note 138, and p. 377. On the authorship of the poem, see V. J. Scattergood, *Anglia*, LXXXII (1964), 137–149. Scattergood has also edited a new text, *English Philological Studies*, IX (1965), 47–83. The iconography of the poem has been studied by David E. Lampe, "Tradition and Meaning in *The Cuckoo and the Nightingale*," *PLL*, III (1967), 49–61.

poem as serving for entertainment on some festive occasion, perhaps an anniversary, for the special benefit of Queen Anne.

Clanvowe's treatise, recently edited by V. J. Scattergood,[53] is
an elaboration of Matt. 7:13–14, two verses from the Sermon on
the Mount:

Enter ye in at the narrow gate: for wide is the gate and broad is
the way that leadeth to destruction, and many there are who go in
thereat.

How narrow is the gate and strait is the way that leadeth to life:
and few there are that find it!

The author discusses heavenly and earthly joys as they are con-
trasted with infernal and earthly pains to emphasize the urgency
of selecting the narrow way. Heavenly and earthly wisdom are
briefly touched upon in terms of I Cor. 3:19, and the author explains that the narrow way begins by fearing God and keeping
the Commandments. The second major section of the treatise is
concerned with the enemies that keep one from the narrow way.
These are the familiar enemies of Chaucer's Melibee—the world,
the flesh, and the devil. Clanvowe's treatment of the world is
especially full. It is here that the charge of Lollardy arises against
Clanvowe, but what he says is that the folk of the world condemn
the meek and temperate as "lolleris and loselis foolis and shameful
wrecches," epithets that are more or less synonymous, in a context based on ideas from I Cor. 1:18 ff. The third and last section
of the treatise explains the Ten Commandments and the fact that
under the New Law they are based on the Two Precepts of Charity. As we might expect, charity, or proper love, is the final lesson
of the treatise.

From a doctrinal point of view, there is nothing odd or curious
about the treatise and certainly nothing that would cause anyone
to think of the author as a follower of Wyclif. It is occasionally
enlivened by vivid imagery, as in a description of a fool and his
bauble, but it is written in solemn cadences frequently joined by
coordinating conjunctions, so that the general effect is somewhat

[53] "*The Two Ways,* An Unpublished Religious Treatise by Sir John Clanvowe," *English Philological Studies,* X (1967), 33–56.

monotonous. If it contains an interesting emphasis that might not have been so great had it been written a century earlier, it is the insistence on the evil of worldliness. This emphasis may easily be attributed to the author's awareness of the increasing greediness that characterized late fourteenth-century society. Clanvowe died, as a good knight should, on crusade. The Monk of Westminster tells us that on October 17, 1391, Sir John, "miles egregius," died in a village near Constantinople. His friend, Sir William Neville, who was with him, fell into an inconsolable sorrow and refused to take nourishment, so that he died also within two days. These knights, our chronicler reports, were "famous and worthy noblemen among the English."[54] In the later fourteenth century England was much in need of worthy knights of integrity and firm moral commitment. There is more than a touch of bitterness in Chaucer's portrait of the Knight he met at the Tabard, who was worthy, wise, and, like Sir John Clanvowe himself, meek and unworldly. This Knight, moreover, could tell a tale emphasizing the efficacy of the New Law under which "the quality of mercy is not strained" and suggesting that Venus and Mars, or concupiscence and wrath, are to be cured by marriage, or the establishment of a proper hierarchy.

Across London Bridge in Southwark, from about 1377 onward, at the Priory of St. Mary Overy, lived Chaucer's friend and fellow poet John Gower. The two poets show certain similarities in outlook. Both were concerned because of the grasping Old Law attitude of much of fourteenth-century society, which frequently evinced a general neglect of spiritual understanding in favor of a lust for visible and tangible rewards; and both showed a strong respect for traditional hierarchical ideals. Gower, like Chaucer, attacked the specific weaknesses of the ecclesiastical and secular orders, devoting special attention to the friars.[55] But the two poets differed enormously in technique. Where Chaucer uses ridicule, vivifying his criticism with exemplification and surface verisimilitude, Gower is direct and forthright and con-

---

[54] Higden's *Polichronicon*, ed. J. R. Lumby, IX (London, 1886), pp. 261–262.
[55] For Gower's attitudes, see John H. Fisher, *John Gower* (New York, 1964), especially Chapter 4.

sequently a little dull. Moreover, Gower very definitely takes the side of Gloucester and Arundel and shows signs of malice toward their enemies. Chaucer was probably considerably more sympathetic toward the Duke of Lancaster, who showed no patience with Arundel in the Parliament of 1397 and who probably regarded Gloucester as a headstrong menace to the peace and security of the realm. However, Chaucer does not attack specific persons but criticizes general weaknesses instead. We can imagine the two poets exchanging information about manuscripts, sharing enthusiasm for books, and comparing evaluations of persons and events. Although Gower was probably far from being as alert as Strode, or as knowledgeable about the world and its affairs as Clifford or Clanvowe, he could very likely offer Chaucer support for his basic attitudes.

London was not lacking in attractions that we might classify as "performing arts." The most important of these were tournaments, which, during the earlier part of our period, were held in Cheap, but later moved to Smithfield. A tournament was not simply a game, but a social occasion of some importance, frequently with diplomatic overtones. Knights and ladies from all over Europe might appear in London for royal jousts, and high-ranking nobles would seek to influence international relations as well as to engage in chivalric rivalry. Historians who have emphasized the "artificial" aspect of fourteenth-century chivalric activity have, perhaps, misled their readers somewhat. The pageantry of tournaments had its counterpart in pageantry elsewhere. Beneath this pageantry there often lay very practical considerations of prestige and influence as well as more material aims. The chivalry of a nation, in spite of the guns and powder in the Tower that looked forward to new ways, was still the key to its military success and a major inspiration to the confidence of its people at home.

The city processionals described earlier were undoubtedly accompanied by minstrelsy and singing. At Midsummer on St. John's Eve the entire population went out into the streets to celebrate. Armed watches were posted in the wards, the houses were decorated with boughs and flowers, and the mayor and aldermen with pageants, minstrels, and torches, marched from St. Paul's to Aldgate, back down Fenchurch Street to Gracechurch Street, up Gracechurch to Leaden Hall, and thence back to St. Paul's.[56] Exactly what the "pageants" on occasions of this kind were like remains obscure, but they were probably elaborate and colorful, involving citizens arrayed in costume to represent a variety of fabulous or symbolic personages. The more powerful misteries probably engaged in similar activities on the festivals of their saints.

In London there are records of dramatic activites at St. Paul's and at Skinner's Well near Clerkenwell. Plays based on the legends of the saints are associated with London as early as the twelfth century.[57] It is said that in 1391 plays concerning both the Old and New Testaments were presented for four days, beginning on July 18.[58] These plays, which do not survive, were prepared and presented by the "parish clerks and other clerks" of the City. When Chaucer has the parish clerk of the "Miller's Tale," Absolon, play "Herodes upon a scaffold hye," he is evidently reflecting a London custom, which may have prevailed in other places. Our knowledge of late medieval drama is unfortunately very fragmentary, but if the London plays were as skilful as those of the Wakefield Master, they were not without some significance for intellectual history.

The plays, like the processionals and other festivities, involved the use of minstrels, who were also employed on special occasions. Thus in 1371 minstrels were paid £16 13s for the celebration of the return of the Black Prince.[59] Great lords had their own minstrels, who might go with them on campaign. As we have seen, minstrels were also employed by the city to assist in the public display of petty criminals. There was probably a fairly large group of minstrels in the city during the second half of the century, and they may have had some kind of organization, although they were not incorporated as a guild until 1469. Ordinary visitors to the city have left some evidence of musical activity. John

---

[56] R. R. Sharpe, *Calendar of Letter Books Preserved among the Archives of the City of London* (London, 1899 *et seq.*), *Letter-Book H*, p. 232; J. Stow, *A Survey of London*, ed. C. L. Kingsford (London, 1908), I, 101–103.
[57] On the plays generally, see Hardin Craig, *English Religious Drama* (Oxford, 1955).
[58] *Ibid.*, 142–143; Monk of Westminster, p. 259; Stow, *Survey*, I, 15.
[59] Riley, *Memorials*, pp. 350–352.

Musical instruments (Pygmalion).

Swetenham of Chester, William Galthorp of Lincoln, and John Picard were arrested on the streets of London on October 20, 1381, "for making a disturbance with giternes at eleven o'clock at night."[60]

Of more importance to the musical history of the city were its ecclesiastical institutions. The choir at St. Paul's probably demonstrated considerable musical sophistication. One of the minor canons in the nineties, Richard Cotell, was the author of a treatise on the elementary principles of polyphony.[61] Sir John Poultney left 10s to the choristers so that every evening after Compline they could go into the chapel he had built and sing an anthem to the Virgin. The fraternity at St. Magnus had the anthem *Salve regina* sung in their chapel every evening, and it is probable that other fraternities in the city sponsored musical devotion. The members of the higher nobility who maintained private chapels in the city probably demanded musical services of some refinement. Altogether, the musical life of the city must have been quite vigorous during Chaucer's lifetime. Some of it is reflected indirectly in his poetry. When *The Parliament of Fowls* was read, it is probable that the rondel with which it closes was sung. The melody, Chaucer says, was made in France, a fact that

[60] A. H. Thomas, *Plea and Memoranda Rolls*, p. 297.
[61] F. Ll. Harrison, *Music in Medieval Britain* (London, 1958), pp. 12–13, 113.

A musical service.

indicates, first, that he was not himself a composer and, second, perhaps, that the court audience had a taste for French music.[62]

We should think of "the performing arts" as an integral part of community life. As F. Ll. Harrison writes, "The life of a medieval musician was always that of a member of a community."[63] The same thing may be said, and indeed should be said with considerable emphasis, about London's most distinguished "performing artist," Geoffrey Chaucer. Since it is quite probable that Chaucer read his compositions aloud, usually before an audience

[62] For some examples of French music of the late fourteenth century, see W. Apel, *French Secular Music of the Late Fourteenth Century* (Cambridge, Mass., 1950).
[63] Harrison, *op. cit.*, p. 1.

that might include royalty, lords lay and spiritual, great ladies, and minor members of the court such as squires, pages, ladies-in-waiting, and clerks, as well as more substantial men of the City, he was a performer as well as a composer. But he was always a member of the court first—whether as squire, customs official, or Clerk of the Works. Like Harrison's medieval musician, Chaucer did not purvey his "talents to an anonymous public." And he was himself not a "private individual." He had the interests of his community at heart and sought to influence it by reminding it of its ideals and by portraying with all the vigor at his disposal what seemed to him to be dangerous deviations from those ideals and, typically, holding them up to ridicule. It was thus that he obtained his early reputation as a "philosopher," for philosophy, in those days, was not exclusively a pursuit carried out in the rarified atmosphere of the schools, but, more significantly, the pursuit of wisdom, which could be a very practical matter indeed. Since Chaucer was a court poet, he was, by virtue of the tendency of the court to center its activities in the London area, a London poet as well.

St. Thomas Becket was, as we have seen, London's most celebrated citizen. The mayor, aldermen, and men of the misteries participated in regular processionals from the hospital of a military order dedicated to him to the grave of his parents at St. Paul's. A magnificent little chapel in his honor stood in the middle of London Bridge, welcoming ships that came up the great highway of the Thames to the city. When Chaucer decided, therefore, to create a fictional pilgrimage to the shrine of St. Thomas at Canterbury beginning on the outskirts of London, he was making a deliberate appeal to the *pietas* of the City of London and, indirectly, to that of the realm as a whole. A journey to Canterbury in search of "the hooly blisful martir" who had helped men to restore their moral integrity "whan that they were seeke," or spiritually diseased, was at once a reminder to Londoners of their highest ideals and an invitation to renewed dedication. To make his point unmistakable, Chaucer begins by describing a knight whose deeds were reminiscent of the great days of English chivalry as he remembered them and who rode humbly and meekly, speaking villainously of no one. When we consider the decay of English prestige after 1369, the factions, the petty quarrels, the malicious slanders that broke out into the open in the Merciless Parliament, or the fruitless expeditions, like that of the Bishop of Norwich, this is a very moving portrait indeed. The portrait of the Squire, a hot lover dressed like pride in a picture, with its suggestion of the Bishop's lamentable crusade, simply drives home the point.

The Canterbury pilgrims are led out of town by a drunken Miller, a man who could "stelen corn and tollen thries," and jangle of "synne and harlotries." He is brutal and contentious. Is this the kind of leadership Londoners have had in their quest to fulfil the ideals of St. Thomas? The jocularity of the portraits of the low characters in the "General Prologue" has led some critics to think of them as "good fellows," fit companions for a gentleman alone with his port, cheese, and cigars after the ladies have retired. More recently, they have become realistic embodiments of "the human condition" to be discussed frankly and with sentimental compassion with the girls over sherry or Martinis. However, for Chaucer and his audience they probably exemplified what Sir John Clanvowe spoke of as those "synful men and wacches [i.e., decoys] of the feend" who are "cleped of the world good felawes." That is, the attributes of the "idealized" figures— the Knight, the Clerk, the Parson, and the Plowman—were designed to remind the audience of those ideals associated with Becket and his memory, while those of the "good fellows" among the low characters were forceful reminders of the decay of the community as a whole. The attributes themselves, whether they are the Knight's participation in the conquest of Alexandria or the Friar's easy penances for money, are, like the distaff in the hand of the rioter in the Stocks in London, keys to ideas, not features of personalities.

The worldliness and greed of the community, supported, as Thomas Wymbledon suggested in a famous sermon delivered at Paul's Cross in 1388,[64] by pride and lechery, are emphasized in Chaucer's portraits. As W. Cunningham wrote long ago, with reference to the period beginning about 1377, "Mediaeval economy with its constant regard to the *relations of persons* was giving place to modern economy which treats the *exchange of*

[64] Ed. Nancy H. Owen, *Mediaeval Studies,* XXVIII (1966), 176–197.

Canterbury pilgrimage badge (copyright British Museum).

things as fundamental. . . . The ordinary object of ambition was not so much that of rising out of one's grade, but of standing well in that grade. . . . Money had come to be a thing for which everyone sought. . . . From this time forward a *desire for wealth,* as the means of gratifying the desire of social distinction and all else, became a much more important factor in economic affairs than it had been before. These changes had a very important bearing on all questions of commercial morality; so long as economic relationships were based on a system of personal relationships, they all had an implied moral character."[65] What was true of economic relationships was true of social relationships as well. To Thomas Wymbledon the disruptive results of the new desire for money were signs of the Last Age. He could see in his mind's eye the Pale Horse of Hypocrisy whose rider is Death looming over the city and the realm. Neither he nor Chau-

[65] *The Growth of English Industry and Commerce,* 5th ed. (Cambridge, 1927), I, 464–465.

cer was aware of the possibility of a new morality based on economic success, or of more recent kinds of morality based on sympathy for the oppressed masses.

In one sense *The Canterbury Tales* is a study of a newly acquisitive society seen against the background of a traditional morality that had its roots in antiquity. The pilgrims tell tales that are reflections on themselves, not as human beings, but as exemplary representatives of either the potential strengths or the potential weaknesses of the groups to which they belong. The idealized characters are humble in appearance and show no appetite for wealth. The others are pretentious, ostentatious, and frequently preoccupied with money. For Chaucer the remedy for all their acquisitive weaknesses was Penance—not Wyclifite contrition without confession, which could easily degenerate into a mere sense of guilt, but Penance as described in the closing tale of the collection by the learned Parson. He was urging his fellow citizens of London and of the kingdom, under the auspices of a martyr who had brought one of England's greatest kings to his knees in repentance, to abandon their ridiculous vices for "lyf by deeth and mortificacion of synne." The Parson's counterpart, the herald of the new age that was already beginning to corrupt the old society, the nemesis of the Knight, the Parson, and the Clerk, was the last pilgrim to be described in the Prologue. The Pardoner had, in a single day, with his false relics

> . . . gat hym moore moneye
> Than that the person gat in monthes tweye.

From Chaucer's point of view, the pilgrimage advocated by the Pardoner, which he follows himself and tempts others into taking also, up a "croked wey" to a hoard of gold, was a pilgrimage to death, not to the inevitable death of the flesh alone, but to the death of the spirit. The Tales are rich in learning, both classical and medieval, reflecting a studious, well-disciplined, and alert mind capable of perceiving in striking ways the operation of general principles in daily affairs. Aside from their superb craftsmanship, they constitute a very substantial contribution to the intellectual history of England. In terms of his own society, which was neither dynamic nor revolutionary in a modern sense, and in terms of his universe of discourse, which was by no means ours, Chaucer's analysis of the ills from which his contemporaries suffered was extremely penetrating.

Perhaps *Troilus* is even more obviously a London production than *The Canterbury Tales*, since London is, by implication, the locale of the action. As we have seen, Londoners regarded their city as New Troy, enjoying the traditions of Old Troy but subject to the vices that left Old Troy in flames. Chaucer had no special interest in a detached history of antiquity and no real interest either in "psychology" for its own sake or in Boccaccio's Trojan poem as a study in the vagaries of sexual love. He was, however, deeply interested in his London community, in the *pietas* of his kingdom, in the manifest decay of English chivalry, and in the beginning of that general decay of ancient *mores* that he was to explore more fully in *The Canterbury Tales*. Boccaccio's poem offered him an opportunity to tell the old monitory story of the Fall of Troy once more and at the same time to emphasize an exemplification of the chivalric weakness that brought it about in the person of the protagonist, Troilus, or "little Troy." The vices of the microcosm were, in effect, the vices of the community as a whole. To give his poem philosophical depth, and greater significance, he adorned it with reflections of Boethian philosophy. Criseyde becomes, because of this philosophical background, not simply a human object of lust, but a figure for misleading worldly attractions of all kinds and an exemplar of their fickleness. The faith of Troilus is thus doomed from the outset, and the more firmly it becomes established, the more he becomes a mere fool of Fortune, subject, like an unreasoning creature, to the forces of destiny, which represents, as Boethius explains, the operation of Providence in particular instances. Hence the appropriateness of the closing admonition to "yonge fresshe folkes" and the concluding prayer. At the end, Chaucer turns to his friends Gower and Strode for correction, seeking approval from the moralist and the philosopher. But his broader aim was undoubtedly an appeal to the chivalry of New Troy and to the realm at whose center it stood to avoid

> . . . al oure werk that folweth so
> The blynde lust, the which that may nat laste.

In the later fourteenth century when, as Peter de la Mare complained at Richard's first Parliament, chivalry "with all other virtue is placed behind, and vice is praised, advanced, and honored," this was not idle moralizing.

If Chaucer had been simply the translator of Boethius and the *Roman de la rose,* the first vernacular work among the chained books in the Sorbonne Library, he would have deserved a significant place in English intellectual history. Neither *Troilus* with its Boethian philosophy nor *The Canterbury Tales* is an insignificant achievement in that respect. But Chaucer was also the author of what has been called "the earliest genuinely scientific work in English,"[66] the *Treatise on the Astrolabe.* He may have also written a translation of another astronomical work, *The Equatorie of the Planetis.* Taken together, Chaucer's works demonstrate a remarkable range of intellectual activity. And this activity would have been possible only in the City of London, with its libraries, its shifting population of noblemen, clerks, preachers, and scholars, and its contacts, commercial, chivalric, and clerical, with the centers of Continental civilization. One might almost reverse the exaggeration with which this chapter began to say that London was the cultural and intellectual center of the kingdom, the place where Oxford and Cambridge met to give whatever useful ideas they produced a practical application, as well as "the capital city and watch-tower of the whole realm."

[66] Derek J. Price, *The Equatorie of the Planetis* (Cambridge, 1955), p. 156.

Bibliographical Note

The most useful general introduction to the content of the records of the City of London in the later Middle Ages is the remarkable compilation of H. T. Riley, *Memorials of London and London Life in the XIII, XIV, and XV Centuries* (London, 1861). A more popular collection that includes materials from outside of London is Edith Rickert's *Chaucer's World* (New York and London, 1948). Guides to the records with summaries of their contents in English are to be found in R. R. Sharpe, *Calendar of Letter-Books Preserved Among the Archives of the Corporation of the City of London* (London, 1899 *et seq.*). Letter Books G and H are relevant to our period. Further records are available in A. H. Thomas, *Calendar of Plea and Memoranda Rolls of the City of London 1361–1381* (Cambridge, 1929), and in the same editor's *Calendar of Select Pleas and Memoranda of the City of London 1381–1442* (Cambridge, 1932). City wills are described in R. R. Sharpe, *Calendar of Wills Proved and Enrolled in the Court of Husting* (London, 1889–1890).

Much material on the topography of the City may be found in Stow's *Survey of London*, ed. C. L. Kingsford (London, 1908). Kingsford's notes often contain material relevant to the fourteenth century. The collection of articles in H. M. Colvin, *The History of the King's Works* (London, 1963) contains an enormous amount of material on medieval buildings. Sylvia Thrupp, *The Merchant Class of Medieval London* (Chicago, 1948) is an astonishing collection of information on a variety of topics, including education, costume, the decoration of houses, and so on. There are many more popular books on the medieval city, but most of them tend to emphasize picturesque detail.

The best history of our period is May McKisack, *The Fourteenth Century* (Oxford, 1959). No one who has made any examination of the primary sources can fail to appreciate her judicious restraint in their use. There is no recent biography of Edward III, although a new one has been promised for the near future. There are two recent biographies of Richard II. The standard work is Anthony Steel, *Richard II* (Cambridge, 1962), first published in 1941. It is a careful and scholarly study, although it sometimes indulges in a rather pious point of view and succumbs to the temptation to "psychologize." A more favorable treatment of Richard is offered by Harold F. Hutchison, *The Hollow Crown* (New York, 1961). This book does not always display firm scholarly discipline, but some of the points in it are well made. The first volume of R. R. Sharpe, *London and the Kingdom* (London, 1894–1895) contains a survey of events in late medieval London in relation to the kingdom as a whole that is still useful. Gwyn A. Williams, *Medieval London from Commune to Capital* (London, 1963) describes the administrative history of the City during the period immediately preceding the period covered in the present book. It is a very thorough study, although somewhat difficult to use. The study by Ruth Bird, *The Turbulent London of Richard II* (London, 1949) is highly technical, but it contains useful specific information about prominent citizens.

Much useful information about Chaucer's immediate background appears in Derek Brewer, *Chaucer in His Time* (London, 1963), a happy exception to the unfortunate tendency of most modern Chaucerians to neglect the society in which the poet lived. The records of Chaucer's life are collected in Martin M. Crow and Clair C. Olson, *Chaucer Life-Records* (Oxford, 1966), a volume that contains useful annotations with bibliographical references. Information about some of Chaucer's more learned contemporaries may be found in A. B. Emden, *A Biographical Register of the University of Oxford to A. D. 1500* (1957–1959) and *A Biographical Register of the University of Cambridge to 1500* (Cambridge, 1963). Those wishing to explore further the general attitude toward Chaucer adopted in this book may find useful the present author's *A Preface to Chaucer* (Princeton, 1962).

INDEX